secure
love

secure love

Create
a relationship
that lasts
a lifetime

JULIE MENANNO

Cornerstone Press

9 10

Cornerstone Press
20 Vauxhall Bridge Road
London SW1V 2SA

Cornerstone Press is part of the Penguin Random House group of companies
whose addresses can be found at global.penguinrandomhouse.com.

First published in the US by Simon & Schuster in 2024
First published in the UK by Cornerstone Press in 2024

www.penguin.co.uk

A CIP catalogue record for this book is available from the British Library.

ISBN 9781529902969

Interior design by Joy O'Meara
Art by NataliaMalikova@Dreamstime.com

Printed and bound in Great Britain by Clays Ltd, Elcograf S.p.A.

The authorised representative in the EEA is Penguin Random House Ireland,
Morrison Chambers, 32 Nassau Street, Dublin D02 YH68

www.greenpenguin.co.uk

Penguin Random House is committed to a
sustainable future for our business, our readers
and our planet. This book is made from Forest
Stewardship Council® certified paper.

For my husband, Mario,
and my children:
John, Clare, Kate, Meg, Sophie, and Lizzie

"Love is a constant process of tuning in, connecting, reading and misreading cues, disconnecting, repairing, and finding deeper connection. It's a dance of meeting and parting and finding each other again. Minute to minute and day to day."

Sue Johnson

Contents

Introduction

i see you

i hear you

i'm safe

i'm on your team

i see you

i hear you

What does a healthy relationship look like?

Many of us have wondered this. But now I want you to forget this question forever. Instead, ask yourself: "What does a *securely attached* relationship *feel* like?"

If you don't know what a securely attached relationship is, much less what it feels like, that's okay. That's why we're here. By the end of this book, you will know about secure attachment, and more important, what it feels like to be in a relationship that is truly fulfilling. You will no longer have to wonder whether or not your relationship is working, because you will find the answers within yourself. If it's not working, you will learn what needs to change and how to go about changing it. If you're struggling in a relationship, you won't have to ask yourself, "Is it them or is it me? Or are we just incompatible?" You'll be able to make distinctions that are clear and that will provide you with the tools you need to create change.

On the deepest level, *all* humans have the same basic relationship requirements when it comes to enjoying a felt sense of safety and closeness with our loved ones. Underneath our different personalities and insecurities and desires, we all speak the same language and each of us can learn to work with our own wiring to achieve the relationship harmony we're yearning for, even if we haven't been able to find it on our own. This truth applies if you're single and seeking a relationship, in a relationship that has been struggling for years or decades, just out of a relationship and looking for answers, or somewhere in between.

If we all have the same relationship needs, why are love and romance so complicated? The truth is, they don't need to be. The problem is that we live in a world where it's rare for a person to be in touch with their greatest, yet most basic, needs. Most of us have never learned how to label our needs, and we've never learned to notice our needs on the bodily level on which they occur. Without that awareness and without those words, it's very difficult to accurately and authentically communicate your needs to someone else. And it's equally difficult to be responsive to the needs of your partner, even if you desperately want to be, if they can't tell you what they need with accuracy and authenticity.

For example, consider how many times a friend has asked you, "Do you feel emotionally validated in your relationship?" Probably never. But emotional validation (along with understanding) is arguably the single most important element of a truly satisfying relationship. And even if some enlightened soul *did* ask if you feel emotionally validated in your relationship, you might not know how to answer.

Feeling emotionally validated is an attachment need—it's one of a handful of essential attachment needs in a relationship. When explaining attachment needs, I find it useful to start with the phrase "to feel close to you, I need . . ." For example, "to feel close to you I need to feel validated"; "to feel close to you, I need to know you appreciate me and see my efforts"; "to feel close to you, I need to know you respect and value me"; "to feel close to you, I need to know my needs matter to you"; or "to feel close to you, I need to know you can understand me." We'll talk more extensively about attachment needs later in the book, but for now it's important to know that each partner must have the *felt sense* of their attachment needs being met in order for their relationship to be close, fulfilling, and harmonious.

But what exactly is a "felt experience"? Think of it like this: You don't merely *know* you're hungry; you also *feel* hungry. Your brain and body work together: your body has a felt sensation and your brain calls it "hungry." From the time you learned to speak, you've been able to put words to your feelings of hunger because you were taught, time and again, to associate the word *hunger* with the feeling of hunger. Thus, you have no problem saying "I'm hungry," and from there formulating a plan to feel the opposite feeling: satiated. The same logic applies to attachment needs. If you were lucky enough to grow up with adults who were relatively emotionally savvy, they were able to recognize your felt sense of emotional pain associated with distress and help you learn to put words to the experience, just as they taught you how to connect hunger the *feeling* with hunger the *word*. They might have said, "Are your feelings hurt? Do you not know that you're important to me right now?" or "Do you feel misunderstood right now?" If you didn't get this experience, you're not alone.

While you may not have words for what your attachment needs are on a conscious level, your nervous system, the most primitive part of who you are, knows *exactly* what they are, and your nervous system will have a strong physiological response when they've gone unmet—your body might tense up, your breath will quicken, your heart rate will increase. Conversely, when your attachment needs *are* met, your nervous system will feel warm and soothed (or at least an absence of tension), signaling to you that you are safe and secure. This is the good stuff.

Through the lens of attachment theory, all relationship behaviors are attempts to experience, maintain, gain, or regain closeness and security with our loved ones. In an environment of attachment insecurity, dysfunctional relationship behavior is a misguided attempt to get attachment needs met. When your needs are met, you feel safe, and that creates an environment of security in your relationship. Underlying every fight, argument, silent treatment, passive-aggressive comment, and attack is an unmet attachment need. You'll learn much more about these misguided attempts as you read this book—you'll begin to understand why your partner yells at you to try to draw you closer or shuts down during an argument in order to try to protect the relationship. I'm not excusing or condoning these behaviors, but understanding them through the lens of attachment is the key to finding better ways to achieve the same goals.

There's much more, however, to this work than knowing about how attachment problems affect your relationship. *Secure Love* is ultimately a book about learning to do what you need to do to create a healthier relationship. This is a couples therapy book, designed to walk partners through the work I do in my practice with couples. Can you benefit from this material if you aren't in a relationship? Absolutely. The material is universal. If you aren't in a relationship, you can use this information to understand how your childhood attachment experiences have shown up in past relationships and/or how they might show up in future relationships. You can use this information to improve your relationship with yourself. After all, self-relationship and self-care are every bit as much of a part of relationship health with a partner as they are a part of self-work. You can use this information as a guide to know more about what you want out of a future partner, and how to give a future partner your best self. Whether you're in a relationship or not, think of this as a relationship instruction manual, and the instructions are written through the lens of attachment theory. After all, *all* relationships are under the influence of attachment energy at some level, and as grandiose as it sounds, I truly believe this book is written for anyone who wants to learn how to connect.

If you grew up having a *felt sense* of your needs being met by your parents or caregivers, as an adult you've likely gravitated to people in the world who know how to meet your needs, and you know how to meet theirs. You do this without even having to think about it. Your nervous system tells you what feels good, and you are free to trust yourself. You have a secure attachment, and you find yourself in relationships that are also securely attached. For those of you who fall into this category, this book will give you more specific details about why you are securely attached, and how to foster even more fulfillment in your relationship. Secure attachment is on a spectrum—no couple has a perfect relationship, and sometimes life stressors come along that make it hard for partners to fully show up for each other, which can impact their attachment bond. My belief is that the more information you have about how relationships work, the more prepared you'll be to navigate the inevitable challenges, and we *all* have room to grow.

If, on the other hand, you grew up in a home where most of the time you didn't feel responded to when in need, that there wasn't space for your feelings, or you felt devalued, unseen, unheard, misunderstood, shamed, invalidated, and/or like your needs were put on the back burner, you likely find relationships that may feel good at first, but eventually devolve into varying degrees of distress. In this case, you have an insecure attachment, and together with your insecurely attached partner (most people with insecure attachments pair up with other insecurely attached partners) you find yourself in a relationship that is stuck. You're probably acutely aware of how painful this type of relationship can be, especially when it comes to conflict and communication breakdowns. At the same time, you might have little sense of what the secure alternative actually feels like. Believe me, you are not alone. Statistically speaking, at least 50 percent of the population has an insecure attachment.

The good news is that if you are insecurely attached, you don't have to spend the rest of your life this way—triggered, distressed, and confused in your relationship, with an overactive nervous system. You also don't have to shut down your innate desire to connect, be close, and get your very human attachment needs met. This book will help you understand what type of insecure attachment you have, why and how it came to be, and how to move into a secure relationship with yourself and your partner. You no longer have to feel lonely even when you're not alone, or that you're broken. You can find a relationship that is nurturing and bonding. I know this to be true because every day I help couples go through this transformation.

When I decided to become a therapist, I adamantly did not want to work with couples. After earning my master's degree, I was enjoying working with individuals, but to earn my full licensure, I needed clinical hours with couples. So I scheduled my first session and felt a little (okay, a lot) demoralized; I didn't realize how hard couples therapy is, how many moving parts there are to manage. The upside to my demoralization was that I felt challenged, and I thrive on challenge. Within a week of that first session, I flew from Los Angeles, where I lived at the time, to Bozeman, Montana, which happened to be hosting the earliest available, entry-level training for Emotion-Focused Therapy for Couples (EFT), a type of therapy created by Dr. Sue Johnson that uses attachment theory to help couples grow toward secure attachment.

While the training was the first step of many more years and hundreds of hours of additional training, individual supervision, and clinical experience, I returned to LA with a passion for the work because I saw the power and incredible results of applying attachment theory to a relationship, and giving couples the tools and words to create emotional safety. During my first couples session after the training, I witnessed the bonding effect that attachment work can have on a couple, even in only one hour. I realized how gratifying it was when a couple leaves my office feeling closer and safer with each other than they did when they came through the door. Working with relationships through the lens of attachment makes this possible.

After returning home from that first EFT training, I stopped accepting individuals as new clients and officially became all couples, all the time.

What I love about EFT is that it's as much about self-healing as it is about relationship healing. I also appreciate that by working with couples, instead of sending my clients home to partners who aren't on the same growth trajectory, as is the case with individual work, I get to send them home with each other, as a couple with a shared experience, a deeper connection, and solid communication skills.

The journey that couples and I take during their course of therapy is similar to the trajectory we'll go through together in *Secure Love*. I first want to know about each partner's attachment history. I'm especially interested in learning about their childhood attachment relationships. Part 1 of *Secure Love* is meant to mirror this part of the process, so that you and your partner can better understand, through the lens of attachment, what each of you have brought to the relationship from your pasts. To make this process even more relatable for you, I've included many case studies from the real couples I've worked with (the stories of the couples and individuals I write about are authentic, though names and most identifying details have been changed, and some examples represent composites).

In Part 2 we're going to learn about how each of your pasts, plus your present reality, come together to take on repetitive, patterned, negative cycles of communication. We'll dig into what negative cycles of communication are, how they work, and how to spot yours. Then we'll look at how to prevent and interrupt your negative cycles, and how to repair from them when they do happen. I'll offer you the tools to create attachment-friendly environments, the kind of environments that will reduce your conflict, create unbreakable bonds, and help you find solutions to your problems.

In Part 3 we'll address some real-world issues that can interact with the negative communication cycle and exacerbate it or perhaps throw a wrench in your conflict-resolution intentions. We'll cover some universal issues, like sex, as well as some unique challenges, such as trauma and addictions. I'll provide you with insight and guidance for how to course-correct if you're not seeing results, and, finally, I'm going to give you some very specific scripts to set up hard conversations for success.

Deep into my couples therapy career, I decided to create an Instagram account as an intellectual and creative outlet, but also because I wanted to share the tools I was giving my clients with a wider audience. With "The Secure Relationship," I offer information that every couple can use, whether or not they are in therapy, covering topics like "are you emotionally available?" "responding to your partner's reaches for connection," and "when I'm sorry might not be enough." I've included similar graphics and easy-to-use scripts in this book to help you digest this advice readily. If my social media posts are quick hits into these topics, this book is the deep dive, but just as simple to put into action.

By the end of this book, you will not *know* you're in a better relationship; rather, you will have learned to find, recognize, and re-create moments of connection, safety, and security. You will have learned how to make this experience the undercurrent in your relationship, so that it exists whether the two of you are on a romantic vacation together, working through a difficult problem, or even when you're simply going about daily life not thinking about the relationship at all. You will also have grown within yourself, so you feel safe and comfortable in your own skin, and you can bring that comfort into all your relationships. This is the root of true connection. This is secure love.

PART ONE

Understanding Your Needs

CHAPTER 1

The Problem Beneath the Problem

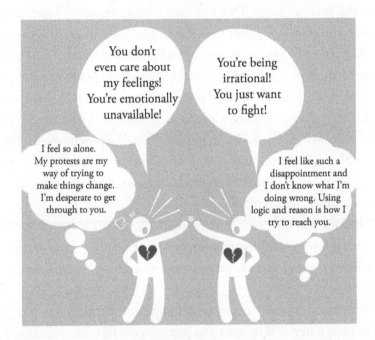

"The problem is not the problem."

Hi, I'm glad you're home," Jen says to her husband, Andrew, as he walks in the door and puts his keys on the table to greet her. "But you put your keys on the table again. I've asked you a hundred times to put them on the hook. That's why we call it the 'key hook.'"

"Really?" Andrew responds. "I just walked in the door. I almost always put them on the hook. You really need to bring this up the second I get home?"

"Almost always? Hardly. More like 'never,'" Jen says. "It might be a small thing to you but to me it's a big deal. I'm the only one who picks things up around here."

You may have heard the phrase "The problem is not the problem" before, especially if you've been in therapy. When partners are fighting—whether they're arguing over money, parenting, where to live, in-laws, sex, or taking out the trash—the conflict is almost never about the issue at hand. Don't get me wrong, issues at hand are important. The trash does need to be taken out, bills do need to get paid, kids do need to be parented, and overall fairness does matter. The bigger problem, however, is what's blocking all of the issues at hand from being worked through in a way that doesn't harm the relationship bond. Only when the bigger problem is addressed can the issues at hand be worked through. The *bigger* problem, the problem underneath the problem, is almost always one of communication, which we see here in a typical argument between this couple, Andrew and Jen.

But it often doesn't stop here:

"Give me a break, Jen," Andrew sighs. "It doesn't matter how much I do, you'll find something to complain about. What about last weekend when I cleaned out the garage? And now I'm in trouble over a key hook?"

"Why do you have to turn everything back on me?" Jen asks, getting more agitated. "Why can't you just own the fact that you don't care about the keys? Or about what I want?"

"Because you're being irrational!" Andrew blurts out.

Jen is infuriated. "Why can't you be more like my sister's husband? He actually supports her!" At this point, Andrew, sensing the escalation, switches gears. "Fine, here, I'll put the keys on the hook. Now can we just move on?"

Jen isn't buying it. She tells Andrew he's patronizing her.

"I give up," Andrew says. "There's no making you happy when you're in one of these moods." Andrew leaves the room, leaving Jen fuming on her own.

I'm guessing you can relate to some version of this conflict, even if the arguments in your relationship are about something entirely different. Andrew and Jen's conversation started out about the keys but in a matter of minutes spiraled into a heart-wrenching battle of emotional weapons and protections, including blame, shame, defensiveness, criticism, and deflection. The episode ended in a silence more deafening than the actual fight. Andrew and Jen may not even remember what started the fight in the first place. What they do remember is how they felt: angry, disconnected, lonely, unappreciated, unseen.

Throughout the evening Andrew and Jen remain disconnected. The next day, when they've each cooled off enough that the immediate tension has lessened, they miss each other and try to move forward. They go through the motions, and although the keys are in the right place, cracks of resentment have appeared in the couple's otherwise solid bond. Still, they don't want to revisit the conversation for fear of another blowup. The fight is over, but the conflict is not resolved.

This episode, or some variation of it, is surprisingly common among couples. Yet, when you're in it, it's easy to feel like you're the only one—that your relationship is doomed; that something must be wrong with you. I'm here to tell you, that's not the case. I see clients in situations like these all the time. You are not alone.

Maybe this type of interaction describes your past instead of your present . . . you used to fight, but you got tired and gave up. Instead of arguing, you and your partner just coexist in the same space. You live in a chronic state of emotional disconnect, punctuated by periods of higher tension. It might seem different than Jen and Andrew on the surface—instead of yelling about the misplaced keys, you are silently resigned to putting them back yourself—but couples in this "coexisting" state are also lost in their conflict. The difference is that instead of addressing their problems with escalation, they disengage. The results, however, are the same: real issues don't get resolved, resentment builds, and connection suffers.

These two situations—constant escalating conflict or persistent disengagement—are what usually drive couples to seek out my help. By the time they're sitting on the couch across from me, the relationship has gotten so bad that they assume they're just incompatible.

The good news is that most of the time, incompatibility isn't the issue at all. Instead, it's about using communication to create attachment-friendly environments and secure attachments. What Andrew and Jen need, what so many couples need, is a way to better reach each other.

The *Real* Problem

Millions of couples are stuck in cycles like Jen and Andrew's. You don't have to share their circumstances—a traditional American heterosexual relationship—to relate to their predicament. Maybe you're in a heterosexual relationship, but you live in India, or Germany, or Argentina, and your relationship has a different cultural flavor than most of the examples in this book. Maybe you're an LGBTQ+ couple. Or maybe there's no way to define you other than as two humans in a relationship who love each other and want to make it work. Every example you will read in this book is specific but is also universal. We all have our own problems and our own circumstances, but no matter if you're gay or straight, in a first marriage, third marriage, or you've never been married, these dynamics will affect you. The truth is, your exact circumstances matter far less than your emotional state.

Couples like Jen and Andrew might fight about parenting, bicker about finances, or disengage completely because they feel so far apart. Some couples read books, learn to use "I-statements," and set better boundaries in an effort to address the problem. Those strategies occasionally work as temporary Band-Aids, but the truth is, we can't permanently fix the surface arguments until we get to the root issue. And that issue, almost always, is attachment insecurity.

Attachment, at its most basic, is the quality of our bond with the core figures in our lives, and it comes alive during each and every interaction. People who are attached, or *attachment bonded*, depend on each other for emotional support. In practical terms, this means, for example, that they know they're seen and understood, they know they're appreciated and valued, they know they can access support when they need it. The most powerful attachment bonds exist between either parents and young children or romantic partners, because these are the people we depend on most in a lifetime. In romantic relationships, where attachment bonds are reciprocal (versus parent-child relationships, where the parent is responsible for the child but not the other way around), the bond is strongest when each party's *attachment needs* are being met. We'll do a more thorough exploration into attachment needs in the next chapter, but globally speaking, this means partners can reach and respond to each other's emotional bids for comfort and connection, and can navigate and resolve conflict with emotional safety. They can give and receive love, and when things get hard, they fight fair. All of this leaves them feeling confident in their connection, and secure in their attachment.

Romantic attachment does not exist in a vacuum, because both you and your partner came to your relationship with baggage from your childhood and impactful adult (or teen) romantic relationships. Nobody escapes it; it's just a matter of degree. Not all the baggage is inherently negative; it just is what it is—baggage. We enter relationships with varying levels of trust of others and of ourselves, met or unmet attachment needs from childhood, communication patterns, self-beliefs, ways of managing our emotions, and learned behaviors. We also attract, more or less, our same level of growth, even when it shows up very differently. Attachment insecurity is on a spectrum and, while there are always exceptions, the degree to which someone has an insecure attachment is likely the degree to which their partner will also have an insecure attachment. But feeling secure in your attachment isn't *only* about your current relationship—your past will always affect your present.

When arguments escalate in the way that Jen and Andrew's did, what couples are really battling is an *insecure attachment*. They are expressing how much they need each other and how devastating it is to be lost, disconnected, and alone. They use surface content—keys, bills, parenting, and so on—as code to talk about the fears and unmet needs that they can't effectively express. Then, to shield against the pain of not getting what they need, partners put up "protective stances"—loud protests, walking away, shutting down—to stave off vulnerability and pain at all costs. But here's the problem: by protecting themselves from pain, they're also blocking connection.

With all that in mind, consider Jen and Andrew's fight in a new way.

Andrew comes home excited to spend the evening with Jen. When Jen scolds him about the keys, he feels deflated, as if he got it wrong again. As a child, Andrew could never "get it right" for his mom, so Jen is hitting a wound. Andrew's body gets tense. His subconscious monologue says, "Maybe if I can convince Jen I'm not the bad guy, I won't have to stand here feeling like she sees me as a failure yet again, which isn't fair considering how hard I work to get it right for her." And so, he defends himself.

But Jen is also excited to see Andrew. She came home early from work to pick up the house so they could relax together. Being organized is part of her self-care. Jen knows Andrew doesn't share her same standards, but it's important for her to feel supported in small ways. She's not asking for much, she tells herself. When she sees the keys hit the table, her own childhood wound—feeling unseen, unsupported, not responded to—flares. She says to herself, "I've tried so hard to get him to hear me. He knows how important this is to me, so he must just not care." Jen feels desperate to get Andrew to see what's really happening so that he'll reassure her.

Jen and Andrew go back and forth, trying to reach each other. Jen needs to know she's cared for and to have her feelings validated. Andrew needs to know that not only does she see him as worthy, but that she trusts his love and care for her are real. Yet no matter how hard they try, they can't reach each other. They are stuck in their protective stances, battling for something that feels like life or death in the moment: attachment security. They are looking for a seemingly simple message: "I'm loved, I'm understood, I'll be responded to when I reach for you, I'm getting it right." Instead they push each other away and reinforce each other's attachment fears.

Eventually Jen and Andrew make up, or at least move on, but the damage to their attachment bond is done and they don't know how to repair it. The same conflict will resurface in the same pattern, indefinitely, until they learn how to stay connected during conflict.

I want you to imagine you're having a conversation with a partner—current, former, or even future. You're talking about a stressful situation at work. After explaining the problem, your partner tells you you're seeing it all wrong—that you should just be grateful to have a job in the first place. You try to protest, but they accuse you of being oversensitive to feedback.

How do you feel? Unseen? Frustrated? Confused? Maybe all of the above.

Now what do you notice happening inside of you? Most people feel a tightening, maybe in their chest or throat. Some report feeling still or caught off guard. This is the felt experience of an attachment rupture. When enough of these ruptures happen in a relationship, when they create a climate of overall unsupportiveness, when they don't get repaired along the way, they reinforce an already insecure attachment.

Some of you reading this book are struggling with more serious issues than where to put the keys: infidelity, chronic physical or mental illness, blended-family issues, military deployment, addictions, extended family concerns, just to name a few. I can't change that reality for you, but what I can do—and what I hope we'll do here together—is help you find a way to buffer your relationship from the negative impact of these external stressors. Why is secure attachment *especially* important when life is throwing curveballs? Because the connection and support that partners derive from a securely attached relationship helps them feel more confident, competent, and resilient. If you want to heal from past wounds and transgressions, I'd like to help you understand what that process looks like. The events themselves might continue to be difficult, but the relationship doesn't have to be. In fact, your relationship can be a source of strength and support as you weather the challenges of life. You and your partner can learn to face the world as a team.

I'm not saying that all couples should stay together at all costs. I don't believe that. Some challenges are too much to overcome. And sometimes, the problem actually *is* the problem. Partners can have disagreements that are true deal-breakers; disagreements where there is no room for compromise. They love each other, but one wants children, the other doesn't; one wants to live in the city, the other wants to stay off the grid; one can't get over a past affair, the other says it's time to move on. Sometimes there is real incompatibility, or the wounds are too great for trust to ever rebuild. We'll talk later about what to do in these instances, but for now I just want to validate that some couples do face insurmountable challenges.

When all outside circumstances are equal, however, some couples will make it while others may not. So what are the surviving and thriving couples doing differently? Multiple factors are at play, but what's certain is that these couples know how to avoid negative communication cycles like the one that plagued Andrew and Jen. That alone dramatically increases their odds. Because no single event takes down a relationship. Negative communication cycles, on the other hand, absolutely do.

Secure Love

Let's revisit that same exercise, the one where you tell your partner about a stressful work problem. Imagine now that as you talk, you can tell your partner is really hearing you. As you speak they reassure you that your feelings are valid and reasonable.

How do you feel? Probably cared for and understood; seen and valued.

What do you notice in your body? When I'm doing speaking engagements and I ask audience members to do this exercise, I get a lot of similar answers: a warm feeling, an ease of tension, a lightening of the shoulders. Sit with your body for a minute. Imagine your partner's loving face as you talk. Notice what happens inside you. This is the felt experience of a secure attachment.

Relationship satisfaction is intrinsically linked to secure attachment. Partners who are securely attached are reliable sources of intimacy, support, and comfort. During conflict, securely attached partners are less negative and reactive. They are able to hold positive images of each other even in the face of distress, and show more warmth and affection than insecure couples. Even their facial expressions are less hostile, and they have more confidence they'll get through the conflict without harming their bond. While *all* couples experience conflict, securely attached couples do so less often because they're less likely to experience missteps as rejections. This is partially due to each partner's high self-esteem as an individual.

In a secure relationship, each partner shows up as their best self, not as a way to get something in return, but out of love and the desire to connect. They share a rich variety of thoughts and emotions with each other and respond to each other with care and sensitivity. They work to meet the other's needs for sexual connection and physical affection, even when those needs aren't the same as their own. Each partner is willing to make appropriate sacrifices for the greater good of the relationship. They support each other's needs for autonomy and the exploration of separate interests. Each partner takes responsibility for their part in maintaining connection and being easy to love. They work to understand each other and validate each other's feelings. They have each other's backs and approach life as a team. They have fun together. Securely attached couples make hard decisions together in a way that might lead to disappointment, but not to resentment. They are each other's primary support system, but each partner also has support systems outside the relationship.

Couples with secure attachments aren't perfect, because no couple is perfect. What I've found in my work is that couples who have a secure attachment, even the ones who don't seem to have a lot in common, are able to draw on the health of their relationship to find ways to meet each other when they don't see eye to eye. Couples with a secure attachment bond generally maintain a felt experience of connection and comfort in their relationship. They're not always thinking about their partner (though when they do, the thoughts are predominantly positive—a natural result of met attachment needs) and they don't spend all their time actively working on and talking about the relationship, either. Rather, they know how to just *be* with each other. They recognize that perfect doesn't exist and so they aspire to something realistic—which is its own version of perfect.

How Do We Get There?

Some of you are in relationships where you feel close and connected most of the time, but when you bump up against hard topics there are explosive fights. Some of you are in relationships with a constant underscore of tension, punctuated by moments of intensity. Some of you don't fight often, but you feel more disconnected than you'd like. And still others of you have your own versions of dysfunction. Regardless of the circumstances, the solution is the same: begin communicating with each other, verbally and nonverbally, in the ways we'll cover in this book. By putting the tools into practice, you can learn to find the connection and harmony you've been looking for *and* begin to solve your "issues at hand" with greater ease. This is the path toward creating secure attachment.

To do this, we must minimize what's not working in your relationship and build up what will. In the chapters to come, we'll examine how each partner's attachment style is showing up in your relationship. We'll consider the attachment bonds from your childhood, which helped protect you at the time, but now need to be rewired. We'll replace old, ineffective behaviors with new productive ones, and all the while build up emotional closeness. We'll learn to communicate from a place of vulnerability, which is the crux of this work. If the word *vulnerability* makes you cringe, know that it doesn't mean opening up in a way that feels inauthentic. Vulnerable communication is simply the opposite of protective communication; you share what you can when you can. You take the risks needed to show up in your relationship in a new way, with less criticism or less defensiveness, even when it initially feels really uncomfortable to do so. Vulnerability heals.

Real relationship change takes place in two ways. The first is a top-down approach, where we change *behavior* in order to improve the *climate* of the relationship. This is the focus of many common forms of couples therapy. Couples are instructed to say and do things in new ways, and by making these changes, they create safety and shift the underlying health of the relationship. The other approach is bottom-up, in which we work directly on attachment gunk underlying the behaviors, in hopes that by healing what's underneath, the behavior will shift on its own.

Which is better? Neither. We need both.

Imagine you're in an argument with your partner. In an effort to prevent further damage, you disengage and walk away, feeling defeated and unheard. This feels horrible. Nothing about it is fulfilling. But it's effective in the moment to protect the relationship from damage inflicted through criticism, yelling, name-calling, uncontrolled expressions of emotion, shaming, and angry rants. Yes, you may have prevented something really ugly, but at what cost? The cost is resolution and connection. If you stop there, your relationship will suffer. Your partner feels unheard, ignored, and abandoned. So if you both engage only in a top-down approach, without diving into the underlying conflicts, healing probably won't happen. But there is a middle ground between fighting and disengagement, and secure attachment lies in this middle ground. When you complement the behavioral work with deeper work intended to help you both understand *why* you go into protective stances and *empathize* with those stances, you can approach the argument and one another with more openness. We can start healing the underlying causes that spurred the argument in the first place. In other words, changing behavior is more about damage control than it is about creating fulfilling relationships, but damage control helps create space to do the deeper work.

I will walk you through both approaches, giving specific advice on what not to do in your relationship and what to do instead. For the work to be thorough, and the change to be lasting, we do the deeper work, too: reframing ourselves, our partners, and our relationships through an attachment lens. The behavioral work prevents damage; the attachment work builds bonds, and bonds build resilience.

Before we can start, we need to "buy the reframe," as we say in emotion-focused therapy. Change can't happen until you reframe your relationship: your partner is not the enemy. Instead, your negative communication cycle is the enemy. Destructive words and behaviors are the enemy. For relationship change to happen, we need to move away from the idea that partners are enemies who must protect themselves from each other. Once you accept this reframe, you can start to see how even the relationship behaviors that look the most vicious on the outside are in fact cries for security and closeness. When we view our conflict through an attachment lens, understanding that ultimately all humans want to bond and feel safe in their relationships, then the magic can begin.

One final note: though interpersonal relationships obviously involve more than one participant, I can't understate the importance of focusing on your own self-growth when it comes to relationship improvement. All of our beliefs about what we can expect from other people are based on past experiences, and these experiences can cause us to react to our partners not as who they really are in the present moment, but as who we assume them to be according to our attachment understandings and personal history. This doesn't always serve your relationship well, so it stands to reason that addressing these self-patterns is a crucial part of relationship healing. But remember, it's not all-or-nothing: you brought your strengths to the relationship, too. One of those strengths is that you're willing to read this book, which means you have grit and a desire to grow. Use your strengths to your advantage and work on the rest.

I offer you now the same note that I always end a couple's first therapy session with: "As we proceed, keep in mind that I'm not going to try to convince you to stay in your relationship. That's not my job. My job is to look underneath the surface, diagnose the attachment issues at play, and help couples communicate about their disagreements in a way that is mutually respectful and emotionally safe. When the communication is cleaned up, then and only then can we know what else might be getting in the way."

Once you learn to communicate with your partner in a healthy way, you can observe and experience your relationship from a place of clarity. When communication is improved and attachment bonds are solidified, partners are far more likely to be able to work through their differences.

I'll end this chapter with a question most of you are asking: How long does it take? The answer to this question depends on the couple. Not only does each couple start this work at a different place, but so does each partner. All relationships can grow. What it takes is access to helpful information, commitment to working on it, and practice. So when you think about how long it will take to see results, which is a legitimate question to ask, think about the following factors: one, if your relationship feels good 10 percent of the time, and that number goes up to 20 percent, that is growth. What I've found is that if you keep doing what you're doing, some growth will usually lead to more growth. Two, growth is never linear; instead, growth happens as a positive trend with peaks and valleys—two steps forward, one step back. Three, each partner will likely grow at different rates. And lastly, when you're putting the right elements into the relationship, especially at the beginning, you might not see results even when the results are there. Think of it like planting seeds. On top of this, sometimes things get worse before they get better because change, even positive change, can make people nervous when it's unfamiliar. Try not to let this demoralize you and maintain your confidence that what you're doing is healthy, even if it's not readily apparent. You're committing to positive change for yourself and your relationship.

CHAPTER 2

Understanding Attachment Theory

your partner needs...

To feel wanted by you

For you to notice the good they do for you

To feel appreciated by you

To know their feelings aren't "too much" for you

To know their thoughts and ideas matter to you

To know you're willing to grow together

To know you'll be there in times of need

To know your heart, not just your head

...and so do you

When you reached for emotional comfort or connection growing up, how were you met by the adults around you? When you were sad, did your parents or caregivers consistently offer warmth? Or rejection? When you felt insecure, did you feel valued? Or pushed away? Did you get the message that your feelings matter and deserve attention, or were you told (if not in so many words) that you're "too much"? Were your feelings validated and tended to? Or were you distracted from your feelings and told "don't cry—here, have a cookie"? Or, a third option, were you shamed and left alone with your feelings, perhaps "you need to go to your room to be angry"?

To understand how you show up in your relationships today, we have to start with your family of origin. The way in which your closest caregivers responded to your emotional needs will absolutely influence how you interact with loved ones as an adult. Childhood experiences set the stage for what you expect, or don't expect, in your most intimate adult relationships, as well as how responsive you can be to your partner. The human brain learns at its most rapid pace throughout childhood, so direct emotional experiences during this time send an important message: "Here's what relationships are like, and here's what I need to do to navigate them. Here's what's necessary to survive this environment." Whether you were raised by caregivers who were emotionally available or unavailable, your brain learned to wade through relationships according to those early templates.

My curiosity as a therapist, when I start working with any couple, is about the *overall emotional climate* during each partner's childhood. How much of the good stuff did you get? Was it enough? How much of the time did you feel a sense of warmth in your home life? How much of the time did you feel anxious and unseen? How often did anyone help you find and put words to your inner experiences like joy, jealousy, rage, excitement? How often were those feelings validated? "I understand you're mad; I get mad, too. I can't let you drive after dark until you have more experience, but your anger and disappointment make sense to me and you're not wrong to feel that way." Did you feel safe and like you'd be protected if bad things happened? Did anyone try to help you make sense of it when bad things *did* happen? Understanding the answers to these questions helps me understand what each partner needs today, and helps us get to the root of any communication breakdowns.

I recently sat down with a couple, Reyna and Sabino, who came to me because they couldn't stop fighting. The cycle was always the same no matter who "started it" in any given moment. Reyna would end up getting mad and lashing out. Sabino would end up getting defensive and eventually shutting down. Early in our session, I asked each partner to describe the emotional climate in their childhood home. Sabino told me he couldn't remember. In fact, he couldn't recall ever being distressed as a child. "If hypothetically, you *did* experience distressing feelings from time to time," I said, "what would have happened if you tried to talk to your parents about them?"

"My mom might have been there for me; it's hard to remember," Sabino said. "Not my dad. My dad would've told me to toughen up. I would've felt like he saw me as a baby. I always wanted my dad to see me as strong. He really valued strength."

"So, you know your dad wouldn't have been a source of comfort, and would've possibly been a source of shame, and you're not entirely sure whether your mom would've been comforting or not," I summarized. "It sounds to me like there's a good chance that talking about your feelings would've put you at risk for feeling rejected. What's it like for you today when Reyna gets upset with you? Does that feel like being rejected, too?"

"Yes," Sabino said, looking down at the floor. "It's awful."

"I'm sure it *is* awful," I said. "But as I learn to know you, it makes sense to me that you learned early on to avoid feeling rejected. That was your young brain's way of protecting yourself. Your brain said 'feelings aren't safe; feelings lead to rejection.' So right here and now, in your relationship with your wife, you're still keeping feelings so far away."

When Sabino told me he couldn't remember having big emotions, what I heard was "my emotions didn't matter from an early age; I stuffed them away before I even learned to talk." After all, why feel emotional pain if nobody is around to provide support? Why not take the second-best option, and disavow painful feelings altogether (albeit subconsciously) and stay safe from the despair of emotional rejection and disappointment? This defensive strategy worked; it protected little-boy Sabino. But the downside is that present-day Sabino doesn't know how to emotionally engage with himself *or* his partner, and it's taking a toll on his life and relationship.

Sabino's wife, Reyna, had a different childhood experience. "My family was dysfunctional, still is," she commented. "I'm really close to my mom and sisters but there's constant drama. I'm trying to set boundaries with them, but they always make me feel guilty if I don't join them in whatever is going on at the moment."

"What was it like growing up?" I asked. "Did things feel chaotic?"

"Yes. My mom was anxious about everything and treated my dad like her servant," Reyna explained. "He did whatever she said, but then would have enough and blow up."

"Could you go to either of them for emotional comfort?"

"No, I was an emotional handful," she said. "Everyone in the family jokes about it. I would get really upset, even all the way up into my teens, and they were always trying to get me to calm down . . . bribing me, punishing me . . . they tried everything. Sometimes my mom could be comforting, but most of the time she just got upset right along with me."

"What happened if you stayed quiet and didn't get upset?" I asked.

"I've never thought about that. Probably nothing. Nobody ever noticed me until there was a crisis," Reyna said.

"So you had to choose between feeling deprived of attention or 'going big' to be noticed?"

"Yes, two bad options," she said. "But it's the same thing with Sabino. I feel like I have to get upset for him to hear me."

Like Sabino, Reyna's childhood attachment was manifesting in her marriage. As a kid she had two options: get big—what she called being an "emotional handful"—or feel emotionally abandoned. It's too painful for children to feel abandoned, so Reyna's childhood brain learned that getting big (which for Reyna meant loud and emotional) was the way to get confirmation that she existed and mattered. It was how she got people to show up for her.

No parent is perfect. Even the most loving caregivers have moments when they are distracted, when they yell and wish they hadn't, when they've had enough and tell their child to go to their room when what that kid really needs is to be pulled closer. No parent responds in the most loving, attuned way 100 percent of the time. And that's okay! According to research, children only need to be responded to with attunement *50 percent of the time* to develop a secure attachment. This is why I focus on overall childhood climate rather than isolated incidents.

The growing child's brain is like a sponge. The child takes in all the information from their surrounding environment, for better and for worse, and it happens almost wholly out of conscious awareness. It's a plan of efficiency—this unconscious learning keeps us from having to stop and ponder each decision and relearn information as we go. Imagine yourself as a four-year-old. By that age, you might have learned that the bathroom is down the hall, the hot water is on the left, the toothpaste in the top drawer. Thanks to your brain's ability to download information and store it for future use, you didn't need to spend precious mental energy considering your every move. Like your physical world, you learned to navigate your emotional world in the same way. You might have learned that when you were frustrated, you could seek help from a parent and feel supported. You might have learned that your dad got anxious when you got sad and so it might be best to hide your tears, or that when you showed your drawings to your mom, in an attempt to be seen and known, you'd feel the warmth of having been responded to. From all this information, you developed a set of emotional rules to serve you throughout life.

When I explain this idea to my clients, they often push back with questions about inborn temperament. Isn't there something to the idea that who you are is a matter of nature, not nurture? Is it possible that Sabino was born with a detached disposition, or that Reyna was sensitive from day one? Yes and no.

We're all born with a baseline temperament, but our environment will determine how that temperament manifests. In their landmark research on the interplay between a child's inborn temperament and the environment they're born into, childhood researchers Alexander Thomas and Stella Chess describe what's called the "goodness of fit" between the temperament of a parent and that of their child. The idea is that in childhood, if you and your father have a "poor fit," for example, then the interactions between the two of you will be strained. Strained relationships create more opportunities for strained communication, which creates a higher likelihood of unmet emotional needs, which will dramatically increase the odds of an insecure attachment. This is by no means the fault of the child, who innocently came into the world with a specific temperament, nor is it the "fault" of the parent, who may lack the skills to work with that challenge. But, while we want to move away from blame and instead focus on responsibility, individual attachment styles *do* develop in response to environment, which is created by adults. Adults are *responsible* for the environment they create, but that doesn't mean they're inherently bad, flawed, lazy, or uncaring people because they didn't know how to get it right enough. They may just not have had the tools. Still, children look to caregivers to teach them how to express and manage their emotions. If a parent isn't able to manage the child's temperament in a healthy way, or even their own, it can create an environment that fosters an insecure attachment.

As we journey into attachment theory together, keep in mind that your parents' behavior did not need to be intentional for you to develop an insecure attachment style. Most parents want the best for their children, but if one or both of your parents didn't have secure attachments of their own, they were limited in their ability to create an emotionally secure environment in which you could emotionally thrive. You may have had extenuating circumstances in your life such as the death or chronic physical or mental illness of a parent, or even a natural disaster that affected your parent's ability to be present for you emotionally. As we proceed through the book, especially as we dig into attachment styles, do your best to find compassion for your parents and for yourself—remember, most of the time we are all doing our very best with what we have. (If you're a parent yourself, as many of you are, and are interested in learning about parenting your own child in a way that fosters secure attachment, I recommend the book *Good Inside*, by Dr. Becky Kennedy.)

Before you can apply attachment theory to your relationship in a practical way, first let's understand the basic concept. Once you understand what attachment theory is, where it came from, and why it's important, it can serve as a guide. You will begin to have a deeper understanding of why you are triggered in certain interactions, what might be going on for your partner when things get heated, and why you might find yourselves in a pattern you're not yet sure how to break. Understanding the *why* behind your relationship behaviors and urges will make change so much easier. It will allow you to approach yourself and your partner with compassion, which is the first step toward finding the relationship harmony you're longing for.

Attachment Theory History

In the mid-1900s, psychiatrist John Bowlby discovered that the "delinquent" adolescent boys he treated at a boys' home in London often had one thing in common: what Bowlby called "maternal deprivation," meaning loss of their mother, repeated separations from their mother, or being passed from one foster mother to another. From this observation he began to theorize that early childhood experiences in relationships can affect a person throughout their life. While this seems obvious to most of us today, it was novel at the time. Bowlby also theorized that we're all born with an "attachment behavioral system" that motivates us to seek closeness with our attachment figures, much in the same way we are equipped with an appetite system in order to seek food.

The biology behind attachment theory is not very complicated, and most of us understand it intuitively: humans need other humans to survive and reproduce. Evolution favors whatever traits support reproduction of a species. Those early humans who had the healthiest and most cooperative relationships with other humans had an easier time getting food, making protective shelter, fighting off predators, and taking care of their young. And not only is it natural for humans to crave and seek out relationships, it's also natural for them to experience high levels of distress when their relationships are under threat. When your partner isn't returning your calls or responding to your texts like they normally do, or when you feel like you're being unfairly criticized, you're not "crazy," irrational, too needy, or otherwise flawed because you feel uncomfortable. In fact, you're *wired* to feel uncomfortable. That said, just because you *feel* an attachment threat doesn't mean your attachment is truly under threat. Sometimes we perceive a threat when in reality there is none. For example, if your partner has a stern look on their face, you might feel triggered and think "oh no, they're mad at me," when they might just be in deep thought (this is why it's so important for couples to learn to communicate through these "misses").

Over time, the psychological community began to accept Bowlby's ideas about the impact of early attachment. In the 1970s, he paired up with psychologist Mary Ainsworth to conduct the formal research that solidified attachment theory as a well-respected and highly useful lens through which to view relationships. This research led to the categorizations of attachment styles: secure, insecure-anxious, insecure-avoidant, and later, the fourth category of disorganized attachment. In the late 1990s, Sue Johnson, drawing on the work of Bowlby and Ainsworth—as well as that of researchers Cindy Hazan and Phillip Shaver, who first applied attachment theory to adult relationships—began researching ways to heal distressed couples using attachment theory. In 1988 Johnson developed what's called Emotionally Focused Couples Therapy (EFT), a road map for therapists to use attachment theory to help couples heal. EFT helps couples understand how each partner's attachment style is driving the poor communication that not only blocks resolution, but does a number on their emotional connection, safety, and support—all the things that give couples resilience to poor communication—and sets vicious cycles into motion. EFT takes the science behind attachment theory and puts it to practical use to help couples not just survive, but thrive. As an EFT therapist myself, I know firsthand how effective it is. For more information about EFT or to locate an EFT therapist in your area, visit ICEEFT.com.

Attachment Needs and Fears

In relationships, what we all want more than anything is to feel lovable for who we are on the inside and worthy for what we do on the outside. Beyond that, we want to use our lovable, worthy selves as a way to connect with the lovable, worthy selves of others, particularly our romantic partners. When we feel as if we're seen by another person as worthy and lovable, we feel safe. Our nervous system says, "This person sees me as worthy and lovable, and people who are worthy and lovable are safe from rejection and abandonment, so therefore I'm safe." For example, we thrive in the workplace when we know our employers and coworkers appreciate our work; it helps us feel worthy of the job. Our family members hopefully meet our need to feel lovable—accepted for who we are more than for what we do. Even if we fail, they will still love us. Virtually all relationship behaviors stem from this need to be viewed as worthy and lovable—or from the pain that arises when we feel we aren't seen this way. These two needs are at the core of any individual's set of *attachment needs*. And, the ability to intimately connect with others *relies* upon feeling worthy and lovable. Why? Because people who don't feel worthy and lovable have to hide to feel safe from rejection and abandonment. Hiding is the antithesis to connection.

If we break down the needs to feel lovable and worthy into workable parts, we have attachment needs (sometimes called attachment longings), which are the building blocks of secure attachment. They are what you need in a relationship for you to feel close to your partner, and likewise what your partner needs to feel close to you. Closeness matters. When you feel close to your partner, you feel supported and safe. When we feel supported and safe, seen and accepted for the lovable, worthy person we are, we want to connect, which leads to more closeness. Connection is fulfilling. People who are fulfilled do better in their relationships and in the world beyond. They have better emotional, mental, and physical health. When we feel supported and safe, we work through life's problems more easily.

How do you know when you're close to someone? You probably haven't thought about this explicitly—you probably "just know." But let's try to pinpoint what's actually required for closeness. Think, for the moment, about your partner. Now ask yourself: "Do I look forward to seeing this person and talking to them? Do I seek them out when I need support? Do I share my thoughts and feelings with them? Do I feel like we're a team? When things feel strained, do I have the urge to reconnect?" If, in the big picture of the relationship, both you and your partner answer yes to these questions most of the time, then most likely you feel close to each other. Closeness doesn't just happen; closeness is earned through the way partners think and feel about each other, in the way they speak to each other, and in the ways they behave in the relationship.

Attachment needs are fairly consistent from couple to couple, although different partners might be more sensitive to particular attachment needs when they go unmet. You might be more sensitive to invalidation if you didn't get enough of it during childhood, or you might be more focused on being seen as successful, because that's how you felt worthy growing up. Some partners have a harder time trusting, because their caretakers often weren't safe, while others are more in touch with their whole selves, and thus have access to a balance of needs.

The following is a list of various attachment needs. To understand your own, I like to use the phrase, "To feel close to you, I need to know . . ."

+ you value me and our relationship
+ you'll respond to me in moments when I reach for you
+ you'll reach to me for support in times of need
+ you appreciate me and my efforts
+ my needs as an individual matter to you
+ you hold me in high esteem
+ you are willing to see and understand me

+ my feelings are valid to you
+ you respect me
+ there's a clear path to pleasing you
+ you see me as a successful partner
+ I can trust your love and loyalty
+ You trust my love and loyalty

When both partners' attachment needs are met, and they trust they'll be met in the future, they have a secure attachment. Conversely, when their needs aren't met, and they can't be sure they'll be met in the future, they have an insecure attachment. Having met attachment needs is what ultimately helps partners feel loved and worthy in each other's eyes, and from there they can experience the beauty of deep connection. If this sounds overwhelming, fear not. Relationships aren't as mysterious as they can sometimes seem. Attachment needs are met through words, feelings, thoughts, and behaviors, and this book was written to help you know exactly what those are.

For now, know that secure relationships are less about how a relationship *looks* and more about how it *feels*, which is why understanding attachment needs on an intellectual level isn't enough. We also need to *feel*, in the big picture of the relationship, that our attachment needs are met. If unmet attachment needs didn't make us feel bad, they wouldn't matter. But they *do* make us feel bad. Unmet attachment needs cause emotional pain, which manifests in our bodies. We tighten up, our throats get tight, we feel heavy, our limbs get tingly, our chests tighten, our heart rate soars, we have a sense of being deflated. This happens even if we might not be consciously aware it's happening. Emotional pain makes us want to yell, tune out, cry, run, call names, hang up the phone, continue to fight, drink a glass of wine, go distract, and on and on.

Once you can articulate your attachment needs, you can begin to understand the awful feelings in your body that arise when they aren't met. Those feelings are literally your nervous system flagging danger. Only when you understand your needs can you communicate them to your partner instead of acting out or saying things that push your partner away and make it less likely your attachment needs will be met. Only when you understand your own needs can you possibly know how to recognize, empathize with, and respond to your partner's needs.

We will all, even the healthiest of couples, experience moments when one partner's attachment needs aren't met. These are called *attachment ruptures*, moments when one or both partners feel misunderstood, disrespected, invalidated, unsupported, unappreciated, or like their needs don't matter. Does this mean all couples have insecure attachments? Luckily, it does not.

I like to use the analogy of climate versus weather. Couples with a secure attachment live in an overall climate of met attachment needs. Most of the time, each partner feels understood, appreciated, validated, and so on. However, even the most secure of couples will experience bad weather. When it arises, in the form of an attachment rupture, it's an isolated event. The couple can make a repair and get back to their climate. On the other hand, when the overall climate of a relationship is such that partners are in a near-constant state of unmet needs, they have an insecure attachment.

This difference between relationship climate and weather can also help explain how you might start a relationship feeling close to your partner and then weeks, months, or years later find yourself feeling far from them. Early in relationships, when couples haven't had enough unrepaired conflict and attachment ruptures built up, their needs are mostly met (and if not, they maintain hope they can figure it out together). But as unrepaired ruptures build up, they begin to take a toll on the relationship, causing even more ruptures, and eventually even feelings of despair and hopelessness. Eventually the moments of bad weather become the new climate.

Let's talk briefly about the flip side of attachment needs: attachment fears. In general, needs and fears are two sides of the same coin. If you need something for survival, it stands to reason you'll experience some level of fear if there is a threat to that need. Think about food. You need it for survival. If your food supply is threatened, it won't take long for fear to kick in. The same is true for attachment. In order to feel safe in relationships, which is tied to our overall sense of safety, you need to have your attachment needs met and feel confident they will continue to be met in the future. When your attachment needs feel threatened in your relationship, you will experience some level of anxiety or fear. Humans will go to great lengths to avoid pain, so it only stands to reason that our attachment fears play an important role: to motivate us to repair our attachment bonds.

Now, for a moment of reassurance: having attachment needs doesn't make you "needy." Clients frequently ask me, "Isn't it codependent to expect my partner to meet all of these needs for me?" But the answer is no. Met attachment needs (and we're only talking about met *attachment* needs, not every single need a person has) are simply what's necessary to feel close to another person. They don't make *you* whole, but they do make a loving relationship whole. That doesn't mean your partner has to love you before you can love yourself. Our partners' love can *help* us love ourselves, or help us expand upon the love we already have for ourselves, but their love can't *make* us love ourselves—that needs to be happening independent of them.

What about codependency? A lot of people erroneously assume that having attachment needs means they're codependent. Codependency is a vague term with multiple definitions depending on who you ask. I define codependency as an overreliance on the feelings, thoughts, and behaviors of others to *feel okay within oneself*. Met attachment needs, on the other hand, are defined by the feelings, thoughts, and behaviors of your partner needed *for you to feel close to them* (and vice versa). If you're worried about your attachment needs being a sign of codependency, ask yourself: "Can I feel close to a person who doesn't respect me or appreciate me? Who doesn't understand me or doesn't even want to? Who can't show up for me when I need support? Who doesn't trust me? Who isn't trustworthy?" Most people will have a hard time feeling close to anyone, especially their partner, when they don't have an overall felt sense of these needs being met. And because the emotional stakes are highest in romantic partnerships, our attachment needs will be highest in romantic relationships.

The Attachment Behavioral System (ABS)

Do you *know* you're hungry or do you *feel* hungry? Your body feels hungry without you ever needing to think "I'm hungry." Most parents understand the importance of teaching their children to recognize their body's signs of hunger: a grumbling belly, irritability, weakness, and food cravings. Why? Because babies aren't born with the words for hunger; they have to be taught.

The same goes for attachment security. The only real difference is that most people aren't raised to have words for our attachment needs. Our bodies *feel* the need, but there's a disconnect between the felt sensation and the ability to communicate the felt sensation. But just like with hunger, sometimes we need conscious recognition before we can intentionally go about getting our need met. Most of us aren't raised hearing the words, "Do you feel invalidated right now? I'm so sorry. Help me better understand your feelings so I can help you with them." Or "Do you feel like your needs don't matter to me? Oh, that's hard. Let me reassure you that they do matter to me very much." Or "I can see you're really upset. Let's talk about what you might be needing right now."

Part of the brilliance of John Bowlby's work on attachment was that he put words to the body's attachment experience. He called it the attachment behavioral system (ABS). Similar to the body's sexual system, which promotes survival by urging us to procreate, and the body's appetite system, which promotes survival by motivating us to eat, the body's attachment behavioral system motivates us to feel emotional distress when attachment is threatened, or when we perceive it to be threatened, and to feel that discomfort until we return to safety.

I mentioned earlier that understanding attachment needs, and being able to put words to them, is critical. The same is true of recognizing and naming your emotional distress. How can you ever learn to self-regulate, or reach for help for, what you can't recognize and name, and instead what you only experience as shapeless "pain"? Imagine you step on a nail. Your body says, "Alert! Pain! It's in our toe! Pull out the nail!"

What if you just felt pain and that was it, with no idea what was really happening? You wouldn't know to pull out the nail, and you'd continue to suffer. The same is true with ABS: you need to be able to understand and name what's happening for you on an attachment level, so that you know what action you can take to soothe your attachment distress.

The Four Cs of Attachment

No two couples struggle with the same surface problems. Your neighbors can't agree on saving versus spending. You and your partner are on the same page about finances, but you often find yourselves feeling emotionally distant from each other. You have a great sex life, but your sister and her partner have struggled with their sex life since their young children were born; yet they work well as a team in other areas, like household chores. You can hear your boss and his partner constantly bickering through the office door. You know they love each other and are highly committed, but things get really ugly when they fight. Your coworker's partner just decided to become sober, but alcohol has been a big part of their recreational time together, and they're struggling to navigate the change.

Each of these couples is almost certainly struggling with communication problems, and those communication problems are both fueled by, and maintained by, underlying attachment issues. But, as the examples show, attachment issues show up differently for different couples. Generally, attachment issues can be sorted into four buckets: Comfort, Connection, Cooperation, and Conflict. I call these areas the four Cs—pretty much any problem a couple struggles with will fit into at least one of them. Some couples will have attachment problems in all four Cs, and problems in one area can certainly bleed over into others. As a result, it's not just important to know about the four Cs, but also to understand how they interact with each other. For example, researchers have found that couples' ability to be supportive to each other (comfort) when discussing personal problems *unrelated* to the relationship predicted less negative emotion during conflict *about the relationship* one year later. That means that couples can increase the quality of emotional comfort outside of conflict to help future conflict be handled in a healthy way.

Understanding the four Cs will help you figure out where to focus your healing and repair; it might also help you better assess the overall health of your relationship, and more clearly see strengths you may have been overlooking.

Comfort

How well do you and your partner comfort each other when one of you is experiencing emotional or physical pain? For example, when you have a tense argument with your brother about something important to you, can you count on your partner to provide you with comfort instead of leading with advice? When your partner feels humiliated by their boss, are you able to manage your own anxiety (which might be motivated by thoughts like "what if they lose their job?") so that you can show up with emotional presence? When your partner is sick, are you able to be sympathetic and supportive? Does it sometimes feel like your partner's overreaction to your distress makes things worse?

When partners have a hard time comforting each other, they each end up alone with their problems. One of the many benefits of a relationship is having support when we're upset. Emotional support might not fix the problem at hand, but it certainly helps us feel less alone and more regulated, which can help us face the problem with better clarity when the time comes—and, importantly, helps us feel close and supported by our partner, which bleeds over into other parts of the relationship.

Connection

Do you and your partner feel emotionally connected? Do you talk not just about the details of events in your life, but also the emotional meanings? I had a client who would come home and tell long stories about his day at work, usually about different versions of conflict with coworkers. His husband would try to stay engaged, but the interactions felt flat, and he would find himself drifting off. When my client noticed his husband drifting off, he felt rejected and alone. I worked with him on talking not just about the surface details of the story ("he said this, I said that") but also to share his vulnerability around the events. He learned to say things like "I felt really humiliated when he said that," which elicited his husband's empathy and helped him stay engaged. Not only did they feel more connected, but by putting words to his feelings, my client was able to better understand himself and start to work through his own role in his relationship with his coworkers. Win-win.

Having fun together is also a great way to connect emotionally. Joy is bonding. This is why any relationship expert will encourage couples to get away from time to time to just enjoy life and each other. In the past, marriages were business arrangements, not love arrangements. Now we marry for love and friendship, and part of that means taking responsibility for our love and friendship. The only way to do this is to make space for connection. Moments of connection help couples be resilient to future stressful situations.

For most couples, physical connection is also vital. This includes sexual touch and connection, affectionate touch from holding hands to cuddling, and everything in between. Some partners feel *most* emotionally connected via physical connection. Sex and other forms of touch help them feel valued, comforted, wanted, and vitalized in the relationship. It soothes their nervous systems. As a couples therapist, I don't want to see anyone *only* able to emotionally connect through sex, but that doesn't downplay the fact that, for many people, direct body connection is as emotional as it is physical. When couples are having problems physically, meaning at least one partner is feeling physically neglected, it can be devastating to other parts of the relationship.

Cooperation

Cooperation has to do with how you and your partner live your lives as a team, make decisions together, and support each other in daily life. This might include keeping the home clean, navigating in-laws and extended family, finances, parenting, or where to live. Given the unlimited number of decisions couples face around these areas, it makes sense that attachment issues show up here. Underlying most conflict or distress that comes up around cooperation are questions like: *Do my needs matter to you? Is your opinion valid to me, even if I don't agree? Are you willing to compromise some of my wants and preferences for the good of the relationship? Am I?*

Conflict

Conflict is about how couples manage when things aren't going well in the other Cs. What happens when you don't see eye to eye about parenting or household chores? How do you talk about it when you feel emotionally or sexually distanced? Are you able to talk about your problems from a place of emotional regulation—meaning you're in control of your emotions, rather than overwhelmed by them—while still staying emotionally engaged? Or do you get stuck in blame, shame, defensiveness, or disengagement? Do you talk through things in a way that is mutually respectful even when you don't agree, or do you find yourself in negative cycles that erode emotional safety and promote insecure attachment?

Every struggling couple will have problems with conflict. But once you learn how to conquer conflict—and you will!—you'll be able to talk about your problems in the other Cs in ways that are far more likely to help you find healthy solutions.

Attachment Styles

Attachment styles largely determine how each partner will go about managing their wants, needs, and fears in the different areas—the different Cs—of their relationship.

How you connected with your parent or caregiver at a young age informs how you show up in a relationship as an adult. In the late 1970s, Mary Ainsworth decided to put Bowlby's theory of attachment to the test and conducted the first study of attachment. From her research, she determined that while we all have the same basic attachment needs, different people have different attachment styles, or ways of *managing* their attachment needs, longings, and fears. These styles, set into motion during childhood, continue to adapt in response to romantic relationships during the teen and adult years. They affect how we love and feel loved, how we fight, how we repair, how we approach life, and how we reach for and respond to comfort and connection.

We're going to do a deep dive into each style, and help you identify your own, in the next chapter. So for now, here's a quick overview of each, since understanding these styles—and how they show up in your relationship—is why we've been digging into attachment theory in the first place.

Secure Attachment

If you're in a securely attached relationship, you probably feel confident that most of the time your partner will respond to you in times of distress. You're able to experience a felt sense of security even when you're separated from your partner, and when your partner reaches to you for comfort and connection, you're able to be responsive in a comforting manner. Securely attached individuals and their partners have a deep emotional bond, so while you experience conflict from time to time, you're able to find repair and resolution. You can set gentle, healthy boundaries when needed.

Insecure-Avoidant Attachment

If you have an *avoidant attachment*, you're probably somewhat disconnected from your own emotions and attachment needs, which makes it difficult to understand and respond to your partner's emotions and attachment needs. You long to know that your partner sees you as successful in the relationship—but you haven't learned all the ways you can make that longing a reality. Sometimes it might seem that no matter how hard you try, it will never be enough. If you have an avoidant attachment, you might handle relationship stress with disconnection, distraction, counterattacks, defensiveness, and even getting overly rational in order to protect yourself from painful feelings of failure or rejection (which probably isn't apparent on the surface). These strategies for self-protection can get in the way of your ability to respond to your partner's distress, and make it harder to form and sustain an emotional bond or engage in healthy conflict. While anyone can have an avoidant attachment, it skews male. Research shows that the majority of avoidant-attached individuals are men—in my clinical experience it breaks down to around 75/25 male/female.

Insecure-Anxious Attachment

If you have an anxious attachment, you probably have difficulty being emotionally or physically separated from your partner, and you likely feel a need to protest when your partner is unresponsive to your distress and bids for connection. You might feel ambivalent about your partner: deeply craving their love and attention, while also experiencing bitterness and sadness over their inability to meet your attachment needs. You might have difficulty seeing how your own relationship behaviors contribute to problems. If you are anxiously attached, you probably attempt to reach your partner with reactive blame, clinging, criticism, and accusations—all because you want to find connection and protect yourself from your fear of abandonment. When you *do* get the connection you're looking for, it's often hard to fully take it in because it can be so hard to trust it will last. While anyone can have an anxious attachment, it skews female. Research shows that the majority of anxiously attached individuals are women—in my clinical experience it breaks down to around 75/25 female/male.

Disorganized Attachment

Even those somewhat familiar with attachment theory may not know about the fourth type, disorganized attachment. The dark horse of attachment styles, disorganized attachment is less common and less easily understood. When compared to those in the secure, anxious, and avoidant categories of attachment, those with disorganized attachment experience more emotional turmoil, fewer coping strategies, and less ability to trust themselves and others. They go to greater (and often more unpredictable) behavioral lengths to manage their attachment distress, including "going blank" or even becoming abusive (although certainly not everyone with a disorganized attachment is abusive). Disorganized attachment is also highly associated with childhood trauma. Many people assume disorganized attachment is a mere combination of anxious and avoidant, but this is not the case. While it's true that someone with a disorganized attachment might be high in both anxiousness and avoidance, the whole is greater than the sum of its parts.

If you have a disorganized attachment you may experience intense emotions and unstable moods and engage in contradictory behaviors that swing between seeking closeness and disengagement. You might experience feelings that alternate between hostility and helplessness, and have extreme fears of rejection. If this is you, you've probably taken drastic measures to avoid pain and seek reconnection with a partner during separations. What do I mean? When someone with a mild anxious attachment experiences an abandonment fear, they might text their partner several times until they get a response. When their partner finally responds, they feel a mixture of relief and anger, but they can more or less cope without becoming dysregulated and/or destructive. If you have a disorganized attachment, this might be even more intense—you might call, text, drive to your partner's work, and maybe cause a scene. On the other hand, you might experience moments, or even stretches of time, of being able to turn off your feelings or go numb.

No matter what attachment style you fall into (and you'll have a better sense of that in the next chapter), it's important to know that you're not alone. You are not broken if you have an insecure attachment—in fact, it's incredibly common. It doesn't mean you necessarily had a bad childhood or that your parents didn't love you or that you won't be able to experience healthy, fulfilling, and loving relationships. You absolutely can, and that's why we're here. In my experience, it's very hard for couples to find a secure attachment without any effort or awareness of the relationship tools we'll discuss in this book. The reason my social media account grew as it did is that hundreds of thousands of people with insecure attachments could see themselves in these definitions and wanted to work on themselves and their relationships. The reason we dig into attachment styles isn't to slap a label on you—it's to create a deep understanding that will ultimately help you get healthier and move toward the connected partnership you know is possible. Once you identify your own style, you can use that knowledge to guide you to improve, and secure, your connection.

CHAPTER 3

Identifying Your Attachment Style

Let's understand *you*: by identifying your own attachment style, you can begin to understand why you show up in relationships the way you do, which in turn will help you make the changes necessary to communicate better, one interaction at a time, and find the secure relationship you're looking for.

While understanding is necessary for change, remember that seeing clearly can be really uncomfortable. As you witness your own patterns emerge, it can bring up a lot of old feelings that you've kept buried for a long time. This is totally normal. As you read through this chapter, please know that this is not the time to be hard on yourself. Instead, it's the time for compassion for yourself and your loved ones. We all come by our attachment styles honestly. No one is born with an attachment style; they are created in the context of relationships. Just like you learned where the toothpaste was in the bathroom (hopefully), you learned how to respond emotionally to the adults in your life, and those became patterns that are still with you as an adult. But today you can choose to understand and move beyond these protective stances—they may have helped you then, but they are likely hurting you (and your partner) now. So your attachment style, whatever it is, is not a value judgment. We investigate our attachment styles not to see how "good" we are at relationships, but because they are at the root of much of our relationship conflict. Understanding where you fall can help you to begin to grow and heal.

Finally, your unique experience with your partner matters more than a label. Although attachment labels will help you get greater insight into yourself and your relationship experiences, you don't need to fit perfectly into an attachment category to improve your relationship. And even if you do fit perfectly into one category, remember that no two insecure attachments are alike. Attachment styles exist on a spectrum. Someone with an avoidant attachment can be more avoidant than another person with an avoidant attachment. Same with anxious attachment. One person might have an anxious attachment that is closer to the disorganized end of the spectrum, while another person's anxious attachment is closer to the secure end. But both people need to move in the same direction by doing the same work. This is key. Attachment styles are not set in stone; an individual can move from any point on the spectrum toward a secure attachment. Also, the premise of *Secure Love* rests on the idea that you need not have grown up with a secure attachment to experience one now. When adults work on themselves to develop the skills and traits of those who had secure childhoods, it's called an *earned secure attachment*.

Consider the following chart to help you visually understand the progression along the spectrum from the most extreme version of insecure attachment (disorganized) to secure attachment.

Attachment Style Spectrum

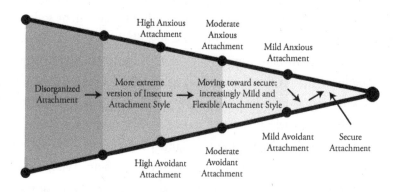

Notice how the arrows begin to shift as the spectrum moves into secure. This is because when a partner's attachment style begins to shift into secure, their behaviors often become more flexible. As an individual becomes more secure, they get better at accessing more parts of themselves. The avoidant partner can access their feelings and become more emotionally engaged. At first, their expression might not be entirely finessed, but with practice they get there. The anxious partner, on the other hand, becomes less overwhelmed and reactive and might start to disengage more than they used to. Disorganized partners develop better coping mechanisms in the face of relationship stress and build trust. Gradually both partners, as they continue to work, find balance.

The icing on the cake is that when partners find security with each other, they begin to see improvement in relationships outside of their romantic partnership—with children, extended family, coworkers, and friends. Why? For one, we all carry attachment "blueprints" within us. Even in casual relationships that don't have the level of attachment bond necessary for a true attachment style to come alive (or don't *yet*, such as in early dating), those attachment blueprints will impact our interactions. You might not have an attachment bond with your employer, but he might remind you of your controlling mother, and so you might react to him in a similar manner. Secure attachment is about learning to truly connect, so it only makes sense that when you learn how to connect with your partner, you'll learn how to connect with the other people in your life (in ways that are appropriate to the depth and role of the relationship).

Attachment in Childhood

Your attachment style was established when you were just a child. Attachment styles can shift throughout adulthood, but most people retain the style they developed during childhood. As you read about each style, you might recognize your own childhood in the descriptions—this can help you identify your attachment style and understand *why* you might feel the way you do. It might hit a nerve! Reliving childhood wounds can be sensitive work, so as you read, I want you to have empathy for the child you once were. I also want you to remember, again, that having an insecure attachment style doesn't mean you were raised with unloving or abusive parents. Most of you with insecure attachment styles were raised by parents who loved you and did the best they could. You may have had an idyllic childhood on paper, and that might be how you remember it. An insecure attachment simply means that your parents weren't able to provide you with the emotional support skills you needed enough of the time. They couldn't give you what they didn't have. This work isn't about casting blame; it's about understanding how your past is impacting your present, in the service of finding solutions.

Once you understand how or why your childhood informed your attachment, we'll discuss how these styles are manifesting in your adult relationships, because childhood wounds almost always carry over into our adult experiences.

Let's start by looking at the three attachment styles that are most likely to cause the relationship problems discussed in this book, and conclude with a look at the ultimate goal for all of us: secure attachment. (If you're interested in learning more about your childhood experiences with attachment, or how your attachment style can show up in your relationship, I've included charts for each attachment style in the appendix.)

Anxious Attachment

The Anxious-Attached Child

My former client Nora remembers fighting with her younger sister a lot, like all kids do, but she also remembers always having to take the blame. Her parents didn't allow her to talk through her anger, or to be heard for how unfairly she felt she was treated and get comfort for how hard these feelings were for her. She didn't receive help to work out her feelings or learn healthy boundaries—instead she was simply told to stop misbehaving and stop picking on her sister. Nora was on her own trying to figure out how to manage her emotions, and because she was ignored when she felt bad, she deduced that "if I have this 'bad' experience like anger, I'm flawed." From there came a logical (if usually subconscious) question: "If my feelings make me flawed and bad, am I even lovable like other kids are lovable?"

Sometimes Nora's parents were able to be there for her, and this is the crux of anxious attachment: they get enough responsiveness to know what it feels like, but not enough to trust it will last. For anxiously attached children like Nora, relationship anxiety is a result of not consistently getting attachment needs met. (Anyone with any attachment style can have anxiety in other areas of life, but anxious attachment is specifically about *relationship* anxiety.) Think of the term *food insecurity*: people with food insecurity aren't starving, but they never really know if they will be in the future. If you were an anxiously attached child, you got enough of the emotional "food" to know it existed, but not enough to relax into the knowledge that it would be there when you were hurting inside and when you just needed to be seen and connect. Instead of your emotional energy being used for your own healthy development, you were busy wondering, "Will you be there for me now? What about now? Are you going to be there for me next time? What about the time after that?" Sounds exhausting, doesn't it?

Fighting for reassurance and validation were Nora's ways of feeling lovable and getting reassurance that her needs mattered. All children are driven to feel lovable. Without even realizing it, they will put everything else to the side to get this need met. If you had to fight to get your emotions validated, you probably found yourself wondering, although maybe not consciously, what it meant about you that you couldn't rely on support and what it meant about those you depended on, that they couldn't always show up for you when you needed them. Could *anyone* be trusted to be consistently there for you? All of this leads to the core fear of the anxiously attached child: a fear of emotional or physical abandonment. The word *abandonment* might sound dramatic, but when we consider that the attachment system exists to ensure our very survival, it's not inaccurate.

Anxious children are also ambivalent about their feelings. On one hand, they don't trust that their feelings are valid or acceptable, but on the other hand, they're still driven to express them. This gets them caught in a cycle of big expressions, being responded to negatively, and then feeling badly about themselves for failing to hold back. This tension between wanting to be seen but also believing they'll be rejected if they try contributes to enormous anxiety.

If you have an anxious attachment, your feelings and perspectives likely weren't consistently validated. In fact, maybe they weren't *ever* validated. Do you remember being told as a child that your feelings made sense and were reasonable, even in times when the way you behaved in response to your feelings wasn't appropriate? If the answer is no, you're not alone. Some of the anxious clients I treat remember getting emotional validation here and there, but many don't remember any at all.

You might be wondering why your parents couldn't consistently be there for you in the way you needed. Maybe your parents were under high levels of stress, lacked parenting skills, had to work long hours to keep food on the table, were dealing with chronic physical or mental illness, had a lack of support for other children or one with special needs, struggled with unresolved childhood traumas or wounds, had to provide care to elderly or sick parents or a spouse, or more. Often they don't know how to meet their own emotional needs so doing so for another person, even a child, is challenging.

So how *did* you get your needs met? If you were an anxiously attached child, you probably had to learn to make yourself as big and noticeable as possible to have your feelings responded to. You may have acted out with tantrums and behaviors that demanded attention, or you may have tested your parents' availability to ensure they'd be there in the future. In a similar vein, some anxiously attached children will become people-pleasers in their quest for reassurance. If you can relate, you drew your value and your sense of safety by keeping those around you happy. Both of these strategies are designed to help the anxious child feel seen, valued, and responded to positively.

Anxious children often have mixed feelings toward their caregivers. They crave love and care and feel driven to seek it out; but they're also resentful about all the times they felt dropped. This tension can feel unbearable and anxiety-provoking . . . wanting to reach in a way that will be successful, but also wanting their hurt to be known.

The Anxious-Attached Adult

I often say that while the hardest thing about working with avoidant partners is getting them through the door, the hardest thing about working with anxious partners is getting them to see their part of the problem. Most of the anxious-attached partners I treat show up to couples therapy because they're certain their partner is the problem, and they need me to fix them. Their search for love tends to be out of balance: a self-focused hunger for love at the expense of an authentic desire to be a sensitive and responsive partner. When we view these individuals through the attachment lens, it makes sense: anxious partners were wired during childhood to be "other-focused." Given the way attachment patterns in their lives have played out, they have good reason to feel let down by others. But that doesn't mean they don't play an equal part in their relationship struggles, a truth they often can't see because of how great their pain is.

Am I saying that partners with anxious attachments are all unreasonable and blind to their own faults? Not at all. Many anxious-attached partners can recognize their relationship faults. They often work on themselves incessantly. They go to personal therapy, they read books, they try their best to follow all the relationship advice they can get their hands on. And when they look up from all their self-work and see their partner doing nothing—no therapy, no relationship books, what they perceive as no attempt at self-growth—they come to the understandable and painful conclusion that "I care; they don't." We'll talk later about why that's usually not the case, but if you have an anxious attachment, the chances are high you can relate.

Also consider that what the anxious partner considers relationship work isn't always effective work. I call this "watering the plant with gasoline." For example, an anxious partner gets a relationship book and learns about healthier communication. They read that partners should share authentically with each other. So when their partner would rather, say, watch football on a Sunday than clean the garage, they "authentically" say "you aren't responding to my needs and that makes me sad." They are "working on the relationship," yes, but are they considering their partner's needs, too? If not, they aren't *really* watering the plant.

Let's go back to this term *other-focused*. If you have an anxious attachment, too much of your sense of self is put into the hands of others—in this case, your partner. You give your partner's experience and behavior significant control over your experience in the world. Say you're out with friends and you text your partner and don't hear back. The meaning you make is they aren't thinking about you. Your anxiety elevates to a level that takes away your presence with your friends. Later, instead of taking some time to feel your feelings about your partner's actions and then sharing your fears with them, maybe asking about their experience and for reassurance, and making a plan for next time, you demand they text you back within a certain time frame because "that's what people who care about their partners do." You're not *trying* to be controlling—only in the rarest of circumstances do I think any partner is coming from a place of consciously wanting to control their partner's every move—but in your mind, you need for them to know how much this hurts so they'll change and you'll feel safe. This is considered an "other-focused" approach because you've led with "what you need to do differently so I can feel okay," instead of going inward and saying, "Hmmm . . . what's going on with *me* right now? What is this all about? What am I needing from myself right now? What am I needing from my partner?" and then "What does my partner need from me?"

When your security is reliant on the words and behaviors of your partner to the degree it is with anxious-attached partners, there *will* be anxiety. Why? Because nobody ultimately has control over their partners. To think otherwise is to give away one's sense of power. Powerlessness creates anxiety.

Remember, none of this makes you bad, broken, or a lost cause. You are whole. Your attachment experiences as a child didn't provide you with the space you needed to develop a healthy, interdependent sense of self. When you experienced a normal feeling like jealousy, maybe you were told that you were "too sensitive" or bad for experiencing an "unacceptable" feeling. In moments when you were needy or angry, you got the message "these feelings are too much, we don't have time for this." Your sense of self manifested as "you define me; your experience defines mine." You became less concerned with "I feel lonely; I feel angry; I feel proud," and more in touch with "*you think* I shouldn't be lonely, *you think* my anger is shameful, *you decide* what I should be proud of," and "if you think I'm too much for having these feelings, I must be too much." Essentially you learned to become disconnected from your own experiences. Your ambivalent mindset—needing others to define whether you are "good" or "bad," "lovable" or "unlovable," in any given moment, but then feeling angry at them for (what you perceive as) having so much power—fuels your relationship expectations and interactions. It also fuels fear-based communication, and you get stuck expending an exhausting amount of energy ensuring your partner will show up in the way that you think will make you feel the least anxious, but in ways that in fact harm the connection you so desperately crave, leaving you feeling even *more* anxious.

In my practice, I see many consistencies among the anxious partners I treat. If you have an anxious attachment, you'll probably relate to any or all of the following: being highly sensitive to any real or perceived threat to relationship safety, or to invalidation; filtering for the negative; having difficulty self-regulating; and feeling a constant need for reassurance at the expense of two-way connection.

"Filtering for the negative" is particularly common among those with anxious attachments. Your sensitivity to anything that might feel threatening to your relationship safety leaves you prone to seeing your relationship through a negative lens, because you have a hard time trusting that emotional support will be consistently available. You probably believe that if you can notice what's wrong now, you can fix it before it's too late. As a result, your partner might do ten things in a given day to show love and care, but due to your need to filter for the negative, a response from them that might be even a little off (intentionally or not) can cause fear to rise up inside you, causing you to go to the extreme: "see, proof that they don't really love me." Quickly, your fear can shift into frustration or anger, and these feelings are going to heavily inform the way you communicate. It's going to make the difference between vulnerable and protective, effective and ineffective.

Your anxious attachment is also going to leave you struggling to feel lovable and constantly pulling for reassurance that your partner will show up for you when you really need them. Your difficulty feeling the love that *does* come your way leaves you feeling chronically dissatisfied with the amount and quality of care you receive from your partner. Those with an anxious attachment often have difficulty trusting that anything good that comes their way will stick around, which may lead you to subconsciously push away the very closeness you pull for. You may end up in long and wordy discussions about relationship problems, peppering your partner with questions (asking the same questions repeatedly, yet not believing the answers), and testing behaviors, which are usually set up subconsciously, in your quest to feel reassured (the idea being "if you can just pass this one last test, then I can finally feel safe").

As an anxious partner, you have a desperate need for love and reassurance, and it can be difficult for you to self-regulate the pain of your unsatisfied longing. Without a source of relief, you might show intense displays of emotion, especially if you're on the more distressed end of the anxious spectrum, which can sometimes overwhelm both you and your partner. You almost certainly have difficulty ending or taking breaks from arguments because fighting often feels better than being alone with your emotional pain.

Just like anxious children, anxious partners are especially sensitive to invalidation, so if your partner responds to you with something along the lines of "you're overreacting," it's going to feel like a punch in the stomach. Nobody wants to hear they're overreacting when they want to be heard, but for you it's a double whammy: the invalidation in the present feels awful *and* it touches a very old, very sensitive wound. You might notice feelings of invalidation as a common entry point into a negative cycle.

If you recognize yourself in this description, don't be hard on yourself. All of what you're doing is for good reason—you're hoping beyond hope that if you can just get it right, if you can just convince your partner to hear you, you'll find the closeness and feelings of safety you may have been yearning for for a lifetime, and you just haven't yet learned another way to get them.

It's also important to not take what I'm describing out of the context of your specific relationship. The majority of partners with an insecure attachment have partners who also have an insecure attachment—together their behaviors reinforce each other's insecurity, and sometimes even worsen it. If you're reading this and thinking, "Of course

I'm going to demand to be heard, otherwise my partner won't pay attention to me," let me say this: I believe you. I believe that your partner does and says plenty of things that leave you feeling invalidated, frustrated, and alone. Attachment styles in relationships don't exist in a vacuum. My intention isn't to shame or invalidate your behavior but rather to shine a light on it so we can make sense of it, and ultimately provide you with a better option, one that will increase the odds you'll be heard without having to exhaust yourself.

Do I Have an Anxious Attachment?

1. In your romantic relationship, do you fear abandonment, either all the time *or* mostly in moments when your attachment safety feels threatened?
2. Do you crave more together time and closeness than your partner seems to?
3. Are you more likely to bring up relationship concerns than your partner?
4. Do you think if your partner would just get it right (in the way you define "right") you wouldn't *have* to protest, get emotionally big, critical, and/or overly demanding?
5. Are you especially triggered when you don't feel emotionally validated or emotionally supported?
6. Do you feel the urge to have things resolved right then and there?
7. Do you find yourself wanting to continue arguments until you find the sense of safety you're looking for?
8. Do you frequently fall into any of the following patterns during arguments: often being the one bringing up concerns (especially pertaining to the relationship), protesting, criticizing, feeling emotionally escalated, crying or feeling rage, seething (maybe with fantasies of leaving them), wanting to make up?

Avoidant Attachment

The Avoidant-Attached Child

My client Jake tells me his parents did an excellent job of caring for his physical, social, and educational needs. He always had the clothes he needed, a stable environment, help with his homework, and he remembers feeling loved. It isn't until we start to dig into why adult Jake is struggling so much in his relationship that he can see a clearer picture. Yes, Jake was well taken care of when it came to his basic needs, which was no small thing, but since he didn't get emotional support from his parents, he tried to push away his need for that support. If Jake felt sad, for example, he would find ways to make the sadness "go away" (usually by pushing it out of awareness and finding ways to distract himself) so he didn't have to deal with two layers of distress: the sadness *and* the painful reality that nobody was around to help him. Eventually Jake, like all avoidant children, told himself (albeit subconsciously) that his bad feelings didn't matter so he might as well just get over them. Jake learned to *deactivate* his attachment needs.

Jake's memory of his childhood is common. Children with avoidant attachment often don't consciously experience stressful childhoods. The avoidant partners I treat often describe their childhoods as normal, sometimes even "perfect." They don't really understand why other people complain so much about their parents. "Sure," they say, "my parents were hard on me at times, but I deserved it." Many avoidant partners don't remember feeling anxious or suffering neglect or abuse. It's not uncommon to learn as the therapy progresses that some of this actually *did* go on. Long-term memories are only stored in the brain when there's a strong emotional component, so children who can push their emotions out of awareness might have fewer *conscious* memories of stressful events. It also stands to reason they don't experience their childhoods as emotionally deprived because they didn't know what they were missing.

Some children learn to become avoidant because at least one parent is emotionally intrusive. In those instances, children have little privacy or are forced or coerced into sharing thoughts and feelings they don't want to share. Emotionally intrusive caregivers don't know how to connect, otherwise they wouldn't need to be intrusive, so kids with this type of parenting end up feeling icky about the topic of "talking about feelings" *and* left without a source of emotional comfort and connection. Another version of this is when children do share what they're feeling and their feelings cause their parents to get anxious, frantic, or overwhelmed. Remember, children need to feel safe, and they don't feel safe if they believe the people they rely on for care aren't themselves safe.

If you were an avoidant-attached child, you had to learn early in life to give up on expressing your emotional needs or distress, and push your attachment longings and emotional needs out of conscious awareness. You might even be reading this right now saying, "I can't relate to this. I never stuffed down my feelings . . . I just never had them." Without access to your feelings, your brain learned to default to logic, reason, and a problem-solving approach to life that comes at the expense of a rich emotional self (along with difficulty connecting with the emotional selves of others). You became emotionally disengaged.

As with the other insecure attachment styles, if you are avoidantly attached, anger wasn't managed well in your family. Maybe you saw family members get big, scary, or off-putting when they were mad, and you came to believe that *anger the emotion* is the same as escalated, *angry behaviors*. Maybe only certain family members showed anger and others pretended it didn't exist and you said to yourself, "I don't want to be the angry one." Maybe you never saw anger expressed at all. Maybe what looked like stability was really a power imbalance, where one parent makes most of the decisions, and the other one goes along with it to avoid conflict. Whatever your experience with anger, one thing you didn't see is two people get mad at each other, work through it, and repair, and you learned to view anger, and the expression of anger, as a shameful experience. While anxious-attached children also feel shame around their anger, they continue to show it. Why? Because for them it's better to fight to be responded to than to be ignored. Avoidant children, on the other hand, would rather avoid the shame they associate with anger by keeping it in.

People often ask me if it's "better" to have an avoidant attachment, so you don't have to feel the pain. I understand the logic. But the truth is that while children with avoidant attachments might not *directly* feel their attachment-related pain, they experience it in other ways, even if it only shows up as a sense of emptiness. Stuffing feelings out of awareness doesn't mean they go away. In fact, when the original study that labeled attachment styles was conducted on children experiencing attachment stress, it was the avoidant-attached children who showed the *least* external signs of stress, but who also carried the *most* signs of stress in their bodies, like elevated blood pressure and heart rate. If you grew up with an avoidant attachment, you had much more going on inside you than you realized then, and probably more than you realize now.

Since avoidantly attached children lack real emotional connection, they are deprived of the assurance that their innermost emotional self is acceptable just as it is. As a result, they work overtime for approval in other areas and are often high achievers. Though in some cases, these children feel as if they're incapable of finding outside approval, develop a fear of failure, and become underachievers. When avoidant children have trouble achieving in the ways that their parents or caregivers value, they might escape their feelings of failure with things like food, hobbies, video games, or even substance abuse.

The Avoidant-Attached Adult

Pete showed up to couples therapy the way many of the avoidant-attached partners I treat do: skeptical. Skeptical of me, skeptical of therapy, and skeptical of the idea that anything can ever be changed by "talking about feelings." His skepticism made sense, given that partners with avoidant attachment approach relationship problems in the same way they approach their non-relationship life: with an overemphasis on logic and reason and an underemphasis on anything emotional. This approach can often result in career success, and it can help avoidant-attached partners get by in relationships to some degree. Oftentimes their ability to suppress emotions can defuse situations that would otherwise escalate. But there is a cost. In Pete's mind, the solution to his relationship problems was simple: his partner, Freya, needed to *stop* being so emotional. If only she could see reason, they wouldn't fight so much. Pete told me, "I do everything I can to be a good partner. I'm loyal and a hard worker. I see these men at work who are all cheating on their wives. I'd never do that to Freya. But she always finds something to complain about and there's only so much that I can 'talk about talking.'" (This was how Pete described Freya's need to talk about the communication problems in their relationship.)

Was Pete stubborn and resistant to change? No, Pete was not broken relationship goods. In fact, he ended up being very successful in therapy. Together we learned that Pete *needed* to minimize Freya's emotional needs because that's how he had made it through life. Detaching from his own emotions that might threaten or overwhelm him, especially during stressful moments, was how Pete felt safe in the world, and he did this without even being consciously aware of it. Freya was initially attracted to Pete's stability and success, which she hadn't experienced much of in her upbringing. In Pete's subconscious mind, if he were to switch gears and start playing a new game he didn't know the rules to, he wouldn't be able to keep up and he'd end up failing himself and Freya. By clinging to the belief that Freya needed to stop being so emotional, Pete was saying, "I don't understand the emotional part of myself and I don't understand how to help Freya with hers, so instead of facing the limitations I'm afraid to see in myself, it's easier to tell myself that Freya's feelings are the problem." Pete wanted a good relationship just as much as Freya did; he just had a very different way of trying to get there.

Another reason those with avoidant attachments can be averse to going to therapy is their belief that they're *supposed* to figure everything out on their own and have all the answers, especially when it comes to relationships, which in their minds should be so easy.

When problems arise, they blame themselves for not getting it right, and nothing says "not getting it right" in a relationship like a fight. If you can relate to wanting to avoid conflict because of the threat it poses to the relationship or to your view of yourself, or because you find it an exhausting waste of time, you might deflect your partner's relationship concerns by saying things like "I don't want to talk about it right now, I just got home." If things get hot anyway, you might tell your partner they're overreacting or getting their facts mixed up. You might get overly defensive, try to stay calm and rational, or you might just say what they want to hear to turn down the heat as quickly as possible.

The "stereotypical" avoidant partner is reserved, shut down, conflict-averse, and connection-averse, but many of you reading this might not be able to relate to that picture. In my experience with real couples, it's not always so cut and dried. Your avoidant attachment might hide behind behaviors that seek connection and resolution in some areas of the relationship (such as pursuing sex), behind romantic words and gestures (especially early in the relationship before negative cycles have set in), behind boisterous personality types, and behind escalated behaviors during conflict.

So what makes an avoidant an avoidant? In my practice I see three commonalities among those with avoidant attachment: a fear of failing, a disconnection from feelings (emotional disengagement), and a fear of being engulfed.

If you fail in your relationship, you'll have to deal with the intense shame of letting yourself down because you've let down your partner, or you've let down others who you fear may judge you for not being able to make it work. Sometimes this fear of failure shows up in what you *do*—deflect or defend so you don't have to be the bad guy—or in what you *don't do*—shutting down, finding ways to distract yourself, or telling your partner what they want to hear, at the expense of being authentic, to keep things from getting worse. While your anxious partner is trying to close the distance in the relationship so they don't feel alone, you try to keep things from getting worse so you don't have to feel the shame of failure.

Avoidant partners often get accused of not wanting emotional connection. I couldn't disagree more. What I've learned to be true is that those with avoidant attachments have simply lost contact with their feelings and with their emotional needs, including the need for emotional closeness. On top of this, they've never had good experiences with connection or intimacy. They've learned to associate them with weakness and dependency, or with expectations they can't possibly live up to, and of course they don't want to feel weak, dependent, and like a failure. My job as a therapist isn't to help avoidant partners start wanting intimacy and connection; my job is to help them clear up their misconceptions of intimacy and uncover the blocks to their desire for connection that already exists. It's not that avoidant partners don't want to connect, *it's that they don't know what it means, and even if they did, they don't know how.*

Anger is probably a particularly complicated emotion for you if you have an avoidant attachment. Many of the clients I treat with avoidant attachment can't admit they're mad, either because they can't recognize their own anger or because they've been conditioned to think anger is a shameful or dangerous emotion. They have bad moods they can't see, but which everyone around them can feel. If you have an avoidant attachment, you might act out anger by shutting down, using mean humor, being passive-aggressive, retreating, or becoming overly frustrated by little things often unrelated to the relationship (a broken faucet, for example, might cause an emotional outburst).

Some of you with avoidant attachments might be thinking, "But I don't always shut down; sometimes I fight." It's not uncommon for avoidant partners to get escalated during conflict, especially when your other strategies to avoid conflict fall flat and you get pushed to your edge. If this is you, you might recognize the following pattern: Your partner makes a complaint about wanting more time together. First you defend yourself and say you spend plenty of time together and list out all the times you've spent together in the last week. That doesn't convince them, so you accuse your partner of never being satisfied. That doesn't work so you stop talking altogether and say something vague like "fine, if you want to spend more time together, we'll spend more time together." Your partner doesn't buy it and the invalidation leaves them angry and coming at you hot and with tears. You feel enraged that what was a perfectly fine afternoon is now a fight and so finally return fire with fire. Afterward, you beat yourself up for letting yourself get mad and vow to "never do that again." Unfortunately, since you haven't yet learned another way, the pattern repeats itself.

If you're avoidant attached, you might find your partner's attempts at emotional reaches stifling and uncomfortable and want to push them away. Somewhere deep inside you, you long for the felt experience of closeness, but when you get it, even if it feels good, a part of you associates it with weakness and dependency, which is, for lack of a better term, a buzzkill. You might associate closeness with a complete loss of self. Instead of facing your own fears, it can be easier to assume that your partner's needs are the problem. You might ask yourself, *why do they have to be so needy?* When you step back, you know this behavior leaves your partner feeling confused and alone, but in the moment your fears take over.

My client Gigi was raised by a single mother who was repeatedly let down by the men in her life. Gigi remembers her mother insisting how important it was for her to grow up to be a strong woman who didn't become reliant on men. This was her mother's way of protecting Gigi from her own painful experiences and Gigi got the message that even healthy emotional *interdependence* with a partner would violate the sense of independence that kept her safe.

When Gigi fell in love with Colin, they ran into problems when Colin had reasonable expectations of emotional connectedness between the two of them. Even on their wedding day, Gigi was reluctant to hold hands with Colin in front of others out of fear that she might be seen as a weak, dependent woman. When Colin talked about feelings or asked Gigi for emotional support, she became annoyed and accused him of being too needy. Naturally this left Colin feeling invalidated and alone and their relationship suffered.

Was Gigi broken and biologically wired to push away closeness? No, she came by her fears honestly, just like you did. And when Gigi was better able to understand herself, connect with her inner world, and use what she found to cultivate true connections, her relationship with Colin (who had his own work to do too) was able to find secure attachment.

Do I Have an Avoidant Attachment?

1. In your romantic relationship, do you fear being seen as a failure by your partner (or a failure at the relationship) more than you fear being emotionally or physically abandoned?
2. Does your partner seem to need more together time and closeness than you?
3. Does too much closeness sometimes feel uncomfortable?
4. Do you tend to avoid bringing up relationship concerns because you either don't have them, or you don't want to talk about them, or you fear it will trigger your partner if you bring them up?
5. Do you often feel unappreciated or as if you're never getting it right for your partner?
6. Do you hold in your relationship anger and try to make the best of things, only to lose your temper later, or in areas unrelated to the relationship?
7. Do you find yourself wanting to be the first to shut down arguments?
8. Do you frequently fall into any of the following patterns during arguments: defending, counter-blaming, appeasing, shutting down?

Disorganized Attachment

The Disorganized-Attached Child

Children in the anxious, avoidant, and secure attachment categories have consistent strategies to get their needs met. Anxious children cry for attention with protest, people-pleasing, or anything that might help them feel seen, valid, and lovable; avoidant children evade disappointment by disconnecting from their needs, and secure children ask and receive (more on this shortly). Due to the consistency of these strategies, the original attachment researchers considered these three groups to be "organized." But there's a fourth category of children who don't fit into any of these descriptions. These children are generally overwhelmed with their inner experiences and have enormous inner conflict. When triggered, their behaviors lack predictability, and as such, researchers have labeled them "disorganized."

If you were a disorganized-attached child, you never felt completely safe. You might relate to feelings of fear and mistrust of your parents or caregivers. The people you needed most may have also been a source of danger. Maybe they were overly punitive, outright abusive, or extremely neglectful. Maybe this wasn't the case *all* the time, but enough of the time to have an impact. If so, it put you in a position of living with a painful inner conflict: an intense, biological drive for emotional comfort and safety, but with no hope of finding it. This is called approach/fear distress: "I need to approach, but I'm too afraid," and the deep sense of despair that accompanies such conflict.

All this inner turmoil would have left you in a state in which your nervous system was activated a lot of the time. You had significantly more difficulty managing intense emotions, which then fueled intense, exaggerated, and often unpredictable behaviors. Your nervous system may have had to learn to dissociate (a sense of leaving your own body) to survive traumatic experiences. Or you may have learned to stuff your emotions so far out of awareness that they practically ceased to exist.

While a disorganized attachment is often associated with trauma and abuse, this isn't always the case. Research has shown that the one thing parents of those with disorganized attachment are found to have in common is unresolved trauma and unresolved grief from their own pasts.

The Disorganized-Attached Adult

If you have a disorganized attachment, your childhood was highly dysfunctional (even if it wasn't obvious on the surface or to outsiders), leaving you with few inner resources to thrive in relationships. You're going to experience higher amounts of attachment distress, your distress will be triggered more easily, and your behaviors to manage all the relationship pain you carry around will be, understandably, more extreme. As I mentioned in the previous chapter, many people erroneously believe disorganized attachment is a mere combination of anxious and avoidant, but this is not the case. While it's true that someone with a disorganized attachment might be high in both anxiousness and avoidance, the whole is greater than the sum of its parts.

Most people with disorganized attachment will relate to the experience of an anxious attachment but with more intensity and less predictability. According to research, this type of disorganized attachment is called disorganized-oscillating.

Those with disorganized-oscillating and anxious attachment styles share a fear of abandonment and rejection, the need to keep partners physically close, frequent dissatisfaction in relationships, and behaviors such as protests and making demands. At the same time, you might find that soon after you pull your partner in, you have the urge to push them away, as if to say, "I need you, but I know you're going to abandon me so I'm going to abandon you before you abandon me. But wait, I need you. Come back." If you find that your current or past relationships are especially tumultuous—fights that might escalate to extreme verbal abuse or violence, impulsive breakups and getting back together, and what we might call high drama—disorganized attachment might be at play.

To say that having a disorganized attachment is a painful way to live is an understatement. If you can relate, your struggle doesn't come from nowhere and you're not broken. You were raised in an environment that left you unable to trust others or yourself. Being able to trust that people exist who can be there for you is required for relationship safety, and safety is required for closeness. Not being able to trust leaves you feeling disconnected and alone, even when you're not physically alone. For many, an ongoing experience of true intimacy and relationship safety might seem like a foreign concept. When the pain is most unbearable, you might take desperate measures to feel better: "text-bombing" your partner, demanding that they engage with you, or overreacting when you think they've been disloyal in any way. Or you might go to the opposite extreme and suddenly "drop" a partner out of the blue, providing them with little or no explanation (especially early into a relationship). The level of escalation can vary from individual to individual, but there is always a flavor of being lost in powerful emotions. And for good reason—in these states of high dysregulation, your alarmed nervous system is driving the car, not the real you.

Those with a disorganized-oscillating attachment will likely relate to going back and forth between moments of intensity and moments of shutting down entirely. This is because if the experience of disorganized attachment is punctuated by anything, it's unpredictability. You have unpredictable thoughts, behaviors, and feelings. What triggers you one day might not bother you the next. You might notice mood swings, even multiple swings throughout the day (not the same as bipolar disorder, where swings are spread over several days or weeks). You might have fits of rage followed by feelings of helpless vulnerability and then back to rage.

I'm not saying this is your experience in the whole of your life. In certain situations where you feel safe and less likely to be triggered, you might feel okay. Some people with a disorganized attachment in their relationships function very well at work or in friendships. But when you *do* feel unsafe and triggered, you feel it so powerfully that sometimes staying in control during the pain feels like an insurmountable challenge. You have a hard time with healthy boundaries: setting and maintaining your own, as well as respecting those of others. You might relate to experiencing others' boundaries as punitive, and be afraid that if you set your own, you'll get abandoned. If you have disorganized attachment and have experienced trauma, which very often go together, you might disassociate (a feeling of leaving one's body) when things get especially intense. It can be easy to confuse dissociation with the typically avoidant behavior of retreating or shutting down, but dissociation is a trauma response, not an avoidant one.

While less common, especially among those seeking relationship help, there's a second subcategory of disorganized attachment that was observed by researchers who conducted the original studies of disorganized attachment. Marked not by high intensity of emotion but by the extreme opposite, the "disorganized-impoverished" category is defined by an absence of emotional expression, or flatness, and is considered to be on the far end of the avoidant spectrum.

The similarities between the disorganized-impoverished attachment and the avoidant attachment are being cut off from emotions and attachment longings, as well as viewing dependency in self or others as weak, but more extreme. If you can relate to this style, you might recognize your need to keep your life safe and small, with measures like keeping a job that is below your qualifications and avoiding novel experiences such as traveling. Deeply buried within you are feelings of inner chaos similar to those with the more common type of disorganized attachment, but further away from awareness. To avoid getting in touch with this place, you work hard to keep a tight lid on it by avoiding stress. You might have rigid belief systems and even avoid relationships altogether.

Do I Have a Disorganized-Oscillating Attachment?

1. Do you find yourself answering "yes" to many of the questions for anxious attachment?

2. Do you experience intense physical and/or emotional abandonment fears in your romantic relationship?

3. Do you struggle with self-regulation when you're triggered, and often feel completely lost in your emotions?

4. When arguments get intense, do you either fight back hard, fall apart emotionally, or run away?

5. Do you get offended or hurt more easily than others?

6. Does anger usually feel like rage?

7. Are you unsure of how you might react to a difficult situation— sometimes you might react strongly, while other times you might not react at all, even when the triggers are similar?

8. Do you often have mood swings that make your life feel unstable and unpredictable?

9. Can your feelings for your partner shift from positive to negative, and vice versa, in a short amount of time?

10. Do you have a hard time trusting your partner's love and/or loyalty even when you have plenty of evidence to do so?

Do I Have a Disorganized-Impoverished Attachment?

1. Do you associate relationship sacrifices with weakness and loss of self?

2. Does the idea of self-reflection (exploring your own thoughts, feelings, and motivations) feel foreign to you?

3. Do you lack curiosity about the inner world of others?

4. If you have some awareness of your feelings, are you unable to put words to them?

5. Do you enjoy work or hobbies more than connection with others?

6. Are you worried that if you commit to too much in life, you'll get overwhelmed and fail?

If you have a disorganized attachment, you can learn many relationship skills from this book. That said, given what you've been through in life, it might be harder for you to self-regulate or emotionally engage well enough in tough moments to put new skills into place. If you're finding this to be true, don't despair. You might need special help working through any traumas that are interfering. I recommend Somatic Experiencing therapy (traumahealing.org), which can help you better access your emotions and self-regulate them and will put you in a much better position to be successful with this work. I'll discuss this type of therapy at greater length in chapter 10.

A Note About All Three Insecure Attachment Styles

If you recognize yourself in any of the three previous descriptions, it's important to remember that having an insecure attachment style isn't a lifetime sentence, and it doesn't mean you're a failure. People with insecure attachment styles struggle in relationships, but find success in other parts of their lives, such as friendships and careers. Sometimes traits of insecure attachment can actually create strengths in other parts of life. For example, a former client of mine, Anika, was a surgeon, a job that required her to push painful emotions away at will. If she didn't, the consequences could be devastating for her patients. On days when she had a fight with her wife or a rough morning with the kids— those kinds of mornings that can leave many people feeling thrown off kilter—Anika's avoidant attachment style gave her an uncanny ability to compartmentalize her feelings to get the job done, and she was known for being one of the top surgeons in the country. What was important for Anika to understand was that while this trait was working for her in her career, it was showing up in her relationship in a way that was *not* working. So we worked on balancing that out, and I hope you will do the same. For Anika, that meant learning to be emotionally regulated enough to do surgery in the morning, and emotionally available with her family that evening.

Secure Attachment

The Securely Attached Child

After reading through all these descriptions of how things go "wrong," you might be wondering what "right" even looks like. When it comes to attachment theory, "right" is what we call secure attachment. As I've mentioned, securely attached children don't live in perfect environments with perfect caregivers; rather, they live in good-enough environments with good-enough caregivers: they have a felt sense of confidence that they can reach for emotional comfort and connection from their caregivers when they need it, that they are safe from harm and abandonment, and that most of the time they will be responded to with love and care.

In the context of the four Cs of attachment, securely attached children get enough emotional comfort when they're in distress (comfort); enough time and attention, including emotional (connection); enough help when things go wrong (conflict); and live in a safe environment where each family member felt their needs were respected (cooperation). What is enough? Let's go back to climate: How much sunshine does a climate need for it to be considered a sunny climate? Do sunny climates have rainy days? Yes, of course they do. Kids can have hard lives—they can experience loss, tragedy, natural disasters, divorce, or other challenges—and still have a secure attachment if they get enough emotional support through the hard stuff.

If you had a secure attachment as a child, you didn't have to spend your energy fighting to get your needs met or pushing them away, because you had an overall felt sense of safety and security. Instead, your energy was free to be channeled into growth and development. You had space to get to know yourself. Just like all kids, you experienced adversity in the world, but because you had a "secure base" to return home to, you were less negatively impacted.

Imagine that you're a child and you get shamed by your teacher in front of the class and you're riding the bus home feeling awful. Now imagine that you don't want to tell your parents about what happened because you know they'll just get mad and blame you, or overreact, or they might not have time to listen at all. Maybe you don't know how they'll respond because sometimes they can be comforting and other times they're angry or unavailable. As you imagine this scenario, what happens in your body when you think about being this child? Maybe you notice subtle signs of sadness or anxiety, like a tight feeling in your throat or chest or tension in your muscles.

Now imagine that you know that later that evening at least one parent or caregiver will be there to listen to you and comfort you. It doesn't take away the pain of the incident, but at least you know you'll be cared for, that someone will be there to hold you and dry your tears. Perhaps just reading about having a caring presence to come home to feels soothing. You can feel a release of tension in your body or a sense of warmth. This is what I mean when I say that security is felt on a physical level. (Parents of securely attached children *do* give advice and guidance; they just don't lead with these things before tending to kids' hurt feelings.)

Without carrying the heavy baggage of relationship anxiety (experienced as a nagging desire to reestablish connection to others) or expending the energy to stuff it away, secure children are free to devote their attention to the rich experiences life has to offer and to feel safe taking the measured risks in life required to build confidence.

If you had a secure attachment, the kind of responsiveness I'm describing helped you know your emotions mattered, that they made sense, and that emotional support was available. From this you learned to honor your own emotions as a useful guide in life, and to eventually develop your own inner resources for self-regulation. Armed with the confidence of being able to reach for emotional support at times when it was available, and to self-regulate when it was not, you developed inner confidence, which reinforced your sense of security.

I once asked my client Jorge to describe a positive experience he remembers with his parents. As the story goes, Jorge was five years old and learning to ride his bike without training wheels. The first time he was able to stay up for several feet was a moment to celebrate. Jorge remembers his parents telling him they were proud of him, but he also remembers his dad asking, "Hey, buddy, are you proud of yourself right now?" which gave Jorge the opportunity to develop awareness of his own experience. By inspiring Jorge's self-reflection, his father helped him develop a sense of self. Jorge was able to say to himself, "It feels good when I overcome a challenging obstacle, not just because others are proud, but because *I'm* proud." In other situations, Jorge's parents might have said, "Look at the smile on your face . . . you're so happy," or even "Uh-oh, it's frustrating when you fall after you've been doing so well, isn't it? Here, let me help you up." Having his emotions reflected to him helped Jorge better understand and express himself throughout his life.

Securely attached children are given space to experience painful feelings. When Jorge was older and didn't get a part in the school play, he was devastated. Instead of telling him not to be upset or that "there's always next year," his empathic parents validated his feelings by saying something along the lines of "I'm so sorry. Of course you're devastated, I know this meant a lot to you." They used an authentic and emotionally engaged tone (which is only possible if the feelings behind the words are real) and if Jorge needed to cry, they held him while he let out the tears. Later when he had vented and grieved his loss, they moved into a problem-solving approach and looked into a community theater program for him to join. But if they hadn't gone into problem-solving mode, that would have been fine, too. Not every problem can be solved.

If you were a securely attached child, you experienced your caregivers as wise and strong most of the time (no parent is perfect), and rarely, if ever, did you feel overly responsible for your caregivers' well-being, emotionally or otherwise. Your caregivers took care of you, not the other way around, but they weren't so protective that they kept you from learning to navigate adversity. Most important, you learned what sensitive and supportive relationships feel like, and what to "feel" for in future relationships.

The Securely Attached Adult

If you have secure attachment as an adult, you know how to reach for emotional connection from your partner, and you know how to respond to your partner's bids for connection. You know what a relationship with met attachment needs feels like and this is your standard. You can access and express your emotions and you're comfortable with vulnerability. You don't fear or push away emotional connection from your partner. You're direct about your wants and needs, are responsive to the wants and needs of your partner, can tolerate disappointment, and have flexible boundaries.

If you have a secure attachment, you don't carry around negative beliefs about yourself like "If I make a mistake that means I'm a failure," or "I'm unlovable as I am; I have to work overtime to be acceptable." Without being burdened with these shame- and fear-inducing beliefs about yourself, you feel more safe to be vulnerable in your relationship. Being vulnerable is by definition risky, but if you have a secure attachment, it doesn't feel like a "life-and-death risk," as is often the case for those who are insecurely attached. Securely attached, you understand that all relationships experience occasional emotional pain, and you're able to successfully navigate rough patches. You're less likely to become defensive in the face of criticism, and you can behave according to your own value system even when your partner does not.

If you have a secure attachment, you place high value on your partner's wants and needs and trust you'll get the same in return. When you don't see eye to eye, you work toward understanding and compromise, rather than trying to convince your partner to see it differently. This isn't to say you give up on the values that are most important to you, or that you don't influence each other, but control isn't at play in the way you manage differences. With a secure attachment, your partner is your number one, your person. But you also have friends and family to go to for connection and support because you know one person in life can't always meet all our needs.

While a secure attachment in your relationship with yourself as an individual and a secure attachment to your partner are closely related, and in fact feed off each other, they are not the same. We're speaking about two different relationships. You might have a very secure relationship with yourself, but if you don't trust your partner to be emotionally available and safe, you can't possibly feel securely attached to them.

Let's take Zoe, a former client of mine, who grew up with an anxious attachment but did a lot of work on herself. Through therapy, self-help, and a commitment to ongoing growth, she learned to better understand and manage her emotions, to trust herself and her worthiness, to better understand what *she* needed to feel close in her relationship, as well as how to be a more loving and attentive partner. As an outgrowth of her authentic connection with herself, she learned how to experience authentic connections with others. While Zoe's secure attachment with herself helped her relationship improve, her partner, Ezra, was struggling with alcohol addiction. Naturally, Ezra's addiction was getting in the way of their connection and Zoe's emotional safety in the relationship. When Ezra didn't come home at night without calling, or picked fights when he was drinking, this understandably left Zoe unable to trust. She trusted Ezra's love, but couldn't trust he would be able to show up for her emotionally in the way she needed. Zoe's secure relationship *with herself* helped her manage her relationship pain and show up for Ezra in the most supportive way possible without compromising her own boundaries. But it didn't help her feel secure in her *relationship* until Ezra was able to start working on his addiction and begin showing up in ways that gradually helped Zoe feel secure in the relationship.

No matter how secure you are as an individual, you aren't going to feel safe and close to a partner who is emotionally unavailable, unsupportive, or disloyal. But, even in this case, you can maintain security within yourself.

Although securely attached partners are more resilient than their insecure counterparts, even the most secure relationships are vulnerable to excessive stress. Extenuating circumstances such as long-term illnesses, trauma, job loss, discrimination, problems with children, or addiction can exceed one or both partners' coping mechanisms. While securely attached partners experience rough patches in the relationship, even sometimes to the degree that their relationship takes on an anxious/avoidant dynamic, they are generally more resilient and are able to bounce back more quickly. If not, they are not afraid to reach for help. Although the divorce rate for securely attached relationships is statistically far lower than those of insecurely attached relationships, secure partners don't always stay in relationships that are no longer working. They are, however, more likely to separate with intention and in a way that maintains mutual respect.

If you have a secure attachment, you aren't perfect and you don't aspire to be. You'll feel insecure sometimes and it won't always bring out the best in you, but these moments are the exceptions rather than the rule. You're willing to be accountable for moments when you hurt your partner, and can make repairs without spiraling into shame or blame.

Attachment with Self

Attachment styles, as we've learned, start with parenting. And, to a large degree, insecure attachment is healed through *re*-parenting, meaning learning to parent yourself in the right way, and by "right" I mean in a way that fosters your secure attachment with *you*. Only when you start giving yourself what you need, meeting your own attachment needs for care, comfort, responsiveness, healthy boundaries, and support, can you ever expect to re-create the same in a loving relationship with a loving partner. This doesn't mean you need to leave your relationship or even avoid relationships until you've arrived at some predetermined level of enlightenment. Not at all. In fact, learning to better show up for yourself will *parallel* how you show up to your partner. Because when you start growing, your relationship will start growing, too.

How secure *is* your relationship with yourself? Are you able to validate your own feelings, treat yourself with warmth and respect, provide self-comfort? Are you willing to understand yourself through the lens of your attachment history instead of through the lens of shame? Do you beat yourself up and constantly tell yourself you're not good enough, flawed, unlovable? Or do you give yourself the benefit of the doubt and accept yourself for *all* of you, even the parts you want to work on? Do you practice soothing your big feelings? If not, you're at risk of having unrealistic expectations of what a partner can provide, and you won't be able to give these things to your partner because we simply can't give to a partner what we can't first give to ourselves.

Also, what are your expectations of others? Do you automatically assume others won't like you or are out to get you? Do you expect more than what anyone can (or should) reasonably give? Do you assume all relationships are doomed to fail? Do you romanticize budding relationships only to feel let down later? Do you believe you're only safe with other people if you're better-than: more attractive, more successful, more intelligent, and so on? The answer to these questions will speak volumes about the working models of attachment within you. If you have an insecure attachment, the work is to begin to shift your relationship with your humanity as a whole.

What about the logistical part of self-parenting: How is your self-care? Do you make an effort to take care of yourself physically (nutrition, exercise, sunlight, etc.)? If not, you're going to be less resilient to relationship stress and more likely to be reactive because it's challenging to show up as your best self when you simply don't feel good.

I wrote *Secure Love* to help you focus on one part of your life, a very big part of your life: your romantic relationship. But there are many other parts of your humanity to nurture. The more you learn to nurture yourself, the more all the parts will work together and feed off each other. So today when you make the choice to eat more vegetables, or tonight when you put the screen down and get an extra hour of sleep, or tomorrow morning when you take five minutes to journal about your intentions, recognize that each of these seemingly small acts isn't just for your own health; they're also ways in which you're actively working on your relationship . . . it all matters.

Attachment Styles in Other Relationships

In this book we're talking specifically about attachment styles as they relate to the parent-child relationships where they were first formed, and the adult romantic relationships where they show up today. Attachment styles show up most strongly in relationships where the emotional stakes are the highest, and emotional stakes are the highest when attachment needs are the highest. Most likely, no matter how much you love your best friend and will experience a strong attachment to them, you will still have higher attachment needs in an established relationship with your romantic partner. What about other, more casual relationships? Does your attachment style show up in these? Yes and no. Yes, in the sense that attachment issues will often impact the way we respond to others even in the most casual of circumstances. No, in the sense that for attachment styles to be most alive, there needs to be high attachment significance in the relationship: the emotional stakes must be high, the loss of the person would lead to intense grief, and you must need to depend on the person for your emotional, physical, sexual, and/or cooperation (sharing a life together) needs to be met.

For example, as I mentioned earlier in the chapter, you might have an employer who in many ways reminds you of your mother. As a result, you might react to his complaints similarly to how you react to your mom's. But while you might rely on your employer for some of your needs, most of us don't rely on our employers to be an emotional support system, or for physical affection. In the event that you were to lose your mother, your grief would be powerful and lasting, much more so than if you were to lose your employer. So while your attachment style may play into your more casual relationships, it will interfere to a far lesser degree than in the relationships we're talking about here.

Attachment styles don't exist in a vacuum. Partners play off each other as if dancing, each responding to the moves of the other. They often show up to the relationship with the attachment styles they developed in childhood, and together these pairs replicate the dynamics they know. But sometimes things aren't so clear-cut and people end up with partners who bring out different sides of them. Or stressful circumstances change present-day relationship dynamics. Let's say, for example, one partner becomes depressed in response to a job loss and emotionally retreats. Their otherwise securely attached partner doesn't understand how depression impacts a person and takes the retreat as a sign of a lack of investment in the relationship. Understandably, this can cause feelings of insecurity and, when the circumstances add up, create an anxious attachment. People with anxious attachments are prone to anxious behaviors. Anxious behaviors motivate the other partner's avoidant behaviors. Avoidant behaviors motivate the other partner's anxious behaviors, and on and on it goes.

But attachment change works the other way, too. When one partner starts to become more secure, they add safety and health to the relationship. Eventually most people will start responding to safety with more safety. This is how attachment security is established to begin with: one person (usually the parent) creates an emotionally safe environment, and the other person (the child) has little need to respond with defenses and protections. Instead, connection and problem-solving are the name of the game.

Identifying Your Partner's Attachment Style

It might be tempting, as you read this book, to want to "diagnose" your partner's attachment style and try to "fix" their insecure attachment. If you fall into the anxiously attached category, this can be an especially compelling approach—you're the one whose style involves trying hard to close the emotional distance in the relationship, so it stands to reason you will be the one actively pushing for change. I like for partners to focus on themselves, but I also think it's hugely important for them to understand their partner. Having a sense of your partner's attachment style will help you understand their core needs and fears, and why they behave the way they do. It will help you see your partner with compassion in especially hard moments, or when they behave in ways that you might find especially difficult. For example, let's say your partner gets defensive when you bring up a concern that's not even related to your relationship. In the past you might have assumed they were simply being dismissive, or even rude. Armed with your new understanding of attachment styles, now you might think, "Hmmm . . . this seems like a moment when they're worried they won't be able to fix the problem and it brings up fears of failing. Maybe it's not about being dismissive at all, but about their need to stay safe with me."

That said, beware of trying to change your partner. It's a losing battle. Instead, I want you to focus on changing the relationship environment. That is an overarching goal of this book and we'll talk about it more and develop the skills for that as we go. Using an understanding of your partner's attachment style to shift the environment, rather than trying to change or even shame them, is the best way for them to change, and that change ultimately needs to come from them. The good news is that the more you work on yourself and your relationship environment, the more likely your partner is to follow suit. Change begets change; growth begets growth.

PART TWO

Understanding How You Conflict–and How to Repair

CHAPTER FOUR

What Is Your Negative Cycle?

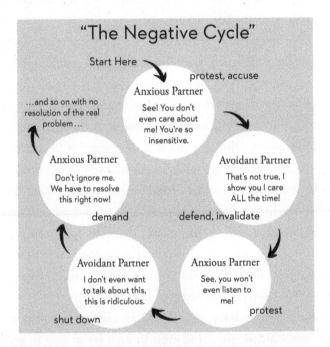

"The Negative Cycle"

Start Here

protest, accuse

Anxious Partner

See! You don't even care about me! You're so insensitive.

...and so on with no resolution of the real problem...

Avoidant Partner

That's not true, I show you I care ALL the time!

Anxious Partner

Don't ignore me. We have to resolve this right now!

demand

defend, invalidate

Avoidant Partner

I don't even want to talk about this, this is ridiculous.

Anxious Partner

See, you won't even listen to me!

protest

shut down

Identifying your attachment style is incredibly helpful when it comes to understanding your core attachment needs and attachment fears, as well as the attachment needs and fears of your partner. It helps put a finger on what you need from your partner to feel close, and what your partner needs from you so that they can feel close. It helps you understand why, when your needs go unmet or when you're afraid they will go unmet, each of you feels compelled to behave in certain ways, even when you think you "should know better." Becoming familiar with your attachment styles provides the first step to improving your relationship.

Next, we're going to look at how you and your partner's attachment styles come together in the relationship as a dynamic. This includes taking a close look at how each of you might be fueling or perpetuating conflict. Armed with a deeper understanding of what is *within* each of you as individuals, combined with the understanding of what happens *between* the two of you as a couple, you can learn to behave in new, more productive ways that will spark connection in the moment and foster secure love in the big picture.

If you have an insecure attachment, it's almost certain that you and your partner have difficulty resolving conflict or reaching for and responding to bids for emotional connection. For anxious or disorganized partners, the desperation to be heard and responded to by your partner will often cause you to blame, protest, criticize, or accuse them during an argument. This is your way of trying to be acknowledged for your pain, create change, seek closeness, and protect how you view yourself. If you have an avoidant attachment, on the other hand, you often feel compelled to defend yourself, deflect your partner's concerns, stonewall (sometimes called "the silent treatment"), or retreat from the relationship. This is your way of trying to protect how your partner views you, protect the relationship from conflict, protect how you view yourself, and/or protect your sense of independence.

Sue Johnson, in her book *Hold Me Tight*, calls these common conflict behaviors "demon dialogue," and even though it's so easy to go there in tough moments, they don't help your relationship thrive. Instead they feed off of each other: Partner A brings up a concern (often in an accusatory manner), Partner B feels attacked and gets defensive, Partner A feels invalidated for their experience and protests back, Partner B deflects the blame, Partner A feels unheard and protests even more, and Partner B shuts down. Resolution is stalled and connection is damaged.

This pattern (and similar variations) is called a "negative cycle."

Most negative cycles will mirror the overall attachment pattern of the relationship. An anxious/avoidant couple will have pursue/withdraw negative cycles similar to the one I've just described (most of the time the anxious partner will be the pursuer during a conflict, but not always). Avoidant/avoidant couples will avoid conflict, but at the expense of resolution of problems and relationship depth. Anxious/anxious couples will have the most escalated and aggressive cycles with heavy blame. (Those with disorganized attachments are less predictable but will typically show up in the anxious role.) While each couple I treat has their own version of this cycle and different topics that will ignite it, you'd be surprised at how consistent negative cycle patterns are from couple to couple.

The negative communication cycle is usually set into motion when two insecurely attached partners attempt to talk about a difficult topic. However, the topic doesn't have to be *that* difficult, as is common between two people who suddenly flare up about a seemingly minor daily routine. Let's see it in action. Marcus and Cassie are working professionals with two young children. Cassie likes to cook and usually makes dinner, and Marcus does the dishes. They share other responsibilities, such as deep cleaning and laundry. Marcus makes sure the bills are paid on time and Cassie does the grocery shopping. One evening, Marcus finishes cleaning after a delicious dinner, when Cassie goes to get a glass of water and notices crumbs on the counter. "I don't understand," Cassie says to Marcus, pointing out the crumbs. "Why won't you just finish the job?"

"It's not a big deal, you're making a problem out of nothing," Marcus mumbles under his breath.

"You never take my concerns seriously," Cassie asserts. "Would it be that hard for you to just do it the way I've asked? Do you even care about what I want?"

Cassie and Marcus go back and forth like this until eventually, Marcus gives up. "Forget it," he says, before wiping up the crumbs, leaving the kitchen, and distracting himself on his phone. Cassie follows him into the other room, trying to continue the argument, but Marcus is done. "I don't want to talk about it anymore," he says. "I'm fine, the kitchen is clean. Let's just drop it."

Cassie leaves the room, and they pass the next hour in separate areas of the house.

Obviously, this argument isn't *just* about crumbs. While this story depicts the facts of what happened between Marcus and Cassie, it reveals only a small fraction of what's *actually* going on between them. Let's retell the story of the negative cycle between Marcus and Cassie through the lens of their unmet attachment needs:

Cassie sees the crumbs left on the counter. Crumbs make Cassie anxious. Since she has repeatedly expressed her need for a clean counter to Marcus, she concludes that Marcus doesn't care about her needs. Cassie, like all partners, longs to feel cared for and responded to. Her attachment behavioral system kicks in (remember, this system motivates us to feel distress when attachment is threatened), leaving her feeling unseen and alone. Cassie's nervous system tries to recover her attachment safety by moving her into anger, which motivates her to take action. She tries to communicate her dejection to Marcus by protesting his behavior, but this leaves Marcus feeling attacked and unappreciated.

In his mind, he's doing his best. When Cassie points out the few crumbs on the counter, he feels like he can't get anything right no matter how hard he tries. Marcus longs to feel appreciated by Cassie and as if he won't be defined by what he gets wrong. He also wants to protect his sense of self, which feels violated when he perceives Cassie as "talking down" to him. By deflecting Cassie's concerns, Marcus is trying to get her to have a change of heart so that he can feel safe in her eyes as well as in his own. But the deflection makes Cassie feel that her distress is unseen and her concerns invalidated. Meanwhile Marcus's stress level is rising, so he tries to keep things from escalating by wiping up the crumbs. He feels defeated, and wishes Cassie would just let things go so they could enjoy the evening together. Cassie, on the other hand, feels abandoned. She wishes Marcus could help her feel heard and cared for. Cassie is mad at Marcus, but she'd rather pull him back in than feel alone—this is why she followed him into another room to keep the argument going—but at this point Marcus has detached from his feelings. He doesn't want to feel worse and has no interest in reengaging.

Here's a visual example of the beginning of the negative cycle between Marcus and Cassie. Notice that Cassie's reactiveness triggers

Marcus's vulnerability, and that Marcus's reactiveness triggers Cassie's vulnerability:

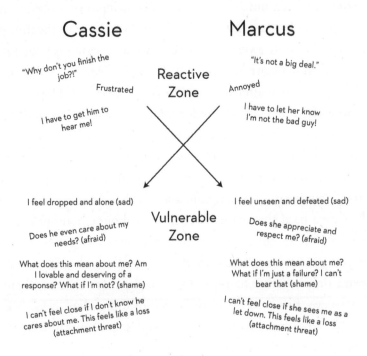

Marcus and Cassie's tension lasts through the night, and the resulting distance feels uncomfortable for both. At some point it becomes too much and they find their way back to each other. They don't explicitly make up—there are no apologies and no discussion of what happened—but they both try to let go of the kitchen incident and move on, because they know they don't have the skills to actually manage the deeper implications of the conflict: attachment safety and unfulfilled longings. Marcus and Cassie feel close again in the moment, but eventually, days or weeks later, they find themselves back in their negative cycle, struggling with the same attachment ruptures.

When you and your partner enter a negative communication cycle, you're managing two problems at once. Your awareness is focused on the surface-level conversation, about crumbs, finances, an affair, breaking plans, or whatever topic creates conflict in the moment. These problems are real, and your relationship won't work unless you and your partner can find ways to resolve them. But that's virtually impossible when another, much more powerful conversation—about unmet attachment needs—is lurking below the surface. Most of the time partners aren't even fully aware this secondary conversation is taking place. The unspoken dialogue here is about big stuff: "Are you going to hear me? Do my needs matter to you? Do you respect me? How much do you appreciate me? Can you understand and validate my perspective? Do you see me as failing you because I got it wrong?"

All couples have topics that are heated for them, and each might be especially vulnerable in one or more of the four Cs of their relationship: comfort, connection, cooperation, and conflict. You and your partner might have a hard time with conversations about parenting styles (cooperation), for example. For you, this hot topic is going to make it more likely you go into a negative cycle than, say, talking about how you like to spend time together (connection). Maybe that's an area where you see eye to eye. But even the most heated of topics don't *cause* negative cycles. Negative cycles happen when couples are communicating with each other in ways that create attachment ruptures. Just because a topic is tough doesn't mean that the discussion around the topic should inspire feelings of being unappreciated, unheard, and invalidated. This is one of the most fundamental differences between insecurely attached couples and securely attached ones. Securely attached couples can work through differences while maintaining safety and connection.

During a fight (if, like Cassie and Marcus, one partner is pursuing and the other is withdrawing—which is the case the vast majority of the time), the avoidant partner's insecure attachment essentially says, "I'm not aware of my own vulnerable feelings so I can't possibly see yours!" This reinforces the anxious partner's fears about being too much, and their insecure attachment retorts, "I'm going to protest this pain you're causing by making you see how wrong you are!" This, in turn, reinforces the avoidant partner's fears of failure. While all this is happening below the surface, above the surface partners are speaking to each other in hurtful ways, causing the tension to escalate. One partner may have "started it"—they may have done or said something, or *not* done or said something, that created potential for the negative communication cycle to be set into motion—but it takes two to engage and keep it going.

For example, let's say on a different day Marcus gets triggered when he finds out Cassie made weekend plans for them without first talking to him. He doesn't want to express his feelings and cause a fight so instead he acts distant. Cassie senses something is wrong and demands to be let in, telling Marcus heatedly that he has no right to shut her out. Marcus continues to say, "It's nothing, just leave it." Eventually Cassie pushes hard enough and Marcus explosively tells her that he doesn't have any say over their lives and that she tries to control him just like her mom tries to control her dad. Cassie cries and eventually Marcus apologizes for overreacting and they leave the topic.

What started this negative cycle? *The way Marcus communicated his trigger* combined with *the way Cassie responded*. They *both* created the negative cycle. Had Marcus managed his feelings about not being consulted by saying something along the lines of "I appreciate the effort you put into making our plans, but at the same time it feels important to me to have more input—can we talk about it?" then the chances are higher that the negative cycle would've been avoided. But even if Marcus expressed himself in the worst way possible, Cassie can still avoid getting sucked into it by taking ownership of her response, which in our example might sound like "I know it can be hard for you to bring up topics that in the past have caused fights, but I'm sensing some distance from you and it's uncomfortable for me. I feel shut out. When it feels safe, I hope you'll bring it up to me. I'm not going to pressure you, but I'll be here when you're ready." This isn't necessarily a magic wand, but it *is* a way to prevent an ugly negative cycle and it will make it more likely they can eventually have a safer conversation around the topic of weekend plans. Either partner can do or say something that makes it highly likely a negative cycle will be set into motion, but ultimately it takes two to make it happen and keep it going.

Once a negative cycle is in motion and nobody is doing anything to interrupt it (we'll learn about that soon), the back-and-forth usually ends in painful disconnection, leaving both partners with a profound sense of sadness, anger, demoralization, disconnection, numbness, and/or mixed feelings about the relationship. This period of disconnection can go on for hours, days, or weeks, until the tension becomes too great and they finally reconnect. Unfortunately, at this point the damage—to their relationship trust and closeness—is already done, and the negative cycle has reinforced their original insecure attachment.

Even the most securely attached partners can sometimes speak harshly, get cynical or critical, roll their eyes, or get overly defensive when presented with a concern. And even the most securely attached partners sometimes have trouble saying to themselves, "I know my partner is just tired and that this moment doesn't define their feelings for me." Even secure partners get reactive. Yes, couples with secure attachments experience fewer negative cycles, and these cycles get less escalated when they do happen, but another critical difference between securely and insecurely attached couples is the ability to make repairs. Secure couples can get out of the bad weather and back into their climate of safety. As you learn how to manage your negative cycle (which we'll get into shortly), keep in mind that we're shooting for progress, not for perfection. Learning to manage a negative cycle happens through practice.

In Marcus and Cassie's case, the argument eventually ran its course and they found their way back to each other. This likely happens to you, too. Fighting is exhausting and upsetting, and when it starts to feel like too much, partners tend to "let it go." But don't be fooled: just because Marcus and Cassie let the crumbs incident go doesn't mean they've repaired. The real problem still exists: Cassie felt unresponded to, and Marcus felt as if he wasn't being treated with appreciation and respect . . . all of which are attachment ruptures that, when repeated over and over again and left unrepaired, can cumulatively do a lot of damage. And on top of that, Marcus and Cassie never came to any agreement about how to go forward when it comes to their differences in cleaning preferences. Negative cycles are notorious for blocking resolution to whatever surface problem kick-started the cycle. For two people—any two people, not just romantic partners—to be able to come together and work through a problem, there needs to be some degree of emotional safety. Negative cycles aren't emotionally safe; *they are the opposite of emotional safety.* How can you and your partner come to an agreement on how to parent, where to live, how to save money, or even what to have for dinner if every time you try to talk about it, you end up feeling unheard, attacked, and invalidated . . . not exactly a breeding ground for sustainable cooperation?

The Anatomy of a Trigger

What exactly is a trigger, beyond the vague definition of "something that makes you upset"?

In short, a "trigger" is when your attachment behavioral system (ABS) experiences an *attachment threat* and gets activated to take action and find safety. It's easy to think triggers are singular experiences, because they happen so fast, in a fraction of a second. But in truth, triggers are a combination of experiences within your brain and body that are set into motion by the *triggering event* (your partner's eye roll, for example), all of which culminate in a reaction.

Triggering events create an overt or subtle sensation in your body (secure, anxious, and disorganized partners are more likely to be aware of their bodily sensations, while avoidant partners are less likely to be aware), and then your brain makes a meaning of the sensation, including the perception that there's been an attachment rupture or unfulfilled longing for closeness. This causes vulnerable emotions such as fear, grief, and shame to well up. Up to this point, much of this is subconscious, especially if you're new to getting to know your inner world.

Since most humans will go to great lengths to avoid feeling pain, your pain will ignite a reactive feeling that motivates you to take some sort of action (words or behavior) to "make the pain go away!" Whatever action you take is intended to help you get back to safety, although it often has the opposite effect. To help you better understand your feelings and name them so that you can start expressing them, which we'll be doing a lot of throughout the remainder of the book, I've included a list of common relationship feelings in the appendix.

While there are many reactive feelings partners can experience in negative cycles, including bitterness, neglected, humiliated, and overwhelmed, a common one is anger (or its other versions, such as frustration, annoyance, or rage). Anger is a strong motivator and it inspires us to do something, anything, to change what's making us hurt. Couples therapist and author George Faller, LMFT, aptly describes anger as that which provides us with the *hope things will change.* This is not to say that getting stuck in anger, using anger as a justification to behave poorly, or showing it exclusively and at the expense of the deeper emotions is a good idea. But when we can reframe anger as hope it becomes easier to validate it, and there's no better way to soothe anger and make space for the deeper emotions than to validate it.

Let's play this out: Your partner rolls their eyes, and you feel your chest tighten. Your brain says, "They're mad and when people are mad that means they don't love me. I don't feel loved by my partner in this moment." Along with this experience comes a sense of loss and fear. As a reaction to this primal pain, your nervous system amps up, this time with indignance, which screams, "You don't deserve to be treated like this, you need to let them know this isn't okay!" Then the anger comes out as a reaction: "How dare you roll your eyes at me!"

But what you're really trying to say is, "Ouch, I'm hurting. I'm afraid you're mad at me and on top of that now I feel unlovable to you. It's easy for me to go there because the wounded part of me already believes I'm unlovable. I need you to know how much I'm hurting, but I don't know how to say it (and you might not be able to hear me anyway). Maybe if I show you how mad I am, you'll get the message and you won't want to hurt me anymore. So I get big and tell you off." But what does your partner see? Not the hurt, not the fear, not the self-beliefs that haunt you, not the attachment longing to feel safe and close. Sadly, all they see is the anger. Most likely it's not going to land well. I'm not asking you to deny the anger part, and we'll talk more about safely validating anger, but problems arise when that's *all* we see, when we only get a piece of the whole picture. When the rest of our humanity, the soft side, the connecting side, gets lost.

Here's a diagram of the full experience of a trigger. This example is relevant to someone with an anxious or disorganized attachment. I've used another example for avoidant attachment in chapter 5:

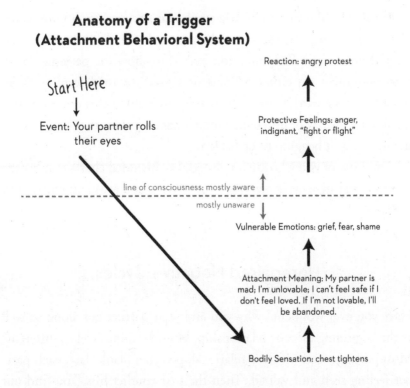

Anatomy of a Trigger
(Attachment Behavioral System)

Reaction: angry protest

Start Here

Event: Your partner rolls their eyes

Protective Feelings: anger, indignant, "fight or flight"

line of consciousness: mostly aware
mostly unaware

Vulnerable Emotions: grief, fear, shame

Attachment Meaning: My partner is mad; I'm unlovable; I can't feel safe if I don't feel loved. If I'm not lovable, I'll be abandoned.

Bodily Sensation: chest tightens

It's important to understand the breakdown of a trigger because understanding what's happening in your brain and body when you feel like fighting back or fleeing will give you something to work with. By recognizing your triggers, you can step back, look inward, and say, "What's going on with me right now? What meaning am I making right now? Is it accurate, or based on past wounds, or a little bit of both?" or "What's happening in my body? I'm holding my breath. Let's breathe for a minute," or "Okay, this is really big. What can I do differently right now instead of reacting in a way that won't get me anywhere I really want to go?" In short, understanding your triggers is empowering.

Now that we have an idea of how a trigger plays out within each partner, let's look at how each partner's triggers play out between the two of them as a negative cycle. Let's revisit Marcus and Cassie's argument over the crumbs:

Cassie was the first to be triggered, and she reacted by protesting. Her protests triggered Marcus and he reacted with dismissiveness, and on and on it went. The intention here is to show the pattern, not to place judgment on either Marcus or Cassie, or to determine "who started it." The truth is that this pattern isn't about this one moment; it's about a history of unrepaired attachment ruptures that keeps showing up . . . as if begging to be healed.

For those of you who are interested, I've included charts that list the common negative cycle behaviors for anxious and avoidant partners in the appendix.

Unrepaired Negative Cycles

Have you ever wondered why you and your partner got along so well at the beginning of your relationship, but now things feel so different? Most partners start off their relationship with a blank slate, each partner feeling seen and valued. Then the first conflict hits. You find out he's still friends with his ex. She's always running late, and you finally bring it up. He snubs your friends. She pouts when you go somewhere without her. If the two of you have relatively secure attachments, you'll work through these conflicts with an intact relationship. Maybe it will take more than one conversation as you learn to navigate your differences, disappointments, and relationship boundaries, but you'll get through it or you'll decide to part ways (which, if done from a place of intention, *is* a version of "getting through it"). But if you have insecure attachments, you're probably going to go into your first negative cycle. The fight or argument will run its course and when it's all over, your need to reconnect will eventually take center stage and you'll make up. But the negative cycle made a small dent in the relationship—not enough to lose all hope, but enough to shake up trust a bit. You each think, "It will be okay. We can prevent that from happening again." But because you talked about whatever the problem was while in a negative cycle, there wasn't space for it to get resolved and maybe the "repair" was just pushing it under the rug. Negative cycles prevent the true repair work from happening and so you start avoiding the problem, until you go out with your friends again and it rears its ugly head.

That first negative cycle also created a bit of distance between you and your partner. Maybe just a morsel, but enough for your nervous system to worry that "if I bring up issues, I'm going to get a response I don't like," or "I won't feel understood if we start talking about hard topics." Still, it's early in the relationship, there's still a lot of trust and hope, and you make your way back.

But then there's another rupture. This time it's a little worse: you go a little bit farther away from each other, because you're not only addressing the new issue at hand, but you're also managing the old wounds from the unresolved last cycle. You come back to each other, again, but the distance has grown. You've lost some trust and maybe hope. You can see how, over a course of weeks or months or years, some couples end up too far away from each other and the distance never gets fully closed.

The Negative Cycle and the Anxious/Avoidant Couple

The vast majority of the couples I treat are in an anxious/avoidant dynamic—it's a very common pairing for a few common reasons many of you will relate to. Anxious partners know they want connection, but don't know what real emotional support feels like to give or receive. Because avoidant partners are often the pursuers during the dating phase, the anxious partner initially feels wanted, but this isn't the same as long-term intimacy. On top of this, avoidant partners like to feel successful, and in the beginning of a relationship when the anxious partner is enamored with them, they do feel successful. But as negative cycles increase, they start feeling unsuccessful and pull away. As they pull away, the anxious partner moves in closer and the avoidant partner begins to feel smothered. Avoidant partners initially enjoy the emotional expressiveness of the anxious partner because it helps them feel things they can't feel on their own. As things progress, the anxious partner's emotions feel less exciting and more overwhelming and the avoidant partner pulls away. The anxious partner is often initially drawn to the avoidant partner's emotional stability, although later it becomes evident that the stability comes at the cost of true emotional engagement. In response, the anxious partner becomes more anxious and demanding. Gradually they begin to resent the very traits in each other that drew them together.

Yet they often keep going despite all of this. Why? Because all relationships do their best to find emotional balance. Relationships that don't settle into a balance often don't last. When two people who come into the relationship lacking emotional balance within (the anxious partner overwhelmed by emotion, the avoidant partner detached from emotions), the second-best version is for them to find balance between them, each taking responsibility for a fragment of the relationship at the expense of being whole selves. In the anxious/avoidant dynamic, the anxious-attached partner pushes hard for resolution or connection, while the avoidant partner pushes back as a protection against conflict neither of them knows how to navigate, as well as protecting against an unhealthy level of "closeness" (which isn't closeness at all, but enmeshment). One seeks whatever connection can be had, while the other works to maintain as much emotional stability as possible. In a healthy relationship each partner works more or less equally for both.

Here's an example of how the balancing act might show up in real life. Imagine a couple having an argument in public. The anxious partner is more likely to become escalated, even at the expense of being noticed by others. The avoidant partner is more likely to try to avoid calling attention from those nearby who might overhear the argument. This is because anxious partners prioritize resolution and reconnection, while avoidant partners are more concerned with avoiding the shame of being noticed by others. Both of them are valid in their needs to feel safe, but when partners are more securely attached they are in touch with each other's personal needs to find reconnection *and* avoid making a scene.

When negative cycles and unrepaired ruptures build up, even partners who don't fit into traditional categories of attachment styles will take on an anxious/avoidant pattern to maintain the attachment balance. This can be true regardless of how you may have shown up in past romantic relationships. If someone has a mild insecure attachment but their partner has a stronger one, the first partner may shift toward avoidance to adapt to the relationship and keep the balancing act intact.

Anxious/avoidant couples are second only to secure/secure couples when it comes to the odds of relationship longevity, and that's *because* of the way their negative cycles play out, not in spite of it. Partners in an anxious/anxious pairing will have constant, highly escalated, negative cycles. Avoidant/avoidant pairings will have fewer negative cycles, but at the expense of resolution and connection. This eventually breeds resentment and harms whatever connection they do have. Anxious/avoidant pairings are like the Goldilocks of insecure couples, the middle ground. If you're an anxious partner bringing up concerns with blame, criticism, and "you need to change or else," you're really trying to close the distance between you and your partner because, well, who else is going to? If you're an avoidant partner invalidating your anxious partner's concerns, saying what they want to hear so it will all go away, you're trying to turn down the heat because, again, who else is going to? In anxious/anxious relationships, there is no one to turn down the heat. In avoidant/avoidant relationships, the lack of heat is the very problem.

Don't get me wrong: having the potential for a *sustainable* relationship doesn't equate to having a *thriving* relationship. Anxious/avoidant relationships work if we're speaking about longevity, but the cost is high. The cost, in the long run, is relationship health. Say you break your leg and can't bear weight for weeks. Your other leg will get stronger to create balance, but healing is when both legs have equal strength. The same is true in relationships: healing is when both partners are secure; not when one is fighting for connection and resolution while the other is fighting to keep things from getting out of control or enmeshed.

Here's a textbook anxious/attached dynamic:

Abhay, an anxious-attached partner, approaches his avoidant-attached partner Divya after spending a weekend with Divya's extended family. "You don't pay attention to me when we're with your family, it's like I'm not even there," Abhay says. Divya instantly makes sense of the protest by reasoning that Abhay is trying to keep her from her family. "I'm just enjoying my family!" she says. "Are you suggesting I shouldn't spend time with my family when we're with them?" Looking below the surface of the conflict, Abhay is fighting to feel valued and responded to and Divya is fighting for her sense of self. Abhay is acting out his anxious attachment with blame. Divya is acting out her avoidant attachment by reacting to Abhay's (poorly delivered) concerns with a lack of curiosity and counter-blame.

While this pattern doesn't feel good for either, to behave differently would mean taking a huge emotional risk. The only way out is for one or both partners to start reaching and responding to the other in new ways. In Abhay's mind, if he quits protesting with accusations and blame, he risks getting no attention from Divya at all; Divya thinks that if she quits pushing back and dismissing Abhay's concerns, she risks losing her sense of self and feeling weak and invisible. So both Abhay and Divya cling to their insecure ways of communicating with each other, to the detriment of the relationship and of their own growth as individuals. To get out of this cycle, they need to improve their relationship environment and shift negative cycles into bonding cycles.

The Real Enemy

When you and your partner are triggered, hurling insults at each other, criticizing, and giving each other the silent treatment, you may look like and feel like enemies. But it's so important to remember that you're not. Your partner is not the enemy; the negative cycle is the enemy.

You're both fighting for closeness, but in conflicting ways that were a learned response from pain in childhood. You want your relationship to work, so by definition, you are not enemies. The negative cycle you're in makes it appear that you're trying to hurt each other, when in reality you're trying to reach each other. In the terribly painful moments after you and your partner are triggered, your attachment fears and activated attachment system are in the driver's seat. You both have unmet attachment needs, you both are hurting, and you both are trying to stay safe with yourself and with each other; you just don't know how. As a result, you devolve into a negative cycle, which is actually the very thing keeping you stuck. Not only are you unable to resolve the problem at hand, but you can't dig out of this place of emotional unsafety and disconnection.

I once received the following in an email from a former client who gave me permission to include it here:

> Something that really helped me when I first learned about the negative cycle, is that my anxious attempt for connection—"reaching out" that was aggressive in a way I was blind to at the time—only made my avoidant partner more scared/avoidant, which in turn only made me more anxious and reach out even more (aggressively), which caused him to retreat even more—and thus the negative cycle intensified and

left each of us feeling so much more alone and isolated when we were seeking connection. It helped me realize how crazy-making the negative cycle is and how useless it is to react from the same place (most days :)) and help break those habits, no matter how hard they are. It later also helped me be able to see my partner's reaction to me as a reflection on what I hadn't resolved yet in myself and where I needed to attend to my needs.

The negative cycle, as my former client so elegantly acknowledged, not only keeps you and your partner stuck in an enemy mindset, it also reinforces each of your insecure attachments as individuals, and the insecure attachment in the relationship as a whole. Negative cycles are like insecure attachment prisons. When Cassie hears Marcus say "it's not a big deal," she thinks her greatest attachment fear has been confirmed: she's unlovable and unworthy of being responded to. It also confirms her attachment fear that Marcus won't be there for her when she needs him. Now that Cassie perceives all of her insecurity within herself and her insecurity with Marcus to have been confirmed, what does she do? She acts the way someone with an insecure attachment would: reactively and with protest. Then the process starts again on Marcus's side. In short, they are each stuck in their insecure attachments. It sounds demoralizing, I know. But it's not, because in this book, we'll walk through exactly how to empower yourself and get out of this trap.

As painful as negative cycles can feel, changing your habits is hard. It can be scary. I don't want to overlook that the work I'm asking you to do takes bravery, especially since these behaviors are often protective measures meant to help us survive. The simple fact that you are here, learning, is a huge step in the right direction. It says that you care, and that you are ready to try something different. And I promise, as difficult as it might be, it will also be empowering and lead you to a place that feels very different and offers real safety and connection, in yourself and in your relationship. When couples can replace the negative cycle with vulnerability and a willingness to take the risks required to get out of each person's comfort zone, the relationship environment will begin to shift and heal. In the following chapters, you will learn to fix the disconnection between what you're hoping for—safety and closeness—and how you go about getting it.

Repeat after me: "The negative cycle is the enemy." Do everything you can to keep this phrase close to your heart. You might even say it to yourself, out loud, during tense moments—this can often create enough of a shift in perspective to regulate or defuse the situation.

From Negative Cycles to Bonding Cycles

Have you ever noticed that during the makeup phase of a fight, you and your partner feel extra close to each other? Sure, maybe you pushed the issue under the rug rather than actually repairing any damage, and maybe the issue will show up again later, but for *this* moment, things feel *so* good.

How can this be when you just treated each other like enemies? Because negative cycles wouldn't exist without emotional investment and vulnerability. For some couples, their vulnerability is only seen during fights and makeups, when it tends to come out whether they want it to or not.

Maybe you've observed this in a couple you know. They seem to be addicted to fighting, which some couples become because that's where the emotional connection is. I know this sounds paradoxical—negative cycles, after all, destroy connection. While there are multiple downsides and I don't advocate for this strategy, the fact remains that fighting can be a way for some couples to close the distance when they don't know how else to do so. At least it's a form of engagement, and for some partners, negative engagement is better than no engagement; also, the makeup phase can feel especially connecting.

When couples can learn how to avoid negative cycles, interrupt negative cycles, and repair negative cycles—all of which you will learn to do in the chapters to come—what they're really doing is learning how to directly access their vulnerabilities and communicate about them in a more measured way than is possible during escalated fights. This communication about vulnerabilities promotes connection, and this is the essence of a bonding cycle. Once you learn to take triggered, vulnerable moments and turn them into bonding cycles, you can begin to feel even closer to your partner, and even more trusting. You will be much more likely to create the space needed for *real* resolution to the problem at hand. Not to mention, bonding creates resiliency for the future. Recognizing, managing, and getting ahead of negative cycles isn't merely a protective measure; it will strengthen even the most secure relationships. All of this is to say, no matter how bad your negative communication cycles might feel, there is hope.

CHAPTER 5

Interrupting the Negative Cycle

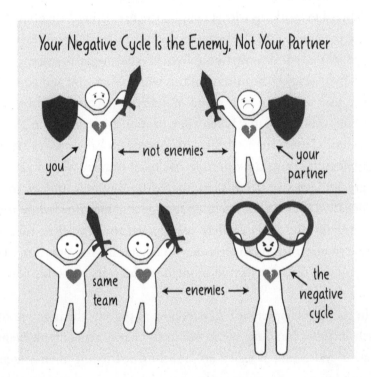

In any given moment in a negative cycle, even when it feels like you're locked in as tight as you've ever been, the truth is that you're not. You and your partner each have an opportunity to interrupt the toxic back-and-forth and stop. It takes two to perpetuate the negative cycle, but only one to *stop*. When you're in a negative cycle, the temptation to protect yourself and let your partner know that everything they're doing is wrong is incredibly strong. It's so hard, in the moment, to be the first one to say, "Let's not let this negative cycle win," or "Instead of saying something I don't mean, I'm going to try something new," or "Let's see if we can get to a healthier place and start talking again in five minutes," especially when you've never learned that sort of dialogue to begin with. But if you can learn to take this step, you may be surprised at how empowering it is, because it allows you to manage the negative cycle with intention, instead of letting it control you with reckless abandon.

When I'm working with a couple, the first thing I do after introducing the concept of the negative cycle is to teach them how to interrupt it. You won't always be able to prevent negative cycles. This is especially true at the beginning of this work, when you and your partner are just wrapping your mind around these concepts, but it will continue to be true later, when your relationship has grown by leaps and bounds. Even the healthiest of couples find themselves stuck in negative cycles from time to time. We're all human. We all get tired, hungry, and stressed. In this chapter we're going to learn how to stop the negative cycle in its tracks once it gets going. But, while there's nothing you can do to entirely prevent negative cycles or to always be able to interrupt them after they've taken on a momentum, there's *a lot* you can do in any given moment to increase the odds you'll be able to do so.

In the next chapter we'll discuss how to prevent the negative cycle, which includes building an environment that is generally resistant to negative cycles (this is called an "attachment-friendly environment"). We're doing it in this order for two reasons. First, it takes time to build the attachment-friendly environment that prevents negative cycles, and even then you'll never be able to prevent them entirely. Also, while we're learning how to prevent the cycles, we need a plan B for when they happen anyway. That's where interruption comes in. Finally, knowing how to successfully interrupt negative cycles is an important component of the attachment-friendly environment that prevents them. So for now, let's focus on stabilization.

Acknowledging the Problem

How do you know when you and your partner are in a negative cycle? Sometimes it will be obvious: you're in a heated argument or fight. Sometimes it's more subtle and you'll need to check in with yourself. If you're interacting with your partner and something doesn't feel right, the odds are high that you're in a negative cycle or you're headed for one. It's important to learn to recognize the first feeling of discomfort. You might notice feeling apprehensive, annoyed, shocked, or let down by your partner. You might feel deflated or blindsided. You might notice thoughts like "here we go again," or "he never does what I ask!" Any thoughts that have a flavor of blaming or of being offended, or that might frame your partner as the enemy, could be indications that you're in the negative feedback loop. It's also important to pay attention to what might be going on with your partner. Are you sensing tension in their words or body language? What's happening with the communication? Are you noticing subtle or overt jabs? Do you feel defensive? Are you needing to get louder to be heard?

I can't emphasize enough how important it is to practice catching these moments. If you can't see them, you can't fix them. When you catch the first sign of a trigger, you have the opportunity to step back and check in with yourself. You might say, "Hmmm, that felt bad, what's going on? I notice I'm feeling flushed. What is my body telling me?" Not only does a check-in help you understand more about what happened, but it also helps you plan your next move with more intention and less reaction. According to psychologist Dr. Viktor Frankl, "Between stimulus and response there is a space. In that space is our power to choose our response. In our response lies our growth and our freedom."

Even if you don't have the capacity to "plan" because you're too dysregulated, catching a trigger can at least buy you some time to do something *less* destructive (progress, not perfection). Even a couple of seconds can be the difference between "I should've never married you!" (when you don't really mean it) and "I'm so angry with you right now!"

If your tendencies are more avoidant, a few seconds of self-awareness can be the difference between "I'm not doing this right now, just leave me alone" and "I'm willing to talk about it, but not right at this second. Give me twenty minutes to gather my thoughts." In the heat of the moment your partner might not like either option, but the latter will be far less triggering.

If you grew up with an insecure attachment, odds are you weren't taught how to check in, feel your feelings, and take space before responding to a trigger. But I can assure you that with time and practice, you'll get better at seeing the signs.

Let's do an exercise to start building awareness. This exercise can be done on your own or with your partner. If you're completing the process with your partner, each of you should complete the exercise and use it to have a conversation when you're finished.

Think of a time when you felt one of the following:

+ Annoyed with your partner
+ Angry at your partner
+ Invalidated by your partner
+ Controlled by your partner
+ Unheard by your partner
+ Unappreciated by your partner
+ Afraid your partner was disappointed or angry with you

Now think about the circumstances surrounding that moment:

+ What did your partner do or say just before you felt this way?
+ What meaning did you make of what they said or did?
+ What happened in your body?
+ In what way did you feel an urge to react? Argue back? Defend yourself? Get critical? Counterattack? Shut down?
+ What did you do next?
+ How would you feel if you didn't do what you did?

+ How might your partner have felt when you did what you did?
+ What did your partner do next?

Here's an example:

Benjamin remembers a moment when he felt annoyed at his partner Lev while they were talking about a recent news event. He recalls a hot feeling rising up in his core. Upon reflection, he remembers that Lev had been pontificating about the issue for several minutes. When Benjamin tried to engage in the conversation, Lev continued on without acknowledging him. Benjamin felt invisible and the overall meaning he made was that Lev didn't value him. Benjamin remembers having an urge to tune out and give up on trying to participate, which is what he did. If he didn't tune out, his annoyance would have turned to anger and he'd rather feel anything but anger. When Lev noticed Benjamin tuning out he said in a snarky tone, "Are you even paying attention to anything I'm saying?" (Of course, Lev had a contributing role in his own disappointment, but right now our focus is on Benjamin's experience.)

Here's a diagram of Benjamin's experience:

Anatomy of a Trigger: Benjamin

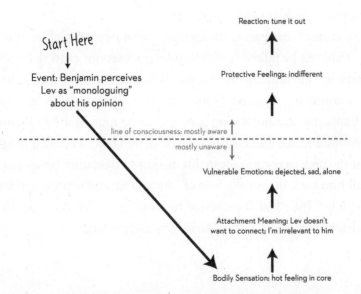

Reflecting on what led to past negative cycles and how you and your partner reacted in those moments can help you understand what triggers the negative cycle in your relationship. These insights also help you recognize what your negative cycles look like when they are happening. Our history and patterns repeat themselves, so if you know that in the past you were triggered by your partner using the word *overreact*, or that your stomach got tied into knots when your partner started heatedly complaining about dirty dishes you left in the sink, you will be better equipped, next time, to recognize what's happening before it gets out of control.

What might Benjamin have done with this information had he recognized it in the moment? There are a few options. He may have interrupted Lev right then and said something along the lines of "Babe, your opinion is so important to me, but I feel kind of invisible right now. Can we go back and forth a bit more?" Or, if their relationship is more direct, he may have said, "Whoa, you're on a roll, but give me some space here" (in a cutesy way, not a demeaning one). Or he may have waited until later and said, "Can I talk to you about something?" Any of those options is better than complete disengagement without explanation.

Now let's look at Lev's experience:

Lev remembers sharing his thoughts with Benjamin about a recent news event. As he talked he felt a sinking sensation, causing his words to break up. He remembers that just before he felt the sinking, he noticed a zoned-out look on Benjamin's face. The meaning he made is that Benjamin was not seeing him and so he must not be valuable to him (ironically, the exact experience Benjamin had). Lev tried to ignore it, but the urge to communicate his distress to Benjamin (in an attempt to pull him back in) got the best of him and he finally protested with a snarky edge. If he hadn't protested he would have felt invisible. Benjamin defensively said, "I was listening to every word."

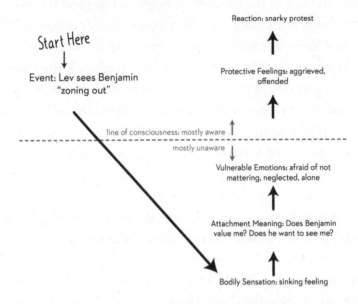

Anatomy of a Trigger: Lev

Start Here

Event: Lev sees Benjamin "zoning out"

Reaction: snarky protest

Protective Feelings: aggrieved, offended

line of consciousness: mostly aware

mostly unaware

Vulnerable Emotions: afraid of not mattering, neglected, alone

Attachment Meaning: Does Benjamin value me? Does he want to see me?

Bodily Sensation: sinking feeling

With more awareness in the moment, what might Lev have done differently? Maybe he could've tried to step into Benjamin's world and reflect on why Benjamin might be *needing* to zone out and asked, "Do I have a role in this?" Maybe he could have verbalized his curiosity with validation: "I can sense your distancing. No shame, I'm guessing there's a good reason for it. Can you tell me what's going on?" Or maybe he could have simply shared his feelings: "I'm feeling unseen right now . . . that always give me anxiety." Again, none of these options will necessarily create the most perfect outcome possible, but they're certainly better than the alternative and when repeated over time will add to relationship safety.

Get Vulnerable

Negative cycles feel awful. But nobody engages in them randomly or for no reason. If you have an insecure attachment, the relationship behaviors that aren't working for you in the long run actually, believe it or not, feel safe in the moment. It might not be good for the overall health of your relationship to deflect your partner's concerns ("What about you? You're not perfect, either") but it can feel safer than hearing things that make you feel like a failure or powerless. If there weren't a short-term payoff to negative cycle behaviors, nobody would engage in them. The short-term payoff? Temporary safety. The cost: long-term relationship health. The solution? Vulnerability.

In the middle of a heated moment, negative cycles give you false hope. While not conscious, your nervous system might be saying, "If I get mean enough, she'll know how much I'm hurting and I won't have to feel alone and unseen." Or, "If I can talk over him and convince him I'm right, he'll see I'm not a stupid, unworthy person."

When I ask my clients to interrupt their negative cycles by doing something different—maybe saying "Let me hear what you have to say" instead of "Nothing is ever enough for you"—I'm asking them to give up their sense of hope, in this case the *false* sense of hope, that if they deflect their partner's concern they won't have to face their own uncomfortable feelings around the topic. Nobody wants to give up their hope, even when it's a false sense, that they can avoid discomfort in the moment. But to make real change you must choose to step away from safety and toward vulnerability.

Many people think vulnerability means sharing your feelings. Sharing your feelings is one way to be vulnerable, but not the only way. Vulnerability means engaging in words or behaviors that *expose* you to emotional pain. Vulnerability isn't about *how* you get vulnerable; that's different for everyone. It's about facing your fears of pain. It's about choosing to stop hiding even when you risk rejection.

I've placed emphasis on the word *expose*, because *expose* is not the same as *guarantee*. Getting vulnerable is not a guarantee you'll be emotionally wounded. In fact, the ultimate goal is to feel better, not worse. But it does mean that you're willing to take the risk of getting wounded, because if you don't take the risk, you *are* guaranteed to miss out on the good things in life: authenticity, connectedness, a sense of empowerment, and/or real resolutions to problems. In my work as an EFT therapist, we like to say "no risk it, no biscuit." Silly, but true.

To be clear, I'm not advising you to repeatedly put yourself in situations where the odds are high that you'll end up feeling rejected or mocked. This work isn't about reckless risk; it's about measured risk. If you never show anyone the authentic you, you never give them the opportunity to accept or reject you and you'll never know if an authentic relationship is possible.

A common confusion around the concept of vulnerability is that it's about your relationship with others. Your capacity to be vulnerable heavily *impacts* your relationship with others and your partner, but ultimately your vulnerability is about your relationship with *you and your own feelings*: How will *you* feel if your partner rejects you after you share more deeply? How will *you* feel if your partner is dismissive when you say something in a healthier way that they aren't used to? How will *you* feel if your partner gets mad when you ask for a break instead of continuing with a negative cycle? Can *you* survive these feelings if you know that facing them can, over time, help your relationship grow?

Imagine your partner has a bad habit of saying a particular curse word you find offensive. One day you're having a nice hike together and they say the forbidden word. You lash out in angry protest because in your mind, lashing out is the best way to be heard, and it might actually work. Your partner might be the type more likely to respond if you lash out rather than saying it more calmly. But lashing out is the easy road. Even if it does get temporary results, they come at the expense of the overall health of the relationship. Interactions like this can, over time, create resentment or reinforce a parent/child dynamic or one in which one partner is afraid of the other. Lashing out is a bad habit, not unlike the cursing you don't like, and what does it mean about the relationship if your partner only responds to aggressive protests?

The vulnerable thing in this situation is to show up less reactively. But for you this is risky; otherwise you'd already be doing it that way. The risk is about *how you're going to feel* if you aren't being heard or responded to. There are a number of reasons why your partner might not be responsive to your repeated requests (and I'm not excusing that), but let's say hypothetically that your partner associates your gentler approaches with a lack of seriousness, and in the past they've just ignored your reasonable tone. It only makes sense you want to say it in the way in which you're less likely to be ignored. If you get ignored, you're going to have to face feelings of powerlessness, rejection, and worthlessness. You might be whisked back to your childhood, when you had to choose between being loud or being invisible.

But the problem with this approach is twofold. Not only is a habit of lashing out not good for the relationship or your own dignity, but it also prevents getting to the heart of the problem: the way the two of you negotiate wants, needs, and requests, which is clearly not working. If the heart of the problem isn't addressed, the pattern—in this case, a lack of responsiveness and aggressive reactions—is only going to show up in other areas of the relationship, even if your partner does stop saying the offensive word.

In order to address the real problem, a deeper conversation is in order. That will require approaching the curse word in a new way when it comes up. And that won't be comfortable. Doing things that aren't comfortable, even when they're for the greater good, requires the willingness to be vulnerable. Do you see the connections?

It's important to keep in mind that choosing to be vulnerable doesn't guarantee a desired outcome. If you could guarantee the outcome, there would be no risk and then we couldn't call it vulnerability.

Here's an exercise that you can do alone or with a partner to help you better understand where you have room to be more vulnerable.

Think of a moment during a negative cycle when you did or said something that wasn't helpful for the relationship.

1. Even if it wasn't conscious, what might you have been hoping for by doing or saying it?
2. What about what you did or said felt safe in the moment?
3. What do you think you could have done or said that would have been better for the relationship?

4. Putting it all together, what was the vulnerable thing for you to do in that moment?

Please note: you might not know what you could've done "better." We still have a lot of skills to learn. Here are some examples to get you thinking:

Shiloh remembers feeling triggered when his partner Tara seemed to be in a bad mood:

> I kept asking her "What's wrong?" and criticizing her for being "dark" even when she said it wasn't about me and just needed space. I was hoping she'd hear me and get in a better mood. It felt safe to keep going because giving up meant I'd be miserable. The vulnerable thing for me would've been saying "okay, I'm here when you're ready" and giving her space because we all need space sometimes.

Tasha remembers feeling triggered when her partner brought up something from the past when she felt let down by Tasha:

> I got angry and told her we've already talked about it and why can't she get over it? I was hoping she would drop it. It felt safe because I didn't want to get in a fight. The most vulnerable thing I could've done was to just listen or even promise her we could talk about it later when I wasn't distracted.

Carol gets triggered when her partner Richard resorts to character attacks when he gets upset such as "you're the type of person who can't handle the truth":

> I usually defend myself by saying things like "That's not true, I'm always willing to hear you out." I'm hoping if I can convince him to see it differently, he'll stop saying it. It feels safe for me to try to make the hurtful words stop. I realize it might be better to

validate him by telling him he's correct that in the past I wasn't always open to his perspective, and that I want to hear him now but I can't continue talking if he's going to attack my character. Setting boundaries brings up my fears of rejection, but by doing it anyway I'll feel more empowered in the relationship. For me, vulnerable is setting a boundary instead of getting defensive.

Self-Regulation and Co-Regulation

"Is it okay to want comfort from my partner?" is one of the most common questions people ask me on social media. Humans are wired to seek emotional support from our loved ones when we're sad, mad, lonely, and scared, yet as society has evolved we've become increasingly hesitant to rely on others for comfort. Phrases like "you're responsible for your own feelings" or "nobody can fix your feelings but you" have been taken out of context to the extent that people worry that seeking comfort from their partner is asking for too much, or even a sign of weakness. Yes, we are all responsible for our own feelings, but a part of this responsibility is asking for help when we need it. Seeking support is self-care. *Co-regulation* is what happens when one partner is in the support role, helping the other feel safe and calm. It is the act of helping your partner regulate their emotions, by being the safe and calm presence. If you're hoping to interrupt a negative cycle as quickly as possible, co-regulation is going to dramatically increase the odds you'll be successful.

Co-regulation epitomizes connection. As such, it is probably the best way to interrupt a negative cycle, because what we're trying to do with this work is replace the negative cycle with a bonding cycle. Here's an example of co-regulation: Vivian and Nala are in the middle of a heated negative cycle about wedding plans. Vivian tells Nala she's being selfish. Instead of responding, "No, actually *you're* the one being selfish!" like she wants to, Nala stops, takes a deep breath, and says to herself, "Okay, this is it. This is the negative cycle that wants to tear us apart. Our attachment fears are flaring. Neither of us is being their best self so I'm going to take the initiative this time to step up and do something new." Then Nala reaches for Vivian's hand, looks her in the eye, and says, "Hey, I love you, let's take a few breaths together. This is hard. I'm right here."

Co-regulation can look like taking deep breaths, changing your tone of voice, talking more slowly, or holding someone's hand. Anything that calms you down, and can create an air of calm in your environment to then calm your partner down, will do the trick.

Another powerful way to co-regulate your partner is to validate whatever is coming up for them. This is especially true of validating anger, which we'll talk about more in chapter 6. When Vivian accuses Nala of being selfish, instead of getting reactive, Nala might say, "I think what you're saying is that you feel like your needs don't matter right now. I get that. Nobody likes feeling like their needs don't matter. How can I help you know that your needs *do* matter so we can feel connected and approach this like a team?" In this situation Vivian was fighting to be seen. When Nala was able to show her that she sees her, Vivian deescalated.

With that said, some partners aren't in the right frame of mind in the heat of the moment to take in validation, and might get annoyed. In that case, it's better to try simple phrases like "I hear you, I'm here" and/or use soft touch. Sometimes your grounded presence can be the most co-regulating thing you can offer.

Maybe you're thinking that this all sounds too good to be true. Your internal dialogue might be saying: "That sounds nice for Vivian and Nala, but my partner tries to 'co-regulate' me by telling me not to worry about it, or by giving me a hug that feels more like changing the subject." But these behaviors are not co-regulation, they are attempts at appeasing, and there's a difference. Co-regulation is motivated by connection, while appeasing is motivated by fear. Co-regulation says, "I want to pull you closer and help you feel safe," while appeasing says, "I want to tell you what you want to hear or calm you down so this uncomfortable conflict will end." One is about going toward; the other is about running away.

In the most successful relationships, both partners can co-regulate, but not always at the same time. Nala was able to show up in our example, but Vivian might be the first to show up next time. My greatest hope is that during a negative cycle, at least one partner will be able to pull back, center themselves, and extend the olive branch. But it's hard to have a thriving relationship if only one partner is always the co-regulator. Still, if that's happening in your relationship, try not to give up right away. While the goal is that *both* partners co-regulate more or less equally but at different times, depending on who is more resourced in the moment, sometimes it takes a while to get there, and the best teaching comes from modeling.

An important caveat to co-regulation is that it can only happen if the regulating partner is self-regulated. What I mean by self-regulated is that you can manage your own emotions—you are in control of your feelings, they are not in control of you. It doesn't mean you cut off your emotions entirely, but that your feelings aren't in the driver's seat. Rather, they're in the passenger seat helping you with directions. In the example above, Nala paused, took a breath, and grounded herself. That was self-regulation, and she was able to pass her "regulated" energy over to Vivian.

Self-regulation starts with awareness. Look inside, get curious, and ask yourself, "What's going on with me right now?" You might notice, "I'm hearing my partner tell me I'm all wrong and that hurts," or "My chest is getting really tight, that means I'm triggered," or "Here comes the abandonment fear," or "I'm worried he's seeing me as stupid and broken."

In order to harness the power of co-regulation to get out of negative cycles and build a strong bond, *both you and your partner must be able to self-regulate.* There's no way around it. This doesn't mean both partners need to do so every time there's a rupture. If that were the case, we wouldn't need co-regulation. But we are relational beings. We need each other's nervous systems to harness the power of connection to others, and we need to be there for our own to harness the power of self-connection. It's not an either/or; it's a both/ and. I believe healthy relationships are 50/50, but I don't believe they need to be 50/50 in every given moment. Sometimes one partner will be more upset over something and sometimes one partner will be less tired, hungry, or stressed, and thus be more resourced in the moment. If neither partner can self-regulate during moments when their attachment systems are sounding the alarm bell, there's nobody to initiate co-regulation and be the comforting presence. Using self-regulation to interrupt a negative cycle doesn't have to be perfect or make bad feelings go away entirely. It just needs to be good enough to help you do something *better*. For example, if you're at a 10 emotionally and you want to throw a plate at the wall, and instead you can get yourself down to a 7 and throw a dish towel, that is better. Better is growth; you can build on better. Maybe next time you can go from a 7 to a 4.

As you think about introducing co-regulation into your relationship, remember that different partners feel soothed in different ways. Some partners like physical touch, some relax with soothing words, others might need something entirely different. Successful couples work together to learn what feels best for each other.

One of the most common questions I receive is "How can I self-regulate?" There are more ways to self-regulate than I can list and what works for one doesn't necessarily work for others. Common strategies include breathing exercises, meditation, physical exercise, journaling, mentalizing, or "feeling your feelings" (allowing them to pass through your body). Mentalization means stepping back and balancing your view of your partner or the triggering situation. When you're triggered and feel threatened, it's all too easy to see the bad in your partner and forget the good. To shift out of this mindset you can mentally visualize a moment when your partner really showed up for you, or a moment when you felt loved and safe. This can signal to your nervous system that there's less of a threat than what it's perceiving, which is self-regulating, and can help you manage whatever problem you're facing with a balanced approach.

Self-regulation starts with awareness, which can be found through practicing mindfulness. Mindfulness is a powerful way to self-regulate and I recommend it as an adjunct to any other strategy you might be using. Sometimes mindfulness is called "body scanning"—it requires stepping back from the situation happening outside of you (what your partner is doing or saying) and into your body. Look inside, get curious, and ask yourself, "What's going on with me right now?" You might notice, "I'm hearing that my partner doesn't care about me," or "here comes the abandonment fear," or "my shame is saying 'you must be stupid.'" Notice where you might feel tension rising. Focus on the tension without judgment. Notice any other bodily sensations such as your heartbeat, tingling sensations, or a tightening in your stomach. Drop into your five senses by asking yourself, "What can I see? What can I hear? What can I taste? What can I feel with my skin? What can I smell?" Mindfulness is effective because it's grounding. It takes you out of the overwhelm of all that is going on outside of you, and into the containment of your physical self. A good question to ask when you're being mindful is "Where are my feet?" which is particularly useful for grounding yourself into the present moment. The very act of being curious about your own experience will help you step back from acting in a way that might not serve you or your relationship. Your curiosity acts like a pause button: "Let me take a beat and look inside before I do or say something I'll regret."

When you ask these questions, *do it from a place of nonjudgmental observation.* Otherwise it won't work and you'll feel worse instead of better. Judging yourself for feeling the way you do will only bring on more shame and add to the problem. You can't fight shame with shame. Next, validate your experience. The importance of validating your experience, whatever it is, cannot be understated because self-validation creates self-acceptance and acceptance is the antidote to shame. Validate your thoughts and feelings which are alive. Here are some examples:

Instead of this self-shaming thought:

"Why can't I pull it together and get a grip on my thoughts?"

Try this self-validating thought:

"Of course I'm hearing my partner say I'm a bad person. I grew up in a home where I got the message that I was 'bad' all the time."

Instead of this self-shaming thought:

"I shouldn't be mad, I'm overreacting. I should just let it go."

Try this self-validating thought:

"It makes sense I'm mad. It's okay to be mad. I have a right to all of my feelings and all of my feelings have important meanings. I can think about the meanings later but first let me take some breaths."

This is where it gets tricky, and you might want to protest by asking "but what if my feelings are irrational?" The truth is that all feelings are rational, simply because they exist. If you step on a nail, you know why you feel pain. If you have a random pain in your abdomen, you may not know exactly what's going on to cause the pain, but yet the pain is real. Your brain creates feelings for a very good reason: to motivate you to take action to protect yourself, or to take action toward fixing a problem or gaining something pleasurable. When your brain is acting out of self-protection, it is either responding to something real in the moment or subconscious memories of past events, or (most likely) a mixture of both. Your perceptions of the situation aren't always accurate. For example, your partner might not really hate you, but it's entirely rational to feel scared if you *perceive* that your partner hates you. Anyone would. When you can validate your experience without shaming yourself, you're going to feel more self-regulated and be in a much better position to react in a healthy way, assess your perceptions within yourself or by checking it out with your partner, and go forward with problem-solving whatever situation led to the trigger to begin with. If you're new to self-regulation techniques, my advice is to try different strategies and create your own list of what works for you. For some people that might be any of the ideas listed above, a walk in nature, dancing, rubbing your hands together, or even shaking your body for a few minutes. It's about dropping down into your body and out of your head—grounding yourself and connecting with yourself in a loving, positive way. Ultimately, you're giving yourself the same connection you yearn for in your relationship. But the best time to work on building your self-regulation muscle is when you're not at a 10. Pay attention to small triggers throughout the day: anxiety or annoyance, for example. Use those moments to practice your skills and build habits that your brain can draw upon when the big triggers come.

Here's a simple breathing exercise called "box breathing." This type of breathing is a way to tell your nervous system, "We're safe. All is well." Inhale for four seconds; hold it for four seconds; exhale for four seconds; hold for four seconds; repeat for a few minutes until you feel your body start to lose the edge.

Name the Negative Cycle

Naming the negative cycle is just that: literally calling it out in the moment to remind you and your partner that something bigger is at play. Naming the negative cycle puts your awareness to use. It reminds your partner and your nervous system that "this is not us, this is something outside of us." This is called externalization, and you can use it to shift the narrative from "my partner is the enemy" to "the cycle is the enemy."

Naming the negative cycle might sound like:

+ "This is our negative cycle. Let's not let it win."
+ "You and this relationship are more important to me than this negative cycle."
+ "The negative cycle is our enemy."

If you're reading this book on your own and your partner isn't familiar with the concept of the negative cycle, maybe ask them to read this chapter. Even partners who might not be ready to take a look at their relationship through an attachment lens are often receptive to the idea of the negative cycle because 1) it's so relatable, and 2) it's de-shaming. For some ideas on how to bring the topic up with as much safety as possible, see chapter 13.

When you get better at recognizing when you and your partner are in a negative cycle, you may notice that you fall into specific negative cycle traps. Similar to naming the negative cycle, naming the traps is also helpful. "Who's the Bad Guy?" "Who Gets to Hurt Worse?" and "The Miss." These "traps" can happen in any type of negative cycle, regardless of the attachment style of each partner or the topic at hand.

Who's the Bad Guy?

"Who's the Bad Guy?" is a blame-blame trap in which each partner fixates on what the other partner has done wrong. If you can relate to blame-blame (and most couples can), remember that you're each fighting to *not* be the bad guy because your insecurely attached wiring has taught you that being in the wrong makes you wholly bad, which is certain to leave you feeling shamed, misunderstood, invalidated, worthless, incompetent, and devalued. You might think, "If I'm proven to be the bad guy here, that might mean I'm not worthy of getting my own needs met." Even when a partner is clearly in the wrong, they may fight hard to prove their goodness. In the moment, not being seen as the bad guy can feel like life or death, and for good reason: you're fighting for your worth as a person and as a partner, because you've been taught that bad guys aren't worthy or lovable. Even if you don't understand why you play who's the bad guy, recognizing that you do it is enough if you can learn to get out of it.

To interrupt "Who's the Bad Guy," name it: "I think we're stuck playing 'Who's the Bad Guy.' What if instead we're both the good guys fighting to reach each other and feel safe?"

Here's an example. Partner A, an anxious partner, tells Partner B, an avoidant partner, that they don't like the way Partner B talks to the kids. The delivery is heated and shaming. Partner B says, "You should hear yourself; you're not exactly Mary Poppins." Partner A responds with "That's not true. I have a great relationship with the kids. They talk to me about everything, including the way *you* talk to them." Partner B responds with "They talk to you about everything because they know you'll tell them what they want to hear." Partner A says, "I was the one who brought it up first. Why can't you just listen?" Partner B says, "Why should I? I never have any space in this relationship to bring up concerns!" And on and on it goes until finally Partner B says, "Forget it, fine, I'll do better. I just don't want to keep going back and forth."

If this sounds more like two anxious partners, that's not necessarily the case. Many anxious/avoidant couples get stuck in this sort of blame-blame cycle. It's just that some avoidant partners will fight harder and/or for longer before eventually withdrawing. Anxious partners, on the other hand, typically feel compelled to keep going until they perceive resolution.

Who Gets to Hurt Worse?

"Who Gets to Hurt Worse?" is similar to "Who's the Bad Guy?" but in reverse. Partners compete for the role of "most hurt," because they believe that only one person can hurt at a time. For this couple, being the hurt one is the only way to feel validated for their pain. Of course, in the context of their negative cycle, *both* partners are suffering with painful unmet attachment needs. *Both* partners are feeling alone and demoralized and, at worst, the despair of hopelessness. The goal is for you and your partner to move away from the belief that only one of you can be hurting at a time, and move toward the belief that you can both be hurting at once. Validating your partner's hurt from the negative cycle does not cancel out your own hurt. Attachment pain is not a zero-sum game.

To interrupt "Who Gets to Hurt Worse," start by naming it: "You know what? We're acting like only one of us can be hurt over this, but that's not true. We're both hurting."

The Miss

"The Miss" is when a couple gets stuck in a loop of misunderstanding each other's intentions. Here's how a miss might play out:

Jayden and Frances find themselves getting stuck in negative cycles around chores. When Jayden feels let down, he often tries to reach Frances (who hasn't historically been responsive to Jayden's expressed concerns) with questions that are thinly veiled criticisms. But sometimes his questions are just . . . questions.

Jayden comes home and asks Frances if she walked the dog. What's going through his mind is, "It's a beautiful evening . . . if she hasn't walked the dog, we can all go together after dinner." But Frances has had enough experience with Jayden's questions to believe there is an underlying criticism. Her nervous system defaults to "Alarm bell, thinly veiled criticism! What he's saying is 'I have a feeling you haven't already walked the dog, in which case you're irresponsible.'"

"What's that supposed to mean?" Frances responds, clearly getting annoyed.

"I was just asking," Jayden states. "Can you relax?" Frances feels invalidated because she's experienced the thinly veiled criticisms many times, so instead of having a nice walk Jayden and Frances get stuck in a negative cycle.

When the Miss happens, name it and get curious: "I think we might be missing each other right now. What are you hearing me say?" When you get to the bottom of your partner's perception, share your own. When you do this, instead of walking away feeling misunderstood and defeated, which is often the way partners end a Miss, you'll make it more likely you'll both feel heard and connected.

Take a Break

In a perfect world, during a heated negative cycle one partner has the capacity to take a pause, self-regulate, and provide the co-regulating energy to both. Like I said, focusing on connection is the best way out of negative cycles, considering that negative cycles are defined by disconnection. But it's also the most advanced and some couples aren't ready for that when they're new to this work. For one, you or your partner might still be learning how to ground yourself and self-regulate in heated moments. Also, being the co-regulator is vulnerable and risky—*what if I get rejected?*—and it can take time to build up to. So what can we do in the meantime?

When you're in a negative cycle and really don't know how to get out, agreeing to take a break might make the best sense. The idea of disconnecting might sound counterproductive after you've read so much about the importance of connection, but taking a break during a negative cycle is the kind of interruption that is meant to protect the relationship. Breaks will help both partners find some space to reorganize themselves around their inner experiences and attachment fears. Breaks give you the opportunity to come up for air, which is especially important for avoidant partners, who often do better facing their feelings in "chunks" instead of all at once.

But breaks aren't meant to be indefinite or open-ended. Agreeing to come back to the conversation is part of the process. If you don't agree to come back to it, that's not a break; that's pushing a hard topic under the rug. In terms of the length of your break, I recommend anywhere from five minutes to one day. Any shorter and you haven't had proper time to catch your breath; any longer and the topic feels too distant. This is a general guideline. Sometimes it will make more sense to table a topic for longer.

Taking a break has to be a team effort. It requires vulnerability on the part of each partner. If you have an anxious attachment, breaks can feel scary and painful. In your mind, it's better to keep fighting or arguing because maybe, just maybe, if the two of you keep at it, you'll finally find the resolution and closeness you're needing. If you stop, then what? You'll have to feel unresolved and sit with uncomfortable abandonment fears.

Breaks usually aren't hard for those with an avoidant attachment. Generally speaking, if you're avoidantly attached, you welcome the space. In your mind, breaks keep things from getting worse. But breaks shouldn't be a means to distract yourself indefinitely. For you, the work is agreeing to reengage. To help your partner tolerate the break, it can be enormously helpful to say, "Don't worry, we'll come back to it," and agree to when, if you're able to do that.

When you need to take a break, you'll have the most success if you use attachment-friendly language. Frame the break not as "you're bad and I have to protect myself from you" but as "our relationship is something to be valued and protected." Here are some phrases to try:

- ✦ "The negative cycle is the enemy right now. Let's take a break so it doesn't win."
- ✦ "This path is going to get us nowhere. How about we take a five-minute break?"
- ✦ "We're in our negative cycle; let's not do this."
- ✦ "I love you more than I love this argument."
- ✦ "This relationship is too important to me to keep going down this road to nowhere."
- ✦ "If we don't take a break, I'm afraid we're going to end up really hurting each other."
- ✦ "I don't want a break from you. I want a break from how overwhelmed I feel."

If you and your partner successfully interrupt your negative cycle and take a break, know that that alone is a huge success. But now what? If you have an anxious attachment, it's almost certain you feel worse. Your nervous system isn't saying, "I'm so glad we took a break and have this space to process our thoughts and feelings so we can come back together and work this out." It's probably crying, "I'm so mad, sad, and scared, and at least if we'd stayed in the cycle I wouldn't have to be alone with it! At least I might get the answers I'm looking for! At least we might eventually find our ways back to each other! Now I'm supposed to just sit here burning up inside?"

It's hard; it hurts. For some people, this can be the hardest thing they have to do in life: face their attachment fears and shame. So what should you do? To start, you don't have to be alone with it. This might be a good time to call a trusted loved one and seek support. That doesn't mean you have to share private details you'd rather keep to yourself, but you can say, "Ari and I had an argument and are taking a break for a couple of hours so we can cool down. I'm having a hard time."

In times when no outside source of help is available, you can try journaling your thoughts and feelings, exercising, breathing exercises, getting into nature, listening to your favorite music, and anything else that might help you ease your nervous system back into a state of regulation. Remember, getting good at feeling your feelings is the path to developing a secure attachment in your relationship with yourself. Learning to take care of you *is* taking care of the relationship.

What if you're the avoidant partner? You might be drawn to distracting yourself or trying to forget about the situation, but the space during the break doesn't let you off the hook. This is your time to dive in and figure out what it is you're feeling. Not just thinking but feeling. When you go back to the situation, my hope is that you go back in with your whole self: a balance of your head and heart. For you, it's less about self-regulation and more about self-engagement. This is the time to tap into yourself and ask questions like "What did I notice in my *body*: Chest tightening? Pressure in my head? Tingling in my limbs? Jaw clenching? Hands clenching? Deflated feeling? Throat tightening? Anything else?" I've worked with countless partners with avoidant attachment who need weeks of practice before they're able to recognize a bodily sensation, so if you're having trouble with this, you're not alone. If you hadn't learned to disconnect from your body, you wouldn't have an avoidant attachment to begin with. I encourage you to put the time into practicing body scanning. It's the first step to understanding your inner world. Once you've been able to locate a physical sensation, ask yourself, "If this sensation had a feeling name, what might it be?" For example, you might call a tightening in your throat "sadness," or a clenching in your jaw "frustration"; a frozen feeling might be "caught off guard."

Connect your feelings with the urge to react. For example, "When I felt this anger, my urge was to defend myself. What did my partner say or do just before I felt the urge to get defensive? What meaning did I make of what was said? Why did I need to get defensive? What was I trying to protect . . . my sense of self? The relationship? Some of both?" If you're able to get your own journal out to help you along, even better. Your partner is going to feel safer and closer if you go back in with more clarity around your emotional and vulnerable self.

Asking for (and Giving) Reassurance

Since negative cycles are driven by attachment fears and shame, asking for reassurance is a quick way to calm fears and de-shame *if your relationship is ready for it.* If you're in the middle of a negative cycle and things are escalating, take a pause and ask yourself, "What am I afraid of right now?" or "What am I ashamed of right now?" Then ask for the reassurance you need to *not* feel scared or ashamed.

Here's an example: Camila and Charlie are going back and forth about her concerns regarding an upcoming vacation. Camila is blaming Charlie for not caring and Charlie is telling her she's crazy, of course he cares. Camila realizes it's the cycle and checks in with herself and realizes she's afraid that if she tells Charlie about her concerns in a way that isn't blaming and accusatory, she won't be heard. Instead of continuing down the same old path, she gets vulnerable, saying, "You know what? Right now we're in our loop of doom [sometimes couples give their negative cycles names] and what's happening for me is that I'm afraid if I don't get big and start blaming you and accusing you, I won't be heard. Can I just get some reassurance that if I shift gears and try this in a new way, you'll be able to hear me?"

You can also offer your partner reassurance even if they don't ask for it. Each of you has the opportunity to shift gears and try something different. Maybe Charlie could've been the one to step back and say, "I think you might be afraid I'm not going to hear you. Can I just reassure you right now that if you can get softer, I will still be able to hear you? Can we try this a new way?"

Or Camila might say, "Charlie, if you're worried that my concerns mean I think you're a bad partner I understand that. I know things have happened between us in the past that makes it easy for you to see it that way. But for me that's not what's happening right now. I see you as a good partner. I have something I want to talk about, that's true, but nothing I have to say can take away from how much I appreciate you and love you."

For some couples, asking for reassurance and responding to a partner's bids for reassurance is too much if they're early in this work, are more sensitive to triggers, can't trust reassurance, and/or are having highly escalated cycles. When it works, it's powerful, but if you try it and it falls flat, don't despair. It's not uncommon. Asking for something is a big risk and even providing reassurance can feel risky. If it doesn't go well, this simply means we need to do some work in the background to build up safety, trust, and the self-regulation/co-regulation skills required to manage the situation when things don't go as planned.

Practice is the best way to build up these skills to help you interrupt your negative cycle. Be gentle with yourself. It takes a leap of faith—in yourself most of all—to change the way you respond. Remember, how you both have been reacting is making you feel farther apart than bringing the closeness you desire. You can change your reaction and underlying assumptions, and it can start with these steps.

But it's also helpful to keep in mind that interrupting the negative cycle is really about triage. You don't want to get stuck in negative cycles as you try to improve the overall climate of your relationship, because as you build the overall climate to increase security and closeness, negative cycles will begin to decrease on their own. It all feeds on itself. We're working this from every angle. With that, let's learn how to build an attachment-friendly climate.

CHAPTER 6

Preventing the Negative Cycle

The Attachment-Friendly Environment

If you can learn how to ward off the negative cycle, well, it's like pre-ventative medicine. As you get better at identifying the negative cycle and course-correcting in the moment, you will hopefully build up to a place where you can prevent it from getting started in the first place. To do this, we need to create what's called an *attachment-friendly en-vironment*.

An attachment-friendly environment is one in which partners have met attachment needs, meaning that in the overall climate of the relationship they each feel valued, seen, understood, and appreciated. In an attachment-friendly environment, partners view each other through an "attachment lens"—meaning, for example, that when your partner gets snarky, you're able to hear it as "you're trying to communicate to me how much pain you're in," rather than hearing blame and shame and the message that "you are the enemy, you are bad, you are trying to hurt me." These environments are more resilient to negative cycles because behaviors such as criticism, cynicism, stonewalling, defensiveness, and accusations are replaced with curiosity, empathy, understanding, and validation. You can use specific skills to create an attachment-friendly environment—and I'll dive into these skills in this chapter—but for relationship change to last, these skills need to be part of a broader mindset to care for the security of the relationship. For example, later in this chapter we'll discuss emotional validation, so that when you say something like, "I hear that you're sad," it's not just empty words; instead the spirit behind the words is "I want my partner to feel seen and accepted for their emotional self right now, because we all thrive when we feel seen. I'm not just speaking the words because a book told me it's a healthy way to communicate. I'm speaking them because they mean something much bigger about the relationship I want to cultivate." To cultivate an attachment-friendly environment, you're aiming to create a felt sense of empathy that drives the words: "I hear that you're sad."

Think of it this way: In the movies, the best actors don't just memorize their lines. They spend weeks or months embodying their characters, even becoming their characters. When the time comes to read their lines, they can show up authentically, because they understand where their character is coming from—they understand the character's motivations, insecurities, and fears. This is what I want for you. I don't want you to just say or do the "right" thing to create an attachment-friendly environment. I want you to understand the *why* so that you can show up authentically in your relationship. My hope is that you will believe in the principles behind the strategies, and embody the spirit of this work, so that in the end you don't even need the scripts.

As we proceed and you learn how to create an attachment-friendly environment, keep in mind that your relationship with your partner is made up of repeated interactions between the two of you, day in and day out, and each of these interactions provides the opportunity to do something profound: to leave each other feeling seen, heard, cared for, and validated. When you learn how to make the most of each interaction, and do it consistently, you will have a healthy relationship.

One note: In a perfect world, creating an attachment-friendly environment is the responsibility of both partners. When I work with couples, I encourage both individuals to practice the skills laid out in this chapter. That's not to say one partner won't grow faster than the other, or that they'll end up at the exact same place. Be patient. My husband will never be as emotionally aware as I am—I'm a therapist who has more time to practice these skills than most people. It's literally my job. But still, my husband is emotionally aware *enough* to give me what I need. That said, you can only control yourself, and it only takes one partner to initiate the relationship change that can lead to a better environment. That doesn't mean staying in a one-sided relationship indefinitely, but for real and lasting change, your work needs to come from a place of "I want to be different even when you can't be." Our own growth needs to be our priority.

Of course we all want our partners to change and grow if we're repeatedly getting stuck in negative cycles. Except we can't want it more than anything else. We have to want our *own* growth more than anything else, because that's the mindset from which real relationship change can take place.

Communicating in an Attachment-Friendly Environment

Imagine a busy restaurant with three tables where couples are sitting. The first couple sounds like this:

Partner A: Wow, this menu is overwhelming. I don't remember it being this big.

Partner B: Why did you want to come here then? You knew how big the menu is; it was your choice.

Partner A: Why are you getting so defensive? All I said was it's hard to decide.

Partner B: I'm not getting defensive. I'm stating a fact.

Partner A: You're being kind of snarky about it.

Partner B: I don't want to get pulled into an argument right now. Let's just eat.

The next couple sounds like this:

Partner A: Wow, this menu is overwhelming.

Partner B: I hear that you think the menu is overwhelming. When you say "the menu is so big," I feel blamed for making a bad decision.

Partner A: That's your stuff. I feel sad that you are misunderstanding me.

Partner B: I feel like you're getting dysregulated, and this is a boundary violation. My therapist said when this happens, I need to take a break and go sit in the lobby until you can self-regulate.

Partner A: I hear that you think your boundaries are being violated. I feel like your narcissism is making me feel abandoned. My therapist says you need to co-regulate me.

The final couple sounds like this:

Partner A: Wow, this menu is overwhelming. I don't remember it being this big.

Partner B: I thought you already knew that before we came. We could've gone somewhere else.

Partner A: (picks up a feeling of being misunderstood by the comment, pauses to check in with self, recognizes the potential for a negative cycle, responds with attachment in mind) I can see why you would think I'm complaining, but I'm not. I really like it here, big menu and all. Anyway, I'm just glad we're together.

Partner B: (feels reassured) Me, too.

Later:

Partner B: Remember at dinner when you mentioned the menu being overwhelming? That was one of those moments when I told myself a story that you were blaming me for getting it wrong, and I felt the urge to get defensive. I appreciate that you were able to respond the way you did.

Partner A: I understand that and I appreciate you bringing it up. Look how far we've come. In the past that conversation could've really derailed us.

While none of these conversations are entirely realistic, they represent three different approaches to the same problem. In the first example, the couple is having obvious conflict; in the second, the couple is having stealth conflict. Though the words might seem "psychologically sound," conflict is conflict. The third has all the elements of an attachment-friendly environment (though you can certainly have this environment without such exaggerated language). This couple managed a trigger without going into a negative cycle like the other two couples. Partner A was able to check in and redirect. They had the attachment savvy to respond without getting pulled into an argument of details. Judging by how they managed it, these two have had enough conversations about triggers to know what each other might be needing. Are they mind readers? No. Rather, they've worked at understanding each other on a deep level, including understanding the insecure parts we all have somewhere inside of ourselves that sometimes need special care. Could partner B have done something differently? Yes, but that's not how it played out here. In another situation partner B might have been the one to catch the negative cycle and change course.

Another important note is that these partners were able to put the trigger aside, enjoy each other, and talk about it later in private. In another situation it might have made sense to talk about it right then and there, but they trusted it could be addressed later without it being ignored indefinitely. And in yet another situation they may not have needed to bring it up again at all. Each situation is unique.

This example shows you what you probably already know: how quickly things can go south. In this case it all started because of a menu. Over and over, couples tell me at the beginning of therapy that "we fight over the smallest things."

"Nope," I say, "you're fighting over something that can feel like life and death in the moment—attachment safety. The content might be inconsequential, but the meaning is powerful. Nothing is small when it comes to attachment."

Attachment Intentions and the Attachment Lens

Attachment theory rests upon the belief that all relationship behaviors have an attachment intention. Every time we snap, defend, shut down, push away, get cynical, sarcastic, use passive-aggressive humor, or call names, it is a misguided attempt to say, "Hear me! Feel some of my pain so you know how much this hurts! Stop treating me like this! See what you're doing wrong so you'll change! See me as good!" And, when distilled further, "I need to feel safe right now!"

Let's say you've tried repeatedly to get your partner to weigh in on whether the two of you should travel to your college friend's wedding. Your partner keeps dodging the issue and you're left in the dark. Based on my experience, the odds are high that the attachment intention is that your partner is conflicted between anxiety about the trip and anxiety about the relationship. Maybe you're trying to save for an upcoming move, so spending money on travel right now makes your partner uncomfortable. That's a reasonable concern, but maybe they don't want to express this to you because they're afraid they'll feel like a failure if they let you down. Their fear might be based on real experience with you in the past, previous relationships, and/or their childhood attachment climate. Regardless, your partner's reluctance to discuss the topic has the *attachment intention* of staying safe with you. If they didn't care about staying safe with you, they'd probably just say "no" to the wedding and leave it at that.

Consider this other example: You're irritated that your partner doesn't tidy up the bathroom after getting ready in the morning, even though you've repeatedly asked them to. When your partner mentions one afternoon that you forgot to close the garage door after getting home from work, you retort, "You're far from perfect—what about how you leave the bathroom every morning?" If your frustration had words, it would say, "This doesn't feel fair and I need to know things are fair between us—that *both* our needs matter equally—to feel safe and close!"

What about big behaviors, like affairs? What's the attachment intention there? We all know affairs destroy attachment, but we also probably know that we all need to feel wanted, accepted, and loved. Our earth is populated by eight billion people walking around hoping to feel this way. When someone isn't getting those needs met, they'll do any number of things to find what they're looking for, including going outside the relationship. I'm *not* excusing affairs—I know the devastation they create, and I know there's a much better way to go about getting one's needs met—but even these destructive choices have attachment intentions.

Keep in mind that positive relationship behaviors have attachment intentions, too. You make your partner's grandma's lasagna recipe because you know they love it. Their happiness contributes to your own happiness and feelings of security. Part of why you keep your living space neat is because it helps you feel relaxed, and feeling relaxed is not only good for you as an individual, but it also helps you enjoy time with your partner when you're together. You work hard at your job to feel a sense of inner accomplishment, but also so you and your partner can be happy and have a good life together. You say "I love you" every day when you part because you want your partner to feel safe and loved.

If you can look at your negative cycle and see the attachment intention underneath the surface conflict, you can start to shift your viewpoint, seeing the situation through an attachment lens. This is very different from what I call the "enemy lens," which is how many partners with insecure attachments view their conflicts—and thus their partner. The enemy lens says, "When my partner says and does things I don't like it's because they're bad, or because they don't love me, or because they want to hurt or shame me." Most of the time, of course, this isn't the case. Ironically, most of the time when your partner says and does things you don't like, they're trying to protect their attachment. Viewing yourself and your partner through an attachment lens, especially in your darkest moments when the most hurtful words and behaviors are flying, is a game changer. It's also critical to establish an attachment-friendly environment.

Adopting an attachment lens is a work in progress. Even as a couples therapist and after twenty-three years of marriage, I still have to remember to reground myself into my attachment lens when there's tension between my partner and me. Nobody is entirely exempt from taking things personally, especially in close relationships where the emotional stakes are the highest. When my husband is in a bad mood, my first instinct might be to think, "You have no right to be grumpy," as if he's contractually obliged to be happy all the time. In this case, my own attachment fears have kicked in: *I feel so alone! What if he stays grumpy forever and never comes back? Will we ever feel connected again?* Or it might be about my own view of myself as unworthy: *If he doesn't care about my needs right now, what might that mean about how much I matter in this relationship? If I don't matter, what does that mean about me? Does that mean I'm worthless?* But the more I do this work, the easier it is to pull back, look through my attachment lens, and reassure myself, "This is about my attachment fears. Let's take a step back and do this differently."

Clearing Out Shame

When I first start seeing a couple, usually each partner is focused on what the other is doing wrong. Such as:

"I tried to tell her I was sad that she didn't support me when our son was being rude. Instead of validating me, she just tried to explain why my way is wrong."

"I do everything I can to be supportive, but it's never enough. I'll never be enough for him."

"She never sees my side of things. Everything has to be her way or else it's a fight. If I try to talk about my side, she gets more upset and we end up talking only about her issues."

"If I bring something up, like how he's always on his phone, he just denies it and blames me for bringing it up, like my concerns aren't real and I'm just trying to pick a fight."

What is the common ground here? Are the protesting partners all bad, uncaring, and self-absorbed? Are the partners on the receiving end unsupportive, overbearing, and unaccountable? Maybe some of their *behaviors* can be described as such, but when viewed through the lens of attachment, each of these "misbehaving" partners is communicating with the same primary goal in mind. Subconsciously, they're trying to stay one step ahead of the shame living inside them . . . the shame that is driving their insecure attachment and leaving them in fear of abandonment and feelings of rejection and unworthiness.

Shame develops during childhood when caregivers send messages, consistently and over the course of time, that some or all of you is bad, weak, selfish, or some other "shameful" descriptor. This might sound extreme, but it doesn't have to be. In fact many decent, loving parents unintentionally shame their children when they're angry or as a means to solve problems. Let's look at an example of how shaming messages, when repeated over time, can lead to bigger problems.

Ten-year-old Peyton asks for a puppy and, like all ten-year-olds, promises to take care of it. But when Peyton makes the request, her dad is indignant. "Why do you think we'd trust you with a dog?" he responds. "You can't even manage to keep your own room clean." It's not a *horrible* thing to say, and all parents can relate to this frustration. But the underlying message Peyton hears is "You should be able to keep your room clean and since you can't that must mean something is fundamentally wrong with you." On top of that, the delivery is not loving and solution-focused; it's cynical. Peyton takes on the self-beliefs that "I'm not good enough because I can't get it right," "I'm not deserving of being spoken to gently," and "Expressing frustration and shaming others is how to work on problems."

This shame-based response can show up in Peyton's life all the way into adulthood. She might become an overly stressed overachiever as a way to hide the parts of her she doesn't believe are good enough. This could be her way of avoiding rejection and maintaining a sense of being worthy of connection. She might try to hide her insecurities by being mean to other girls at school, the subconscious idea being that if others feel weak and unworthy, she won't have to. Instead of learning how to express her frustrations in a healthy way, she might hide them underneath cynicism just as she saw her dad do.

Let's contrast this with an alternative response: "I'm concerned about a dog being too much responsibility for you. Right now you're at the age when you're learning how to get better at taking care of the basic things like your room. Let's focus on that for a while before adding something else to your plate." This response achieves the same "no" for Peyton's dad, but suggests *growth*. It tells Peyton that her father believes she'll be able to handle these responsibilities one day. That she is good enough, and deserves to be spoken to with respect.

When children pick up shaming messages they learn to hide parts of themselves they believe are bad or unworthy. Humans are driven to connect, so it only makes sense that you're going to hide the parts of you that you believe aren't worthy of connection.

But it doesn't have to stay that way. There's a *lot* you can do to create your own low-shame microenvironment in the safe confines of your relationships with your loved ones. The antidote to shame is acceptance, and the hopeful news is that when you view your partner through the lens of attachment you can accept *them* without accepting all of their *behavior*, and they can do so for you. By separating the behavior from the person, shame will, over time, begin to dissolve. When Shonna chronically breaks her promises, instead of her partner Ariana saying "You're irresponsible and selfish," she can say, "I understand how much you have going on and how easy it is for you to overcommit right now. At the same time when you say one thing and do another, I feel left in the dark. I need to know your words mean something. What can we do here?"

When Shonna reflects on her behavior, shaming herself, "I'm so bad, why can't I get it right?" it's only going to bog her down with negative, unproductive energy. But healthy guilt, on the other hand, which might look like thinking "I'm a good person and a good partner, but I'm letting Ariana down when I break promises; this is something I need to work on," is going to be a much healthier way to motivate herself to make changes without making her want to hide away and avoid connection.

Let's say your partner seems resistant to change when you've tried bringing up your relationship struggles. So now, when you recommend a relationship book you've been reading, they push it away and say, "We don't need that, we just need to be nicer to each other." In my experience, what this partner is really doing is rejecting their own shame, saying, "It's too unbearable to think I can't do this on my own. Normal people make their relationship work; they don't need help from books." Again, shame is saying, "If I can't figure it out on my own, *I* am all wrong, broken, or unworthy." Push away the book, push away what the book represents: shame.

People with insecure attachments are walking around the world trying to keep the idea that they are bad or unworthy at their core—their shame—at bay. This requires them to engage in all sorts of ineffective communication patterns and behaviors to keep a lid on the shame they so fear being exposed.

Here are some examples of how shame shows up in relationships:

Overreacting: Shame says, "I carry a self-belief of unworthiness, so anything that comes along to confirm what I already fear to be true is going to overwhelm me with the painful shame in me. When that happens, I have to get as big as possible to fight it away."

Blaming and Defensiveness: Shame says, "It's too painful to own my flaws. People who mess up are unworthy. So I have to convince you that you're wrong and then I don't have to be the bad one. If I'm not the bad one, you won't see me as unworthy."

Rigidity: Shame says, "I can't be open to your ideas about parenting, there's too much on the line. If I mess up as a parent, what does that mean about me? I'm too afraid to mess this up and let down my family and feel like a failure. I need for you to see that I'm in pain, too, but I don't have awareness or words for it. Your parenting ideas feel like a threat to my safety, so I have to shut them out."

Withdrawal: Shame says, "I don't know what to do to make this better right now and if I can't fix it, I'm a letdown. I feel so powerless. I'd rather go hide than stand here feeling defeated and broken."

Criticism: Shame says, "I'm telling you exactly what I need, but you won't do it. You must not love me. Am I worthless to you? Feeling worthless is too painful; at least if I keep telling you what you're doing wrong, maybe you'll finally hear me, and I'll know I'm valuable."

Not only does shame block communication and resolution of problems, but it also blocks connection. When people carry shame, they want to hide themselves. They say, "I can't get too close. I can't be seen. It's not safe. All these bad parts of me are shameful and so I have to hide them. If I don't hide them, I'll be rejected." People who have insecure attachments are so mired with shame that they end up hiding so much of themselves they have very little authenticity left to connect with.

You can do a lot to get the ball rolling to create a shame-proof relationship. Dissolving shame isn't a quick fix, but when you begin to use the strategies in this chapter authentically and consistently, shame in your life—both for yourself and in your relationship—will diminish. When you spill a green smoothie all over your light carpet, you can say to yourself, "Well . . . I'm rushing around a bit. Good for me to notice I need to take a breath and pull back," instead of "I'm so angry with my-self! I can't even manage the simplest things. Why can't I be like other people and hold it all together?" When you give this gift to yourself it's much easier to show up gently for your partner or other loved ones when they drop the ball.

Shame is minimized through safe communication. First, keep your attachment lens on. Shame interprets your partner's behavior as "You're bad and wrong for what you did," while the attachment lens comes in and says, "I don't like what you did, but I can see that was your way of staying protected from something you didn't want to feel. Let's talk about it so maybe it will play out differently next time."

Let's say your partner is trying to get you to open up more about your relationship with your parents. They say, "You never talk about your relationship with your family and I don't get it. You must have feelings about them. Why won't you share with me?"

You respond with: "There's nothing to open up about. They're my parents, that's all. Why are you always pressuring me and trying to cre-ate problems that don't exist?"

This touched your shame, setting off alarm bells in your nervous system. What's happening underneath could be "I don't know how to talk about feelings, and my relationship with my parents is complicated but I don't want to be seen as a bad partner for not being able to open up, so the best I can do is turn it back on you and call you the problem so I don't have to be the shameful, unworthy problem."

But by pushing your partner away, you're sending the message that there's something wrong with *them* for wanting to know *you*. That their desire to connect is too much. That *they're* too much.

How might this situation play out in a nonshaming way?

Your partner is asking to know more about your relationship with your parents. You have the urge to get reactive but instead you look through your attachment lens. You can see that your partner isn't trying to be invasive. They want to connect with you and they want to know they're valuable enough to you to be let in.

Now from this softer place you might say something like "I understand you feel left out. It's not that I don't want to share with you. It's that I don't have the words."

An important caveat: nobody can *make* someone else's shame go away. What we can do is *help*, by doing our part to create a shame-free environment.

Moving out of the shame cloud is harder for some of us than others. It starts with a focus on connection, which is infinitely easier when you're able to look through the attachment lens. Shame says, "I'm not worthy of connection," so when communication is centered on connection, the message is just the opposite: "You *are* worthy of connection and that means you *aren't* shameful." Let's say your partner is staring at their phone instead of talking to you. How can you tell your partner you want them off the phone without shaming them ("you're always staring at that screen!")? Focus on connection first. Ask yourself, "How can I create an invitation instead of an accusation?" Then try, "I enjoy talking to you. Do you think you can finish up and put your phone away so we can chat?"

Creating the Attachment-Friendly Environment: EVVICT Shame

The following strategies are all intended to help you establish an attachment-friendly environment in your relationship by "EVVICT-ing shame": Empathy, Validation, Vulnerability, Influence, Curiosity, and Tolerance. Keep in mind that while they are described separately, all these skills work together. The better you get at one, the easier the others will be. Before we jump into learning how to EVVICT shame, let's revisit the idea of self-regulation, without which none of these strategies will be possible.

Self-Regulation

When it comes to personal and relationship healing and growth, self-regulation is paramount. When partners don't work on self-regulation, the environment they create is reactive, which is not attachment-friendly. And reactiveness is not easy to overcome (but very possible). A trigger is called a trigger because it tells your nervous system to take action or freeze. In a triggered moment your nervous system believes that you are under threat and in danger. Remember, attachment threat is an existential death fear. Your nervous system's "keep us alive at all costs" logic means the priority becomes survival. You aren't *supposed* to pause and think through a situation when you're under threat; you're driven by instinct. This is why triggers feel so powerful. They are meant to be heard and obeyed, no questions asked. This is why overreaction is so easy.

But only in the most extreme situations do we completely lose ourselves into sheer panic when triggered. Most of the time we still have some, even if only a little, capacity to ground ourselves—or in other words, to self-regulate. As we discussed in chapter 5, ways to self-regulate include taking deep breaths (deep breaths with slow exhales signal safety to your nervous system), journaling, using mentalization and mindfulness, and/or saying soothing phrases to yourself like "I'm safe. I've got this." This is how self-regulation works—it gets you out of a place of reactiveness so that you have more control over what you say or do.

Consider the Four Fs

Marriage and Family Therapist Pete Walker, in his book *Complex PTSD: From Surviving to Thriving*, has what I've found to be a useful take on how we respond to triggers: Fight, Flight, Freeze, or Fawn. Most partners have a go-to response when triggered in their negative cycles, which usually corresponds to one of these four F types.

Some partners are more likely to fight: criticize, accuse, judge, attack, get defensive, or do something with the intention of aggressively changing a situation. Others are more likely to respond to triggers with flight: avoiding the topic or getting out of the situation as quickly as possible so they don't have to feel overwhelmed. Some are more likely to freeze: go numb, shut down, or go blank. Still others are more likely to fawn: appease (say what their partner wants to hear without really meaning it), people-please, or offer praise, compliments, or anything else to say "I'm safe!" for the sake of safety but at the expense of authenticity or healthy self-interest.

According to Walker, some people go back and forth between opposite extremes: if fawning doesn't work, they flip to fight (or vice versa); if flight doesn't work, they flip to freeze (or vice versa).

The concept of the four F types has been talked about extensively in the world of psychology, but Walker takes it a step further and offers helpful tips for how you can manage your predominant F type(s) (your predominant F type is the one you're most likely to employ when you feel threatened). To start, each F type operates on a spectrum—there's a healthy version and an unhealthy version of each type. Take "fight." On one end of the fight spectrum is the aggressive version, but on the other end is a healthy assertion. The same is true for the other F types:

+ The healthy version of fight is assertion.
+ The healthy version of flight is removing yourself from an unsafe situation.
+ The healthy version of freeze is to take a pause and consider your next move before overreacting.
+ The healthy version of fawn is to defuse a situation with calm and/or kindness.

Reflect on your negative cycles. How are you most likely to respond to being triggered by your partner? In other words, what are your one or two predominant F types?

Once you've figured this out, identify the healthy version of the opposite F type—again, fight and flight are opposites, so are freeze and fawn—and try to do *that* instead. Here are some examples of how this strategy can play out in your negative cycle:

When your partner tells you they're bothered that you forgot about their work holiday party and then acted surprised when they reminded you, your urge is to get defensive, which is a fight response: "You probably told me when I was half-asleep. Why didn't you text me? You know I won't remember things unless you text them." For you, the opposite is a healthy version of fawn, which might sound like an authentic validation of their feelings before going further: "Honey, I'm sorry. I know that's super frustrating, especially considering how important this event is to you. I'm going to get it sorted out."

What about if you're *already* a fawner, and your partner says, "You can't remember anything! It's so annoying; it's like you're always stuck in your own world," your go-to might be somewhat frantic, "You're right, I'm just an idiot . . . I can't believe I forgot. You're so wonderful to want me there with you, and here I am dropping the ball." In that case, you might need to adopt the healthy version of fight, which is assertiveness: "Okay, I hear you and I know it's frustrating when I forget. But can you please say that to me more kindly because it's hard for me to hear you when it comes at me like that."

What if you're the one trying to bring up the concern and your partner comes in hot, saying, "I wouldn't forget things if you thought about *me* every now and then." Your urge might be flight: "Never mind, you're right, I shouldn't have brought it up," and disengage. For you, it might be useful to try the healthy version of freeze: taking a pause before immediately giving in to your urge to back down, and giving yourself a second to respond.

Last, if your urge is to freeze, you might consider doing the healthy version of flight, which is to remove yourself from the situation. Take a break, with the intention of coming back to it in the near future.

Now that we've reviewed the importance of self-regulation, let's move forward with EVVICT-ing shame from your relationship.

Empathy

Empathy is created when you allow yourself to feel some of what your partner is feeling, particularly their vulnerable emotions such as fear, anger, grief, shame, and even joy (doesn't it feel good when someone laughs with you?). This will elicit compassion, and you are far more likely to be responsive to your partner's reaches for help, comfort, and connection when you come from a place of compassion.

For many people, empathy is there but it gets buried. Sometimes people think they're being empathic when really what they're being is anxious, or rather their empathy gets intertwined with anxiety. You can tell the difference because when you're being empathic you're meeting the other person where they are . . . holding their hand (metaphorically or otherwise) as they experience pain. When you're overcome with *your own anxiety about their pain,* you'll try to move them away from their pain as a way to soothe your own anxiety but in a way that leaves them alone. Another way to tell is if you're wholly giving up your own self-care or needs in an attempt to rescue your partner from their feelings. Of course nobody likes seeing their partner suffer and sometimes there *is* appropriate action to take to help. But often there's not. Some problems can't be solved and we just need to show up and *be* with them. It's not always black or white, either/or, but it's something to be mindful of. Research shows that when a partner brings a nonrelationship-related problem to their anxious partner, the anxious partner often reacts in a way that leaves their partner feeling worse, not better, and that's certainly not the goal. Let's say your partner had a bad day at work and they come home feeling down. An anxious response is a frantic-flavored "What's wrong? Why are you upset? What happened? Are you going to lose your job!?" An empathic response is an authentically delivered "I'm so sorry you're feeling down, do you want to tell me about it?"

For others, difficulty accessing their empathy stems from never learning how to tap into their own feelings (you can't understand someone else's feelings if you've never even investigated your own) or because they've been so stuck trying to protect themselves from the painful feelings of their insecure attachment that they can't possibly step out of themselves. Partners with avoidant attachment often fall into this category and have a tendency to respond to their partner's distress with a lack of visible emotion, from a place of heady problem-solving, or indifference, none of which fall under the rubric of "empathic emotional presence." This does *not* mean those with avoidant attachment lack empathy; it's just that it can be hard to see. The good news, however, is that accessing and communicating empathy is a learned skill. As avoidant partners learn to emotionally reengage with themselves, empathy only gets easier for them to share.

When you and your partner are in touch with your own emotional experiences, while also open to each other's emotional experiences, you are emotionally present with each other. You can feel each other, but without losing yourselves. Sometimes it can be helpful when your partner is upset to visualize one foot in your partner's experience and one foot grounded in your own experience. This might feel like "I'm mad at my partner for saying mean things, but I can also feel how desperate they are to be heard." You aren't losing your own anger, which will help you problem-solve and set healthy boundaries when the time comes, but you can also feel your partner's vulnerability, which will help you problem-solve and set those boundaries from a place of love. This might look like saying, "I love you and I can see how painful it is for you when you feel unheard. At the same time, the things you're saying to me are really hurtful and this has to change. It's not good for either of us."

Empathy can be regulating during conflict, because feeling your partner's pain will tell your nervous system, "My partner is safe" instead of "My partner is a threat." That said, it does require some self-regulation to allow empathy in. You have to get yourself settled enough inside, and then the empathy will settle you even more. And remember, everything you do will impact your partner's experience and behavior, so empathy can get you and your partner into a loop of connection instead of a negative cycle.

Validate

Between my second and third children I experienced a miscarriage. I found out very early on, at eight weeks, meaning I had only known I was pregnant for four weeks. Still, I was devastated. Many well-meaning people in my life comforted me by telling me it was meant to be, that at least I wasn't further along in the pregnancy, and that luckily I had two other children to be grateful for, all of which were true. My husband was there for me, of course, as he always is, but he wasn't affected in the same way I was and couldn't relate to my pain. I understand that and feel nothing but appreciation for the people in my life who did their best to say what they believed would help.

At the time, I didn't know what I needed anyone to say. I only knew I was hurting and that I felt alone with that hurt. But now, eighteen years later, when I look back through the lens of attachment, I know *exactly* what I needed: validation. I needed for someone to hear me when I said, "I know it was only four weeks and that it wasn't meant to be and that I have a wonderful husband and two children who I love more than anything, but for four weeks I *believed* I was going to have a child. For four weeks I bonded with a life growing in me. I bonded with the future I imagined for this baby. It was real. It meant something to me. And the loss hit hard."

What would've helped me feel less alone in that situation was to hear someone say, "The way you're describing this to me is really helping me understand you. For four weeks you bonded with something real. All of the other things are true too and the rational part of you sees it . . . the loss was meant to be, you were barely pregnant to begin with and you are lucky in so many other ways . . . but *still* this life meant something to you, and *still* you feel devastated and *still* the pain is real. And it doesn't matter how much it makes sense to me or anyone else because it just is. The pain just is. Your heart was broken and I'm so sorry that you're hurting."

That is validation. Imagine having someone show up for you with the type of validating response I just provided, and you might feel how powerful it can be. Admittedly, what I've just described are validation skills spoken by someone who's been doing this professionally and personally for many years, but trust me when I say that everyone, with practice, can learn to be good at validating, including you and your partner. You know how badly you need empathy and understanding from each other, if for no other reason than because you know how bad it feels when you're not getting it. Validation is an extension of empathy and understanding because it puts these two important experiences to words so that you communicate the experience. Empathy and understanding are internal experiences that exist *within you*; validation is a communication of the internal experience and exists *between you and your partner*. It's nice when your partner feels empathy for you and understands you, but it's more soothing and bonding when they tell you about it: "I can see this is really bothering you right now and it makes a lot of sense to me. This is a tough situation you're in. It hurts me to see you hurt, but I'm right here to walk through this with you."

I want to distinguish that validation is not the same as agreeing with facts or circumstances the other person offers. Here's where people really get stuck and it often prevents them from validating another. You might say, "How can I validate her when she's telling me I make terrible financial decisions when I know for a fact I've made some good ones? I can't validate that. It's not true." And you're right. It's probably not true that every financial decision you've ever made was a bad one. But in this situation your partner is saying something else—now's the time to get out your attachment lens. What she's really saying is "I'm scared and I feel out of control. I don't know any other way to get through to you how insecure I feel about money. I'm worried that if I let you handle it, something bad will happen, so I'm going to show you all the ways you've been wrong and then we can do things my way and we'll be safe." Through that attachment lens, what do you see? Vulnerability. I'm not asking you to validate the facts; I'm asking you to validate the vulnerability. Validate what you want to grow.

Here's what invalidation sounds like in this situation: "You're full of it. This is what you do: you look back at a few mistakes and then I get defined by that. Do I do that to you? Do I make lists of all the ways you've been wrong over the years?"

Here's what validation sounds like: "I understand where you're coming from and that you're scared. Our financial safety is understandably important to you, and you feel desperate to get it figured out and you're trying to make sense of it in the best way possible. But I don't like the way you're telling me. It feels unfair and leaves me feeling unseen and alone. Underneath all of it, I can see *you, the real you*, the caring and responsible you. And of course you're scared. But we've got to learn to talk about this differently because I need to feel safe, too."

What about validating anger? For most people validating "softer" emotions such as sadness and fear will come much easier than validating anger. It's easy to assume validating your partner's anger will make things worse, but most of the time the opposite is true. Without validation, anger will harden; with validation, anger will soften. Think of a time when you were mad at your partner. Try to conjure up the angry feeling in your body. Next imagine your partner invalidating your anger by saying something like "you're overreacting," or "you have no right to be mad, you do the same thing to me." Now imagine that instead your partner says, with authenticity, "I hear you. I hear how mad you are and it makes sense to me. I would be mad, too, if I felt like my needs don't matter to you." A lot of the time this creates a "mic drop" moment because when anger is heard, understood, and validated, it no longer needs to fight for those things. Your partner doesn't need to agree that your needs don't matter to them, but they can agree that in a similar situation, if they believed that to be true, they would be mad, too. It's hard to validate anger, really hard. Anger can be scary for many people. But I can tell you with confidence that until anger is validated (even if just by the person feeling it), it's not going anywhere. Once anger is settled, and it might take some time and space, conversations are more likely to move forward. And keep this in mind: nobody likes the idea of validating another person's anger. But *everybody* wants their own anger to be validated. *Everybody* wants to be heard and understood when they're mad. "Golden rule" moment.

We have to be careful not to use validation as a way to manipulate a person or situation. Manipulation isn't validation. Saying what you know someone wants to hear in order to shut them up or get your way is not the same as validation, and most people can easily feel the difference. But when it's real, validation can have a powerful impact on the emotional safety of a hard conversation. It can help you get back, often relatively quickly, to the real issue—in this case, finances—and chances are you're going to get further than you did the first time. Will it be perfect? Probably not. But it's a better path that will lead to better places when you keep at it. And if you're new to validation, you'll be surprised to see that a little bit will go a long way.

Vulnerability

Vulnerability is effective in interrupting your negative cycle, and over time it can even help you decrease the frequency of the cycle or prevent it. In fact, your relationship will stagnate unless, in good time, both you and your partner are willing to be vulnerable.

Let's say your partner gets a promotion at work and you feel threatened. You don't want to feel threatened, but you do. It's scary to you. You grew up watching one of your parents get promotion after promotion and with each one you saw them less and less. So when your partner shares the news, you get triggered. You don't want to bring it up, that's too vulnerable, but you know they can sense that something is keeping you from being fully happy for their success. They might think you're mean or selfish or uncaring. After all, "What kind of person isn't happy for their partner's successes?" you ask yourself. You recognize you're triggered when you probably don't want to be, which is bad enough, but on top of that you're shaming yourself for being so. So, you do what you've been doing for a long time to manage pain: you get distant to protect the relationship from your "bad" feelings. Steering clear is your comfort zone. But what would it be like to do something new? What would it be like to go to your partner and say, "Hey. I'm sure you've noticed my distance and I'd like to explain. I've been distant about your promotion because part of me is so proud of you and happy for you, and this other part is scared. A part of me worries that your success in your career will become so important to you that you'll abandon me." Instead of leaning out, what do you imagine will be different if you decide to take the risk to lean in?

Here are some other examples of vulnerability:

+ Setting boundaries and telling your partner you'll have to leave the room if they keep saying mean things and "hitting below the belt," even when you know they'll be even more mad at you when you walk away.
+ Being honest about going over your budget and purchasing an expensive item, instead of being secretive to keep your partner from being disappointed with you.
+ Sharing with your partner how humiliating it felt when your employer disrespected you, instead of just complaining about what an awful person they are.
+ Speaking your truth, showing your deepest feelings, and being your authentic self, even at the risk of rejection. Yes, rejection hurts. But it doesn't hurt as much as the loneliness of spending a lifetime hiding, especially from your partner.

A lot of couples new to therapy tell me how vulnerable they think they already are. "I cry all the time," one might say. Or they tell me they're an artist so of course they're vulnerable. A lot of the time the very same people, while often highly emotional, aren't as vulnerable as they may think. In fact, if you have an anxious attachment, you might be surprised to learn that vulnerability is likely to be as uncomfortable for you as it is for your avoidant partner. You just manage the discomfort very differently.

People often confuse emotional outbursts such as inconsolable crying and long, wordy rants with vulnerability, the idea being "I'm not holding back my emotions, so that means I'm being vulnerable." These things are emotionally expressive, yes, but unless they involve stepping out of one's comfort zone for the greater good, they are venting, not vulnerability.

While crying is not necessarily an emotional outburst, I've treated many partners who believe that because they cry in front of their partner, they are being vulnerable. But while crying always comes from a valid and worthy emotional experience, it is not always vulnerability in and of itself. Sometimes crying can be tears of angry protest. In this case, to be truly vulnerable, it might mean getting through the angry tears and down into the deeper part: "I am so sad right now and I feel so powerless." That is true vulnerability. Sometimes what's vulnerable, especially if you grew up in a home where tears were acceptable but anger wasn't, is to talk about the anger. Sometimes vulnerable tears don't involve words at all, but the felt experience of vulnerability is palpable. Again, vulnerability isn't objective; it's about stepping out of your comfort zone and authentically sharing your subjective experiences, which in a given moment are going to be different from person to person.

Influence

In a healthy relationship, you mutually influence each other. You motivate each other to grow and to be your best selves. But—and it's a very big but—you *don't* try to control each other. Controlling tactics, including stealth ones, create insecure environments. Nobody likes to feel controlled. It's shaming and demoralizing. When someone is trying to control you, the message is "you're less than, you're not an adult, you don't have a say." There's very little room for control dynamics in relationships that are supposed to be founded on intimacy, cooperation, and connectedness.

So what's the difference between influence and control? Control demands instant gratification; influence is willing to let things sink in and simmer. Control gives away your power; influence is empowering and recognizes its own limitations. Influence is confident; control is scared. Influence is about self-expression and cooperation; control is draining and fear based.

Influence puts the immediate goal of behavior change to the side in order to focus on connection. Let's say your partner has a hard time opening up about their feelings, leaving you feeling shut out. A controlling approach is to say, "Why can't you just tell me how you feel? It's not fair for you to just shut me out right now. If you're not willing to work on your avoidant attachment and start talking about your feelings, I don't even know if I want to be in this relationship." In this situation, you're trying to control your partner and demanding change right now.

Instead, from an influence perspective, your approach might be "I feel shut out, but I don't think that's your intention. I think maybe something else is going on. Maybe you're afraid to share your feelings. I don't want to put feelings on you that aren't yours, but I also want you to know that I don't think this is about you being stubborn."

In the second example, you're creating space for exploration instead of hoping for instant gratification and then getting frustrated when that can't happen just yet. You're not saying, "I need for you to do it this way or else." You're saying, "I'm impacted by this, but I also understand there's deeper stuff here than what can be solved in this moment. Let's keep talking."

Curiosity

When you ask, "Hmmm, what's going on with me?" instead of "I shouldn't be upset about this," you're stepping away from self-judgment, which is shame inducing, into a place of understanding. The same is true when you're curious about your partner's inner experience—instead of sending the message that they should feel differently, which again comes from a place of judgment as opposed to acceptance, you send the message that they are worthy of being understood and that you want to learn more.

Curiosity can be especially effective when you are triggered. If you can notice your alarm bell putting you on high alert and can respond by moving into a curious mindset, you'll actually move yourself out of the scary emotional center of the brain, where a lot of old fears linger, and into the rational center of the brain, enabling you to access both emotion and reason at the same time. When it comes time to respond to a relationship trigger, a balance of reason and emotion is your best friend. It's the difference between a stale "I feel offended. I am sad. I need an apology," on one hand, and an emotionally charged "How could you say that to me?! You'd better apologize right now or I'm leaving," on the other. Somewhere in between is the sweet spot, which might sound something like "Honey, that really hurt. What's going through your mind right now because that felt really harsh and I know that's not how you meant for it to land?" Curiosity doesn't ask that you change anything, only that you observe what's happening. Nonjudgmental observation often naturally ushers in compassion. Compassion, whether for yourself or others, is regulating because it removes threat, which facilitates safety. When you're self-regulated, there's a good chance you'll soften to your partner. When you *feel* softened, you will communicate more softly.

Curiosity also fosters connection because it will give you and your partner a chance to know each other's inner worlds, not just what you see and hear on the surface. It leads to understanding, and feeling understood is medicine for us all. Who doesn't want to be understood?

We need to be careful not to confuse curiosity with what I call "peppering with questions." Curiosity is a mindset. You can be curious without asking a single question, and you can ask questions without really being curious. If you find yourself peppering your partner with questions, you're probably trying too hard to manage your own anxiety. The kind of curiosity I'm referring to is more about seeking understanding.

Curiosity is always important, but in the context of negative cycles, it's the most reliable guide when you feel a relationship trigger—that moment when your partner looks at their phone when you're talking, or tells you you're overreacting, or blames you for leaving the refrigerator open. In this moment, ask yourself, "What's happening inside me? What am I thinking? What meanings am I making? How am I feeling? Is there tension in my body? If so, where is the tension sitting?"

Curiosity for your partner sounds like "I want to understand you. I'm not concerned right now with agreeing or not agreeing, I'm concerned with understanding *how* you came to think the way you do, and I'm curious about how you feel. Tell me about your intentions. Help me step into your world so that I can see you and see through your eyes.

I want to understand the experiences you've had that have led you to this point."

Let's play this out using the example of the refrigerator door. Before you react with "I didn't leave the door open, you did. Stop blaming me for everything," check in with yourself. Get curious. Maybe you can say something to yourself like "Wow, I'm triggered. I feel unseen and misunderstood and that hurts." Then see if you can step into your partner's world and get curious about them. "Okay, clearly something's bothering you. What's going on? Is this about the refrigerator or are you upset about something else? Help me understand." Maybe it's about the refrigerator, maybe not, but you're far more likely to get to the root of it with curiosity than you are with a battle. Of course, there needs to be space for you to say, "Hey, can you bring this up to me in a different way next time?" but your first goal is to create safety so that in the bigger picture, *both of you are more likely to be heard and understood.* And if you're the partner who's annoyed about the refrigerator? Instead of blame, maybe try "I'm really trying to cut back on our electricity bill. I think you may have left the refrigerator open. No judgment, just reminding us both to stay on top of the little things." Perfect? Maybe not, but it's *better* than coming in hot with blame and *more likely* to help you feel heard.

Tolerance

Nobody is perfect, especially not partners in relationships. Everybody gets tired, hungry, disappointed, overwhelmed. Everybody has bad moods. Nobody thinks exactly like you, makes meanings of events exactly like you, or handles situations exactly like you, and that doesn't necessarily make them "wrong," just different. Intolerant environments are reactive environments and reactive environments aren't safe. This is why developing the skill of tolerance is especially important. When your partner does something that triggers you, a very important question to ask is "Can I let this one go?" Because a lot of the time when you look back, you'll wish you had. If however you look back and say,

"I shouldn't have let that go," you still have the opportunity to bring it up, and it might even be better to bring it up after the fact. I'm not saying to let things go that are very important; sometimes it's best to speak up in the moment. But before you do, double-check to see if you're responding or reacting, and how useful it will be to address it then and there. Take a breath or two, check in with yourself, and ask "What's the best long-game way to handle this?" Also consider the four F's discussed earlier in this chapter. If your tendency is to let things go, you might want to practice speaking up; if your tendency is to react instantly, you might want to practice letting it go in the service of creating a more tolerant environment.

Vulnerability Exercise

I'd like to close this chapter with an exercise that can help you better communicate understanding, empathy, and vulnerability to your partner, all of which, as we've learned, are the hallmarks of an attachment-friendly environment. As with all the exercises in this book, do your best: progress not perfection, and any amount of curiosity about your inner world and/or that of your partner will only help you get to know yourself and each other better—and you can build on that over time.

Use the following template:

When you see me (1) _____ , inside of me I'm feeling
(2) _____ because (3) _____ ,
and I can see how that leaves you feeling (4) _____ .

1. What reactive behavior or words did your partner see you do or say?
2. What were the deeper emotions underneath your words and/or actions?
3. What unmet attachment needs (or other experiences) were at play?

4. What inner experiences did your reactiveness inspire in your partner?

Here are a couple of examples:

"When you see me (1) *getting big and protesting*, inside of me I'm feeling (2) *desperate to be seen and heard* because (3) *it hurts so much that I can't reach you*, and I can see how that leaves you feeling (4) *attacked and feeling like a failure*."

"When you see me (1) *getting defensive*, inside of me I'm feeling (2) *afraid* because (3) *I don't want you to see me as failing you*, and I can see how that leaves you feeling (4) *unheard and alone*."

You can also use the exercise as a template to express your needs:

When you (1) _____ instead of (2) _____
I feel (3) _____ and am more likely to (4) _____ .

1. What can your partner do or say that would feel good for you?
2. What words or behaviors can this replace?
3. What attachment needs might get met, or what positive feelings might you experience?
4. How might you react differently?

Here are a couple of examples:

"When you (1) *validate my feelings when I'm upset about something* instead of (2) *first trying to fix the problem*, I feel (3) *heard, seen, and comforted* and am more likely to (4) *eventually settle into a problem-solving mode*."

"When you (1) *share your fear and sadness when you get triggered* instead of (2) *showing me only your anger*, I feel (3) *more empathic, understanding, and safe* and am more likely to (4) *respond to you in a way that feels good for both of us*."

CHAPTER 7

Reaching and Responding

relationships . . .

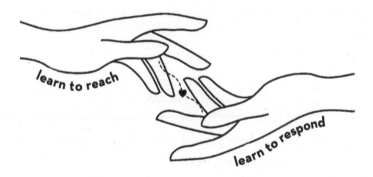

learn to reach

learn to respond

. . . and the rest will fall into place

All couples will have times when they need to initiate hard conversations. There will be topics where you don't see eye to eye, the ones that bring up the biggest fears, anxieties, anger, and old wounds. These are the conversations that have never gone well, but still have to be addressed. Sometimes they're obviously big topics: when to start a family, relocating, where to spend the holidays, attachment ruptures from the past, ex-partners, substance abuse problems, healing from an affair, a child struggling with a health issue. Sometimes they're big topics that aren't so obviously big, but have taken on "bigness" because of the unmet attachment needs surrounding them: keeping the house clean, what vehicle to buy or not buy, where to plant the garden, where to go for lunch, what to pack for the trip, chronic lateness, not texting back, and so much more.

All of these conversations involve some level of reaching and responding. One partner needs to reach by bringing something up, and the other is put in the position to respond. The way you reach and respond in your relationship, especially when it comes to these difficult topics, can go a long way toward building an attachment-friendly environment and helping to prevent negative cycles. Below are some guidelines to help the conversations go in a better direction than they have in the past, and help you plant seeds for a better relationship future.

Self-Focus

Coming from a place of self-focus is especially important when bringing up a concern or initiating a hard conversation. Some relationship experts call this strategy "I-statements," but try not to get hung up on the "I." You can say "I." Or you can skip the "I" and still maintain a self-focus. You can even say "you," depending on how you use it. (It's better to default to authenticity over semantics.)

If you bring up a concern in an other-focused way, it sounds like "You ignored me at the party." Versus the self-focused approach: "I understand you wanted to catch up with friends, and I want that for you, too. At the same time, I felt lonely a lot of the time. How about we try to strike a better balance next time."

Notice the shift between the two. One doesn't include or imply protest, accusations, shame, demands, or control. Instead it offers validation, vulnerability, sharing how you were impacted, and suggesting a solution.

Coming from a "place of self" doesn't change the fact that you want something to happen or change, but it's a way of taking ownership of your own needs instead of trying to get someone else to do things or feel a certain way so that your needs are met. When a person is communicating from a place of self, they are saying, "Here's what's going on for me. Here's what feels good. Here's what doesn't feel good. When something doesn't feel good, I'm going to reach out to you for help. When you're unable to help me with something, here's how I'm going to take care of myself."

Concerns vs. Criticisms

When your partner brings up a concern, what feels better? To hear "you're irresponsible" or "you said you'd be home at seven thirty, but I didn't see you until after eight, let's talk." I'm guessing the latter. It's important to deliver problems as a concern, rather than a criticism. Concerns address the behavior; criticisms attack the person. Concerns are solution-focused; criticisms are shame-focused. When tensions are high, if a problem is being addressed in a way that makes your partner feel attacked as a person, it will likely trigger them and make it harder for them to be open to your message.

This doesn't mean there's no room in relationships for constructive criticism. This is one way partners help each other grow. We just need to make sure your attachment-friendly environment is being protected. Here are some examples of voicing concerns instead of resorting to criticism:

Instead of:
"Why do you have to be such a slob? How hard is it to pick your stuff up as you go?"

Try:
"When your things are left on the counters, I have a hard time feeling settled. It's overwhelming. Can we talk about this and try to come to a solution?"

Instead of:

"The problem with our relationship is that you're emotionally unavailable. When I try to ask you about your feelings, you refuse to share anything with me."

Try:

"I understand that it's hard for you to share feelings, I really do. But I'm left feeling lonely when I can't reach you in that way. Now that I'm starting to learn more about my own feelings, I'm starting to realize how important it is for me to also be able to connect with yours. I'd like for us both to somehow figure out a way to feel more emotionally connected."

Include "Attachment Language"

Sometimes you can meet your partner's attachment needs while bringing up a concern at the same time. Since most concerns are attachment related, I encourage couples to use this to the advantage of their relationship, especially when bringing up a tough conversation. By phrasing things with an attachment angle, you're letting your partner know that you're not the enemy, that you love them and want to feel close. This strategy also adds emotional richness to the relationship.

Instead of:

"You didn't text me back and I was really worried. What happened?"

Try:

"I know you get busy and don't want to be glued to your phone, but I got worried when I didn't hear back because of how important you are to me [attachment meaning]. Can you remember to get back to me when you say you will?"

Instead of:

"We never agree about anything."

Try:

"I know it's frustrating for both of us when we don't see eye to eye. But the way you see things is very important to me *[attachment meaning]* and even when I don't agree with you, I still respect you *[attachment meaning]*. I need to know the same because that's part of what closeness is to me."

Use Validation

To feel emotionally safe going into a hard conversation, each partner needs to have confidence they'll be heard and understood. Partners spend an incredible amount of energy trying to be heard and understood, so much so that until both partners are confident in this fact, the conversation really can't proceed productively. By validating your partner's experience while bringing up a concern, you can save a lot of time and energy. Show your partner validation by letting them know that, at the very least, you can recognize how they feel and think. If you can take it a step further and show that you not only recognize how they feel and think, but you can *understand* the way they feel and think, you will be able to create even more safety. By leading with validation, you are doing what therapist and author George Faller, LMFT, calls "creating invitations instead of accusations," in other words pulling your partner in instead of pushing them away.

Especially remember to validate anger. You don't have to agree with the *why* or tolerate poor behaviors like yelling or name-calling, but making space for anger is important *especially* if you're hoping to help it defuse.

Instead of:

Why did you sign up for more guitar lessons when we need to be saving money (in an accusatory tone)?

Try:

"I know how much joy you get from your music, and it makes me happy to see you happy. At the same time, I'm concerned about the new classes you signed up for because of how much we need to cut back on our spending."

Instead of:

"You shouldn't be mad about that. You know I'm doing my best."

Try:

"I get your frustration. You have every right to feel mad and let down. I'm not willing to stand here being spoken to disrespectfully, that feels bad and humiliating, but I *can* handle you being mad at me."

Instead of:

"You never want to watch Netflix with me at night anymore. You're always too tired to watch anything."

Try:

"I know how hard you've been working to get your project done at work and how exhausting it's been. One of the things I appreciate so much about you is your dedication to quality in everything you do, and I don't want to take away from that. At the same time, I feel filled up when we make time for each other and miss our time together. It will help me if I can get some reassurance that when you get through this, we can get back to our routine."

Lead with Appreciation

Before making a complaint, lead with appreciation. It sends the message that "I see your worth and value. I care about your feelings. Even though I have a concern, it doesn't take away from how much I appreciate you as a partner." When you do make the complaint, your partner is less likely to feel unappreciated, and less likely to be triggered.

Instead of:
"You weren't being very friendly to my mom."

Try:
"I really appreciate how hard you've worked to have a good relationship with my mom, and that's a lot because I know how difficult she can be. You've been amazing. I noticed you seemed tense around her tonight. Was something going on you want to talk about?"

Avoid Controlling for a Certain Response

When trying a new method of communication, it's easy to believe that it's only successful when your partner responds in the way you'd like. But this belief stems from a place of control and inner insecurity—it doesn't reflect real, authentic communication. Often anxious and disorganized-attached partners in particular will believe that unless something is resolved right then and there, there's no hope that anything will ever change. This lack of trust shows up as a desperate need for a quick fix instead of giving it time. We all want our partners to respond in the way we'd like, but we aren't always going to get that. Don't let this be a reason to give up. You can't guarantee your most desired outcome, but by cleaning up your side of the street, you can plant seeds for the future and increase the odds of attaining the relationship closeness you long for. Also, in moments when you get vulnerable and start showing up in newer, healthier ways, and your partner doesn't respond positively, you have an opportunity to work through the painful feelings which come up in a new way. Often we want to control our partner's responsiveness in order to prevent feelings of grief or a sense of powerlessness. But there is enormous growth potential in facing your innermost pain and not reacting in ways that will damage your relationship. And when you grow, the relationship grows . . . *even in moments so painful that it's hard to see the bigger picture.*

Let Go of the Need to Agree

No matter how compatible you are in some areas of the relationship, you're still two separate individuals. You're going to bump up against differences around certain decisions. Maybe you get stuck in courtroom-style arguments trying to, what I call, "out-attorney" each other with facts and evidence in the hope of convincing the other person to see it your way. The problem is, nobody likes to be told their ideas and opinions are wrong, and it can often lead to one or both of you doubling down.

Instead of hoping to always agree, try making the goal that both of you be willing to hear each other's perspectives. If anyone is going to change their beliefs, it's more likely to happen when you feel heard and respected. Sometimes, though, you'll just have to agree to disagree and go from there.

Instead of:
"That's an inappropriate movie for the kids to be watching. I think it's irresponsible of you to allow this."

Try:
"In my eyes you're a great dad and that's something I appreciate about you. At the same time, there are some areas where we don't agree, and to feel safe in the relationship I need for us to be able

to talk about those things. One thing in particular is the movies we agree to let them watch."

Prioritize Meaning Over Details

Hands down, the place where I see couples get the most stuck during communication is getting lost in the details.

Take Layla and Omar, a newly married couple who have recently started to argue a lot. During our session, they start arguing about Omar's mountain biking. Layla thinks Omar spends too much time biking, and is maybe even addicted. Omar thinks all he's doing is decompressing after a long workweek. Layla brings it up by telling Omar he spent "five hours riding yesterday." Omar says that's not true at all, it was more like "two hours." Then Layla reminds him that she was out from noon to four and he still wasn't back when she got home, while Omar interrupts saying when she was gone he mowed the lawn before his ride. Layla says when she came home the lawn wasn't mowed and that he didn't mow the lawn until after she got home, but Omar said he mowed the backyard while she was gone, not the front. And on and on it goes.

What do I, as a therapist, do with this?

Me: Layla, do you feel neglected when Omar is riding?
Layla: Yes.
Me: Then let's not get lost in the details and instead focus on your feelings of neglect. Omar, do you believe that Layla is being unfair to you about this?
Omar: Yes.
Me: Then let's try not to get lost in the details and instead focus on how it is for you to feel like you aren't treated fairly.

The bigger meaning here is that Layla is walking around the relationship feeling neglected and worried about whether or not her husband has an unhealthy preoccupation with bike riding, and Omar is walking around feeling like he should be able to enjoy his downtime as he wishes and that Layla is treating him like a child. Who is right and who is wrong? That's not really for me to decide. But these two will never figure out a solution to their problem until they focus on the bigger meanings in order to identify the real problems—feelings like resentment, loneliness, powerlessness, and maybe even despair—and find a way to talk about these without getting hijacked by details. The details are pitting them against each other like battling attorneys, and blocking emotional safety.

When Layla tells Omar, "The bigger meaning for me is that I miss you when you're out riding and away from me. I feel lonely and I want to know you can see that, maybe even more than I want anything to change," Omar is much more open. When Omar tells Layla, "When I don't feel like an equal in your eyes, it's lonely for me, like we aren't partners. I feel less than. That's when I feel the most alone," Layla is also more open.

Avoid "Always" and "Never"

This one is pretty straightforward. The words *always* and *never* can take conversations down a dead-end road, because when someone is making blanket statements, it's easy to argue for the exceptions. *Always* and *never* will also leave partners feeling boxed in, and the original issue gets buried, with no resolution. Also, *always* and *never* are often not true. Stick with what's true.

Instead of:
"You always leave your stuff on my side of the bathroom sink."

Try:
"I noticed your stuff was on my side of the sink again. Can you work on that so we both have our space?"

Instead of:

"You never make time to spend with me in the evenings."

Try:

"Let's try to spend more time together in the evenings. The time together helps me feel close to you, and I've noticed when we make time to connect we argue less. What are your thoughts?"

Loving Listening

So far we've covered skills to bring up your concerns in your relationship in the most attachment-friendly way possible. Now let's address the other side of the conversation, when you're on the receiving end.

"I really need to talk to you about something that's been bothering me" is a statement even the most securely attached person might bristle at. It's never fun to be forced to face one of your flaws or discuss a topic that brings you anxiety. If you have an insecure attachment and struggle with shame, being on the receiving end will be even more uncomfortable, because you're already struggling, to some degree, with a fear of being unworthy or with a belief that parts of you are unlovable. In these moments, everything in you might want to say "Shut it down!" or "Turn it around" or "Defend before this gets worse!" But you and I both know this kind of response won't get you the secure attachment with your partner you're looking for, so let's learn what will.

Hopefully, your partner brought their concern to you in a way that helps you feel safe and validated. Unfortunately, that won't always be the case, especially when this work is still ongoing for the two of you. When your partner comes to you with a concern in a triggering or blaming way, see if you can give them some grace and do your best to listen anyway. I'm not saying to accept extremes such as yelling, name-calling, and other especially destructive behaviors, but when it comes to imperfect deliveries, remember that this entire process is about working together and sometimes that means picking up the slack for each other.

Of course, there will also be times when your partner delivers their concern in the most perfect way possible and you're still triggered because, for one, it's hard to talk about what you're getting wrong, and two, you're still working on yourself.

Most of us are familiar with the idea of "active listening," and that it's the key to good relationships in our personal and work life. On paper it sounds so easy. *Just listen. Nod. Ask clarifying questions.* How hard can that be? But when we look at listening through the lens of attachment, active listening can feel insurmountably hard in the moments when your partner wants to discuss something you don't want to talk about. If you struggle with listening, instead of talking about why you *should* listen, let's talk about why it's been hard for you to listen. Because I'm confident that your authentic self genuinely wants your partner to feel heard in the relationship, just like you want to feel heard.

The problem is not how you feel now. The problem is how you feel when you're asked to listen, especially when you already feel triggered and unsafe. In that moment you're not hearing your partner say, "I love you and I love this relationship and something happened that hurt our bond and I really need to reach you so I can feel safe again." What you're hearing is "I think you're all wrong, I don't appreciate anything you get right, and now I'm going to tell you all about it. And I need for you to just stand there and listen." If that's what's going through your mind in that moment, of course you will have trouble listening and a strong urge to react with counterblame or defensiveness.

But what if your difficulty listening isn't really a difficulty with listening at all? What if the real problem is that you haven't yet learned how to listen in a way that can actually feel good?

Listening is about connection. If you have an insecure attachment, you were raised in an environment where true connection wasn't valued, and shame and control were. This bled over into listening. For you, listening during moments of conflict meant feeling shamed, misunderstood, unfairly blamed, invalidated, and/or unheard. Now when you have a hard time with your partner bringing up a concern, even if it's delivered in the most attachment-friendly way possible, you're not really blocking out your partner; what you're really blocking is feeling shamed, misunderstood, blamed, invalidated, and unheard.

When people say things like "successful relationships require good listening skills," the message is that listening is a chore, or a box that needs to be checked before you can finally be heard. That doesn't have to be the case. When you start to view listening as a legitimate emotional support skill, it can feel really good. You know how giving someone a gift (especially when you know it's something they've been wanting) can feel just as good as, if not better than, getting a gift? It's the same concept. Listening is a way to love. For this reason, I'm going to change the term from *active listening* to *loving listening*. I want to help you move away from the idea that listening is only beneficial to your partner, and lean into it being for you, too, and your relationship. Listening is a connecting point. Show your partner you are lovingly listening by minimizing interruptions and distractions (put down your phone), using eye contact, reflecting back to them what you're hearing and clarifying with them that you're hearing correctly, validating their concerns, and trying to understand how they might be feeling.

Problem-Solving

Negative cycles usually come up when couples are trying to solve a problem—whose family to visit at Thanksgiving, how much to budget for groceries, what to do about a misbehaving child, what to cut from the budget after a loss of income, which city to move to. After you work on your negative cycle repair, you might feel bonded but you still need to make a decision about that major purchase or whether or not we should move to Montreal. I get that. The repair process is meant to reestablish emotional safety and attachment security in order to establish a healthier platform for problem-solving. It's not meant to solve the problem itself; it's meant to create an environment that will make a problem-solving conversation likely to be more comfortable and productive.

When you're trying to solve a problem, what is considered a solution? I consider a solution to be a mutually agreed-upon decision that might leave one or both partners feeling disappointed, but that doesn't create long-term resentment for either partner. Disappointment is fine and normal (as long as the same partner isn't the one disappointed with every decision); resentment is a problem. Lingering resentments will bleed out into the relationship as bitterness and create blindsiding negative cycles.

Some solutions might be a compromise of the wants and needs of both partners, while other solutions mean one partner gets things their way and the other doesn't. This is going to happen sometimes. Part of being in a long-term relationship means that at one time or another each partner will need to concede.

No matter what problem you are working through, the most important thing to remember is that the felt experience of intimacy and partnership is more important than the end result of most decisions. On your deathbed, you won't be thinking about what couch you two decided to buy decades earlier. Instead, you'll probably be thinking about how well you were able to love and be loved.

Here are some tips for effective problem-solving:

Find Confidence

Some partners struggle with feeling confident about their ideas and perspectives. We second-guess ourselves, even when deep down we know what we want. Then, when it comes time to talk about our preferences, we lack assertiveness, which makes negotiation difficult. If this is you, you might end up agreeing to something you don't really agree with and then resenting your partner later. It's really important for partners to be flexible and open to each other's perspectives, but some partners, especially those vulnerable to people-pleasing at the expense of their own needs, are *too* open. Be clear within yourself about what you want and need, and advocate for it with confidence.

Genuinely Listen to Your Partner's Perspective on the Topic

It's easy to become so stuck in our own perspectives, and the feelings we have about our perspectives, that we have difficulty truly listening to our partner's ideas. For the health of your relationship, it's really important that each partner feels heard, especially when it comes to high-stakes topics. If your partner can tell you are genuinely listening, they will be more likely to feel safe and understood and appreciated, which in turn will help them be able to hear you and help you feel safe. In this case, you're both more likely to drop your defenses and be more open to compromise when it comes to problem-solving.

If you're having a hard time listening to what your partner has to say because you have so much to say on the topic yourself, self-regulate by being mindful of what's happening in your body . . . tension? tightness? . . . and breathe into it. It's possible to listen to your partner's words and soothe your own body at the same time, and it will help you with urges to interrupt or tune out.

Clearly Deliver Your Perspective

When you are solving a problem, it's important that you are communicating your perspective in a way that is clear and honest. Be as concise as possible, but if you're confused about your thoughts and feelings, say so: "I'm still trying to work out how I think and feel, but here's where I am right now." Remember that the overriding goal is to express your position and feelings, not to get your partner to agree (more about this soon). Speak from yourself by using phrases such as "This is how I see it," instead of "Here's why you're wrong."

Be mindful of not ranting and/or repeating yourself as this is the best way to lose your audience. Instead, figure out what it is you're trying to say and what it is you're needing before you say it (anxious partners often process as they talk, so breaks to sort through your feelings and thoughts can be helpful here). If you're on the receiving end of a partner who is repeating themselves, you might try pausing them and saying gently, "You're repeating yourself. That tells me you're worried I'm not hearing you. How can I show you that I'm really listening?"

Be Flexible

Healthy relationships require the ability to be open to your partner's perspective. This isn't easy, especially when triggered; it can feel like a direct confrontation to your perspective. But if you want to solve a problem, you need to try to let go of the idea that your view is the only true reality.

If you were raised with an insecure attachment, your goal was to stay safe, and one way to stay safe was to try to gain control over your environment. Don't get me wrong: taking control over your life where you can and should is empowering. But those with insecure attachments often learn early on to be overly rigid about the way they do things, think about things, and want others to do things. It only makes sense . . . this is their way of feeling secure. As adults, this can show up as black-and-white thinking and inflexibility, which can get in the way of compromising with a partner. You might think you have to have the same ideas about parenting, politics, ways to navigate extended family relationships, whether or not to save for the future or enjoy yourself now, ways of eating, and on and on it can go. If you can relate, it's important to the harmony of your relationship to open yourself up to consider your partner's perspectives. That doesn't mean you have to entirely let go of your value system, or the things most important to you, but if rigidity is getting in the way of truly hearing what your partner has to say, this can interfere with problem-solving and connection.

Validate Your Partner's Perspectives and Feelings

You'll need to be able to validate each other as you work toward a solution. Again, validation does not mean agreement. It means you're able to understand the other person's perspective to some degree and, more important, that you understand their feelings about the issue. Here's an example of validation in a problem-solving context:

> *Instead of:*
> "Getting a dog is a bad idea right now. What would happen if we want to go away for the weekend at the last minute? I just don't understand why you'd want that on our plate."

> *Try:*
> "I can't say I agree this is the right time to get a dog, but I understand why it's important to you. You love animals. That makes sense."

Don't Try to Convince

Assertively presenting your argument is a healthy part of finding a solution, and that might mean trying to get your partner to see that your idea is a good one. Sometimes you'll be successful—securely attached couples often have more capacity for flexibility when it comes to decision-making. But sometimes you won't be and your partner won't agree. We all have certain strong opinions that are unlikely to change. Your partner might feel just as passionately that their idea is best, as you do about yours. All couples will have these sticking points somewhere, and that's not a bad thing; it's just life. In fact, having a partner who has their own ideas is a sign of authenticity and inner strength, both attractive qualities in a person.

The key here is not to get stuck trying to convince your partner that your idea is the best one. When it's evident that you see it differently and that's just the way it is, the best thing you can do is find mutual respect for each other. Ideally you'll be able to validate each other's feelings, express disagreement, and move into navigating a solution. Sometimes it takes time to build mutual respect in the relationship in a way that each partner trusts, before trying to find solutions to your most challenging topics.

Instead of:

"Keeping sugar out of the house is only going to make the kids want more and sneak around. Studies have shown that depriving them is the worst way to go about it."

Try:

"I know the kids' health is a priority for you and I admire that about you. Their health is a priority for me, too, and I'm glad we both care so much. It's been tempting for us to try to convince each other where we don't see eye to eye, and I'd like to move away from that and see if we can find a way to make decisions based on mutual respect. After all, we both have the same goal of having healthy kids. What are your thoughts?"

Remember That Some Decisions Take a While

This can be hard to accept in our instant-gratification culture, but most things don't need to be resolved overnight. Some decisions, especially the big ones, take weeks, months, or even years to make. Resolution sometimes comes at the end of many, many conversations. Having multiple discussions about tough topics allows space to slowly get to know each other's perspectives, build mutual respect, and maybe even warm up to them. Resolution eventually evolves from there.

Understand That Not All Problems Have Solutions

Some decisions have deep ramifications and represent major differences in values or desired lifestyle. The most common example of this is when partners feel differently about whether they want to have children, either when or at all. Sometimes couples want dramatically different lifestyles and that significantly impacts their compatibility. Sometimes partners will be able to work through the differences, and sometimes they might decide that they aren't lining up in crucial areas and it will be best to separate. My goal for couples in this situation is to be able to separate from a place of clarity and emotional health. When couples can discuss these big topics outside their negative cycle, they are far more likely to walk away from the relationship feeling confident about their decision. And, as always, when a situation feels bigger than a couple is resourced to navigate, professional help might be warranted.

There you have it, the skills that both reflect and fuel an attachment-friendly environment. If you have an insecure attachment, whether anxious, avoidant, or disorganized, your childhood was lacking in many or all of these crucial relationship elements. You are not broken, flawed, or less-than in any way if these skills don't come naturally to you. It's just that *you haven't yet learned how.* There's no shame in this. You can learn now. You *can* create an attachment-friendly environment for you, your partner, your relationship, and your children if you have them.

If you wear eyeglasses, you probably have moments when you don't have them on and someone wants to show you something. Do you go ahead and look at the distorted image and assume it's inherently distorted? Or do you say, "Hold on, let me put on my glasses so I can see clearly"? What we are doing here is building that pair of glasses. The next time you get triggered, step back, take some deep breaths, and say to yourself, "Hold on, let me get out my attachment lens." You will never regret taking the extra moment to choose connection.

CHAPTER 8

Repairing After a Negative Cycle

No matter how much your relationship grows, negative cycles will sometimes get the best of you. Growth means they will happen less often and be less intense when they do. Still, when a negative cycle sneaks in, all is not lost. You can make full repairs.

One of the most, if not *the* most important parts of your relationship lies in your ability to repair from ruptures. It is the difference between a successful couple and an unsuccessful couple. When you can fully repair from ruptures, you and your partner will build trust; trust builds and reinforces attachment-friendly environments; attachment-friendly environments minimize negative cycles. And that's not all: successful repairs will make space for you to harness the bonding potential of vulnerability and give the two of you the opportunity to choose each other again and again.

Often when couples are humming along and feeling increasingly confident in their relationship, they'll get blindsided by a negative cycle. When I'm seeing a couple, they may go weeks without much more than the small arguments they've learned to navigate on their own and then they'll come back one week feeling wholly demoralized. "We had a big one," they report. "Now what? Are we going back to square one?"

The answer, of course, is no. Setbacks are a normal part of the growth process.

Often these unexpected blowups happen around a topic the couple has been trying to avoid. It's as if their nervous systems are saying, "We're healthier now. It's time to take a pass at that topic we've been dodging."

Spotting Subtle Ruptures

Most of the time, if a repair is needed, you'll know. Most negative cycles are obvious arguments, and if you didn't have a chance to interrupt the cycle before it got too far out of hand, you'll need to repair it. But some negative cycles are more subtle. If the climate of your marriage is pretty warm and sunny, you might be able to say to yourself, "I know I'm loved, I know I'm appreciated." But what about today's weather? Are you carrying around an air of hurt? Are you feeling slightly annoyed but can't say why? Does something feel off and insecure? Is there unspoken tension in the air? Some of this might be normal relationship friction you can handle on your own by, say, shifting your perspective without necessarily needing to bring it up with your partner. Not every little thing needs to be processed. Sometimes partners just get in bad moods and it can be easy to start looking for something (or someone) to blame. But sometimes it *is* about the relationship. If the feelings aren't going away when you have a meal or get some sleep, or if they do go away but keep resurfacing, or especially if they're accompanied by resentment . . . these are signs that a reparative conversation is in order to restore closeness.

Negative cycles are fueled by a host of inner experiences, vulnerabilities, and meanings, all of which have one thing in common: an unmet attachment need. In other words, there's been an attachment rupture. Another way to know you need to work toward a repair is if you're feeling any of the following (some of these experiences aren't technically feelings, but I'm describing them in this way to bring the concept of attachment needs to life):

+ I don't feel like my needs matter
+ I don't feel valued or wanted
+ I feel disrespected
+ I don't feel like an equal
+ I don't know that you trust me
+ I don't know that I can trust you
+ I feel like you weren't there when I needed you
+ I feel like I can't get it right no matter what I do
+ I feel unappreciated
+ I don't know that I can ever get it right for you, no matter how hard I try
+ I feel like I'm letting you down
+ I feel emotionally invalidated
+ I feel misunderstood and unheard

. . . or any other moment when an attachment need is perceived to be unmet.

If you live in a sunny-climate home but are experiencing any of these feelings, try not to get stuck in a battle with yourself. Don't try to convince yourself out of your emotions. It's tempting to say, "I *know* I'm valuable to them, and most of the time I feel that . . . maybe I should ignore the fact that I don't feel valuable right now." Or "I *know* they see me as a good partner, so why do I feel like they see me as a complete letdown in this moment? I must be crazy." You're not crazy. You're experiencing an attachment rupture. Your relationship is saying, "Hey! Over here, can we look at this so we can get back to our warm, safe and secure climate?" That is the goal of repair: to get you back on track.

Mending Fences

Nothing feels quite as good as a successful repair from a negative cycle. When I work with couples, I place a heavy focus on reparative conversations. I guide them through the work to better understand, feel, and share all the deep, rich, previously unknown material that came alive within each partner during the rupture—so much more than what they alone could see on the surface—and help them connect from this place of vulnerability. At the end of the sessions, couples leave feeling close, connected, and hopefully much better than they did when they came in.

The reason repairs are initially easier to achieve in a therapist's office than at home is that the work has to happen within the safe confines of an attachment-friendly environment. (Behavior change takes less work and self-discipline than you might realize when the environment is ripe for change.) This environment includes listening, validation, and staying out of negative-cycle behaviors like blame and defensiveness. Since distressed couples don't yet know how to create this kind of environment, it's my job to help them do just that so that they can make repairs at home. As couples and I travel through the repair process session after session, they gradually learn to create attachment-friendly environments and repair on their own, until I've eventually worked myself out of a job.

I'm sharing this process because I want to help you do the same thing at home. This book isn't therapy, but the work I do with couples doesn't need to be confined to a therapy office. Like the couples I see in person, you can learn the process of repair well enough to put it into practice in your relationship.

Alejandra and Ryan are a couple I worked with to help them learn to repair. I'd been seeing them for seven months and they were doing really well in therapy. Not only were they able to interrupt negative cycles, but they were being more vulnerable with each other in general. Instead of coming at Ryan with protest and accusations when she had a concern, Alejandra was able to say, "Here's what's going on with me and it feels important that we talk about it." Ryan learned to really hear and respond with presence and validation (even when he had a different perspective of the situation). Rather than harboring resentment by avoiding charged topics, Ryan was also starting to bring up his own concerns with attachment-friendly language like "I feel hurt about something. Can we talk about it?" Alejandra was also increasing her capacity to listen with love. They were both learning to be more flexible and willing to understand each other.

One day they entered the office feeling obviously demoralized. They'd been doing so well, they told me, and then bam, out of the blue, two days before we met, they found themselves in a negative cycle over something that "shouldn't have even been a big deal." One minute they were talking about how to care for houseplants and the next minute they were hurling accusations in desperation to be heard and building walls in an effort to hide. They were still reeling from the fight.

When couples bring me examples of negative cycles from their week, my response is always "Let's work to better understand what happened." My intention is never to *get* them to repair. I *hope* they'll repair and leave feeling better, but that's not my goal. My goal is to create understanding and empathy. I know that if I can help them see the negative cycle for what it really was—two people trying to reach each other and stay safe—repair will emerge on its own. In other words, my job is to *create space* for healing, to set up the right environment for it to happen naturally, not to *force* healing. Try to apply this logic to your relationship . . . don't try to make healing happen, try to create the right environment where healing is most likely to emerge on its own.

Let's take a quick look at what happened before Alejandra and Ryan got lost in their negative cycle: Ryan moved one of their houseplants to a new location. Alejandra thought the location he chose wasn't optimal. "What did you put it there for?" she asked. "Devil's ivy likes little sun . . . you'll fry it." Ryan responded that Alejandra was, "once again, the expert on everything." From here, both partners got heated and a negative cycle ensued.

Since Ryan was the first one to get triggered in this particular situation, I asked about his experience in the moment when Alejandra asked him why he moved the plant. What was really going on with him when he sarcastically accused Alejandra of being, "once again, the expert on everything"? As Ryan and I explored his experience, it gave Alejandra a chance to see new parts of Ryan, view him through an attachment lens, and either understand him in a way previously unknown to her, or hear him learn more about himself.

Underneath his snarky comment were the vulnerable parts of Ryan that were hiding and afraid to be seen. Vulnerable Ryan didn't hear Alejandra say, "What did you put it there for? Devil's ivy likes little sun . . . you'll fry it." Instead, he heard his dad say, "What's wrong with you, Ryan? Why are you so stupid?" In a fraction of a second, shame welled up in him, and he felt the raw sting of betrayal. And then anger. It hurt so much to think Alejandra could talk down to him like this, like he was nothing (which wasn't Alejandra's intention, but the perception of Ryan's nervous system's experience with past attachment wounds). From there his attachment system kicked in to say, "I have to let her know how much I'm hurting so that she'll see me and she'll have compassion for me, and she'll want to help me . . . and I can only do that by making her hurt, too. Then she'll be able to feel some of what I feel." It goes without saying that his strategy backfired.

I worked with Ryan to uncover his deeper fears and other feelings. I used my own relationship with him to start. I helped him to realize that through *my* eyes, nothing about him was shameful. In fact, to me, everything that happened between the moment of Alejandra's comment and the moment when Ryan protested back made so much sense considering his past experiences. Hearing me say this was a game changer. Ryan, like many of the people I've worked with in my career, had never once in his life experienced being validated in this way.

That is connection.

The next step was to take the connection between Ryan and me and move it over to Ryan and Alejandra. I asked, "Ryan, would you be willing to share with Alejandra what we've talked about? What feels important for her to know right now?"

After a pause, Ryan turned to Alejandra: "I want you to know that when I get mad like that, all you see is the anger. You see me saying hurtful words, and you see that look on my face, and I know you get caught off guard. But what's really happening underneath it all is that I'm feeling like I'm worthless and I'm scared that you're seeing me in that way, too. It hurts so much. I just want you to see how much it hurts. And I'm so sorry that's how I tried to show you."

When Ryan had finished speaking, we all sat quietly. As you can imagine, these are very powerful moments. Eventually Alejandra, very softly, and with Ryan's hand in hers, responded, "Thank you for sharing all of this with me. Thank you for letting me in. It all makes sense to me."

You'll notice that she didn't say anything like "it wasn't my intention to upset you." Talking about intentions are important, as are upheld apologies and commitments to change (when relevant), but the process I'm describing is not just about explanations, apologies, and commitments to try harder next time. Repairs, at their heart, are about creating deeper understanding. When these conversations all play out in the way that I hope, repairs contribute to greater levels of connection, and connection is far more likely to create relationship resilience than a simple "I'm sorry. I'm going to work harder."

Next, I went through the same process with Alejandra. In my sessions, I help each partner share with the other because I want them to really see the other, to see what they couldn't in the moment things got tense: their true selves, the people they really are underneath the protective walls and accusations. By facilitating this deep level of communication, I'm also helping couples build a powerful bonding experience . . . and this is my goal for you, too.

When Alejandra and Ryan left my office, they felt much closer and connected to each other than when they arrived, because both partners were willing to be vulnerable, and vulnerability breeds intimacy.

You might be wondering if, or why, Ryan's inner hurt excused him from his outer rudeness. It didn't, but I get this question a lot. "Just because Ryan was hurting inside, that makes it okay for him to say whatever he wants?" No, definitely not. Although my focus is on inner experience, I'm looking for behavior change as much as everyone else. If I thought it would work to simply tell someone, "Your behavior is atrocious and you're going to push your partner away if you don't change, so stop that," I would do it. What I've found is that real relationship change takes place more effectively and sustainably when motivated by empathy and understanding than it does when solely motivated by reasoning and fear of consequences. If this weren't the case, Ryan and Alejandra would've found their way out of negative cycles long before coming to me.

Repair Exercise

Before you can show yourself, you have to know yourself.

Now it's your turn. I created this exercise to help you understand the real, authentic, vulnerable you that gets hidden during negative cycles. If you're working through the book on your own, complete your side as a way to get to know yourself better and connect with yourself. If you're reading this book as a couple, each of you complete your side. When working as a couple, my intention is for the two of you to share with each other what you find about yourselves. My hope is that by working through this exercise, you'll be able to say to each other, "Here I am. Here's the 'me' I wasn't able to show you in that moment." I want to help you piece together the puzzle of yourselves and each other, so that you can truly see each other.

To start, come up with an example of your negative cycle. Pull up the event in your mind and try to re-create it as vividly as possible.

Now, each of you pick a moment during the negative cycle when you can recognize being triggered. Instead of remembering the cycle as a whole, pick one small moment: a word, phrase, behavior, or body language (you could also include a shift in energy, or an awareness of tension in the air). Stick to one specific moment only. If you try to look at the negative cycle in its entirety all at once, you might get lost.

During this exercise, you won't be perfect. This is an exploration process, a jump start on curiosity, not an exercise in perfection. You might not be able to answer some of the questions, and that's okay. Anything vulnerable that you share with your partner during a repair process is far better than nothing. The last thing I want is for someone to give up on sharing themselves more authentically with their partner because they can't answer all these questions with perfect accuracy.

Here's the chart from chapter 4 to help you visualize the process:

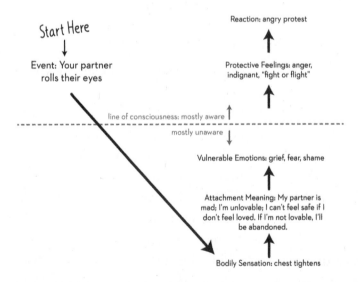

**Anatomy of a Trigger
(Attachment Behavioral System)**

Start Here

Event: Your partner rolls their eyes

Reaction: angry protest

Protective Feelings: anger, indignant, "fight or flight"

line of consciousness: mostly aware

mostly unaware

Vulnerable Emotions: grief, fear, shame

Attachment Meaning: My partner is mad; I'm unlovable; I can't feel safe if I don't feel loved. If I'm not lovable, I'll be abandoned.

Bodily Sensation: chest tightens

Now that you have your moment, grab a notepad and use the following prompts:

1. *Describe the moment.*

What did your partner do or say? Was it a word, a phrase, behavior, and/or a facial expression? Were you suddenly aware of tension? If you're having a hard time remembering, ask yourself, "What happened just before I noticed being uncomfortable?" Try to be as specific as possible.

2. *What meaning did you make of your partner's words or behaviors?*

Remember, these are perceptions, not necessarily reality. For example, if the meaning you make in a tense moment is "they must be mad," that doesn't mean your partner was actually mad. It means that's how you perceived it in the moment, and this awareness will help you unlock what may have automatically come next.

3. *Dive into your body and see if you can remember any physiological sensations you felt in that moment.*

Did you notice tightening in your chest, tingling in your limbs, pressure in your head, a clenched stomach, shallow breathing, or any other physiological sensation? Think of how you feel when you're relaxed and note how different it felt in your body during this moment. Often it's easier to notice an uncomfortable feeling by focusing on the contrast.

4. *What were your unmet attachment needs in that moment?*

Think about what you believe your partner's words or behaviors meant. How did that make you feel? Did you perceive being invalidated, unappreciated, abandoned, or unaccepted, misunderstood, like you can't get it right in your partner's eyes, or any other attachment-related distress? Do you recognize these experiences from an earlier time in your life?

5. *What vulnerable feelings seem to have welled up?*

Consider how helpless you may have felt, the desperation or confusion present. Perhaps you sensed loneliness, fear, shock, a sense of betrayal, or even grief. It could have been deeply rooted anger (the kind that's about more than just the moment), or a sense of abandonment, or shame. As you consider these feelings, take some deep breaths, tune in with your body, and see what awareness comes up around how the moment made you feel on a deeper level.

6. *What is your childhood-rooted shame telling you (or shame stemming from past adult relationships)?*

Have you felt these feelings before, or did the situation seem familiar, even if it was about something quite unrelated in topic? What's happening below the surface, regarding the needs you have but don't feel are being met, or perhaps even invalidated or under threat? Examples: I'm unworthy of really being loved. I'm stupid. I'm a loser. I'm unworthy if others are unhappy with me. I'll never get it right. I have to hide myself to be acceptable. Having strong feelings is weak. Others don't care about my feelings. I have to be small and quiet to be acceptable. I'm a burden.

7. *What protective feelings came up?*

What we often don't realize is how much our subconscious moves to protect us. Its overriding goal is to motivate us to take action . . . any action to prevent the deeper experiences of vulnerability such as fear, despair, and shame. We might feel anger, frustration, desperation, overwhelm, powerlessness, humiliation, irritation, jealousy, and more when we perceive an attachment threat. Refer to the feelings chart in the appendix if you need help narrowing down your protective feelings.

8. *Did you fight, flight, freeze, or fawn?*

Recall earlier in the book where we discussed the four Fs:

Fight: Did you get bigger to be heard? Did you protest to show your anger? Did you blame to say "change!"? Did you criticize to make them see they're wrong? Did you defend yourself or deflect concern to change their mind? Did you make accusations?

Flight: Did you say, "I don't want to talk about this right now" (as a way to avoid, not to take a break)? Did you try to avoid the conflict by convincing them to see it differently? Did you deflect their concern to change the subject and avoid the conflict?

Freeze: Did you shut down? Did you go numb?

Fawn: Did you say what they want to hear to get the situation to end? Did you try to make them happy to change the subject?

9. *How might your partner have been impacted?*

Did your partner get left with an unmet need? What might have happened in their body? What meaning did they make: being unheard, invalidated, misunderstood, blindsided, unappreciated, attacked? Did their shame get tapped into? Did they feel unlovable or unworthy in your eyes? What did they do next? Did they fight, flight, freeze, or fawn?

Next, write down your experiences in a narrative format. Here are some examples:

1. My partner was complaining about something I did, repeating the same thing again and again. No matter what I said, they just kept going. I don't remember what happened in my body, but I know I was thinking, "Here we go again, I'm being bulldozed." I felt overwhelmed and frustrated. In that moment, I didn't know if my needs mattered. I have deeply rooted anger around this. I grew up in an environment where I felt powerless to say I wasn't okay with the way I was being talked to. I got overwhelmed and started to tune them out. I was trying to stay safe and not let anger get the best of me so I didn't say something I regret and make things worse. My partner saw me disengage as if I just didn't care. I can see how that could have left them feeling desperate for a response.

2. When my partner was late getting home and didn't tell me in advance, I felt my body get tense and heavy. I said to myself, "They don't care to respond to my needs." On the deepest level I felt abandoned, defeated, and crushed. Also, I got really scared that nothing will ever change. The pain hurt, so my fight response kicked in and I felt enraged and desperate to be heard. In my desperation to be heard, I kept telling them what they were doing wrong. I thought, "If only I could say it in the right way, they'd finally get it and help me not have to feel so abandoned and scared." What my partner saw was me being angry and saying the same thing repeatedly. I can see how that left them feeling overwhelmed and then they disengaged.

3. When my partner was talking to my child in a way that I thought was too harsh, I felt panicky. My heart started to race. I thought, "My child's going to suffer, and I can't prevent it." I get scared that my child's needs will go unmet and everything will fall apart, like when I was a child. My worst fear is messing it up as a parent. I also felt angry at my partner for not helping me feel safe, since they know how much I care about this. I felt alone. I angrily took over this situation. All my partner could see was that I was being angry and unsupportive and then they went to their protective place.

4. My partner asked me if we could help friends move over the weekend. I had my own reasons for wanting to say no, but I was too afraid to say no. I grew up thinking people who say no are mean and shameful. I said to myself, "I don't want to help someone move this weekend, but if I say no, my partner will be mad at me." It felt like they were putting me in an impossible position. Now I know that's not true, but at the time it made me think my needs didn't matter to them. I felt caught off guard, alone, and defeated. My chest felt tight, and I noticed a deflated feeling. I said yes even though I meant no. When the time came to help with the move, my resentment overpowered me and I was

snarky the whole time. This was my way of saying, "I'm angry, but I'm too afraid to talk about it." All my partner could see is me being cynical for no apparent reason. I can see how that left them feeling confused, alone, and treated unfairly.

5. My partner said something that made me think that they think someone else is physically attractive. I felt threatened and my stomach knotted up. My mind said, "This is it, I'm being betrayed." I've been cheated on in the past, and it was devastating. I can't bear to feel that way again. I felt scared and a sense of loss. I felt angry and I just shut down and disengaged because I was afraid to let anger seep out and push them away. All my partner could see was the silent treatment. I can see how that left them feeling confused and shut out.

If you and your partner are doing this exercise together, it's time to share with each other. I suggest taking turns sharing in the following way:

Partner 1: share your narrative
Partner 2: respond
Partner 2: share your narrative
Partner 1: respond

Keep responses short, validating, and focused on your partner. We aren't trying to find a solution or correct for accuracy right now. This exercise is less about exact wording and more about seeing and understanding more about each other. Learn how to be together in this discomfort, how to hear each other and share. For it to be successful, we really need to make space for vulnerability. When your partner shows their vulnerability, it's so important to treat it with care. Remember how scary it is for you to share vulnerably. Keeping some of these in mind when you respond can help:

+ Show appreciation that they were willing to share with you.
+ If you feel close to them as they share, tell them how close you feel.
+ Don't apologize or explain yourself, just sit with them.

◆ Hold their hand, or make another physical connection.

◆ Validate: *It makes so much sense, you make so much sense, I understand your feelings, I understand you.*

◆ Keep it short and simple. Aim for three sentences.

Here are examples:

Thank you for letting me see you. I feel let in and close. You make sense to me.

Thank you for trusting me with all this. Nothing about your vulnerability is weak. I see you as strong right now. What you're sharing with me isn't too much. I want to see all of you.

Apologies and Behavior Changes

For many of today's adults, one of the hardest parts of this approach is forgoing the immediate need for an apology. This generation grew up in a world where apologies were paramount—your parents likely focused more on "say you're sorry" when things went wrong than "let's understand why you did that." Don't get me wrong: I think apologies are very important. When you apologize to your partner you're saying, "I see how what I did hurt you and it hurts me to hurt you." Apologizing shows your willingness to take accountability, which shows a willingness to work on the behavior. The words "I'm sorry" are important and sometimes they're enough. But there will be times when triggers are more powerful and wounds are deeper, and the "I'm sorry" will be much more effective when delivered in the context of a full repair conversation.

Also, apologies are more meaningful when you take the time to understand how your behavior impacted your partner and then share your understanding. A sincere "I'm sorry I said that" is meaningful, but "I'm sorry I said that. I can see how that left you feeling really hurt and betrayed," or "I'm sorry I said that. What did that feel like for you?" is even more so.

What if you're thinking that it's nice to understand what's going on beneath, but what you're really interested in is making sure things change so that it won't happen again? This work all exists for the overriding goal of closeness and harmony, both of which ultimately hinge on behavior change. Behavior change is a crucial part of the repair process. No amount of insight, empathy, and understanding matters if a couple can't shift out of behaviors that damage attachment safety and erode trust, and into those which foster connection and trust. Your relationship simply can't thrive when damaging behaviors aren't improving. But behavior change can't happen in isolation. Safe and healthy environments create space for safe and healthy behaviors. And even in the most attachment-friendly environment, behavior change will not happen right then and there.

Real and sustainable change takes space, time, and consistency. This book aims to teach you how to create the space.

CHAPTER 9

Attachment Injuries and Repair

Most of the examples of conflict in this book so far are hard but relatively commonplace ruptures around topics like finances, extended-family issues, misunderstandings, and big decisions that need to be made. But what about those of you who are dealing with bigger wounds, ones that have had a greater impact on trust? Conflicts like this could include an affair, a serious lie or chronic dishonesty, failure of a partner to show up in a key moment (a hospitalization or giving

birth, for example), abusive behavior, ongoing substance abuse problems, especially damaging fights, or anything else that has a theme of
betrayal, has deeply impacted the trust in your relationship, and is still
alive in the relationship today, sometimes even years later.

These types of issues are more than just ruptures; they are *attachment injuries*. Attachment injuries can be recognized because they have
such a profound impact on trust and connection that without healing
(which I define as reestablishing trust), it might be impossible for the
relationship to thrive. They are also characterized by a strong feeling of
betrayal. Some couples are struggling with multiple injuries. Often injuries are one-sided (in the examples above, one partner is the "wounding partner" and the other is the "wounded partner"), but both partners
can have attachment injuries in the relationship, and sometimes even
over the same event.

If you've been on the receiving end of an attachment injury, you
probably know what I'm talking about. The memory of the event is
likely entering your mind as you read this, and perhaps you can even
feel your body react. Maybe you notice your chest get heavy, your jaw
tightening, or suddenly you can't concentrate on what's in front of you.
Attachment injuries are subjective: what one person experiences as a
betrayal, another person might not. Like all traumas, attachment injuries are defined by the *meanings* of events and the impact, not by the
events themselves.

While your attachment injuries might be "bigger" than the more
day-to-day ruptures referenced throughout the book, they share an
important commonality: attachment injuries *can* be healed. They can
even create opportunity for deeper levels of growth. But the process is
a sensitive one and before any healing conversations can even begin,
certain baseline criteria need to be met.

My former client Leah was a trail runner. One afternoon she slid
down a muddy slope and ended up in the ER with a tremendous
amount of pain and a broken leg. Her partner, Max, didn't show up to
the hospital for several hours because of a work crisis he felt he couldn't
interrupt without serious repercussions at work. Leah, alone and in

pain, was devastated and felt deeply betrayed. Clearly this was an at-tachment injury, but it wasn't an isolated event. Leah had long felt that Max put work first. Still, this hospital moment was the last straw for Leah. When it *really* mattered, Max wasn't there for her. At first Leah wasn't sure she could stay in the relationship.

Max didn't get it because his sense of safety in the world—including the safety of Leah and their relationship—was rooted in being success-ful at work. To fail at work was to fail everything, to *be* a failure. In Max's mind, Leah wasn't alone on a hill after her fall; she was getting medical care and had doctors and nurses helping her. Max knew he'd get there eventually, just as soon as he could. I'm not excusing Max's behavior, but it's important to understand that what can appear to be callousness is often its own version of a trauma response, in this case resulting from toxic messages from childhood centered around Max's worthiness, which drove his desperation to "keep it all together," even at the expense of the attachment security of his relationship.

With the relationship on the line, Leah and Max both decided they wanted to make it work and to go to therapy. I let them know that we had a wound to heal, and they both agreed to try to work through it. Could we, as therapist and clients, work to prevent situations like this in the future? Yes. But first we had to approach the situation with openness to understanding all the moving parts. For Max, going for-ward meant that he had to be willing to consider Leah's experience of the event, even when nothing in him ever meant to intentionally leave Leah feeling so betrayed and with shattered trust. He had to agree and accept that an attachment injury had occurred.

Once we established that an attachment injury *had* occurred, I explained to Leah and Max that the only way through the healing would be to process the injury in an attachment-friendly environ-ment with safe, reparative conversations. Safety isn't only important for the protection of the wounded partner; it's also important for the protection of the *wounding* partner, meaning just because the offend-ing partner behaved in a way that created a lot of damage, this doesn't mean they deserve being on the receiving end of insensitive, mean, or abusive language. Safety for both parties means avoiding statements like "How could you be so insensitive? Are you some kind of sociopath?" "You're being a little dramatic, you know I did the best I could," "Why can't we just move on?" or "I hope our children don't turn out like you."

I also explained to Leah and Max that the process takes time. If our goal was to rebuild trust and safety in the relationship, the best we could do was to create the right conditions for healing to emerge naturally and gradually. We couldn't force or shame it into being. The nervous system has its own time line. As hard as it is when you miss your partner and long for the safety and closeness you once had, try to think of healing these wounds as a *process* rather than a one-time event. It's not about being done or not done (either you heal or don't; either you forgive or don't; either you get over it or you don't). You won't have one conversation and feel suddenly healed. Instead, when things are going in a healing *direction*, one day you will realize, "Oh, wow, I don't think I'm as affected by that event as I used to be." This, as you probably can imagine if you've ever experienced an attachment injury, is huge.

Healing Conversations

The conversations for repairing an attachment injury are similar to those for repairing a rupture; they need to include healthy amounts of vulnerability, validation (including validation of anger), and empathy. But because the wound is deeper, so too must be the healing.

Here is a step-by-step guide for a healing conversation for an attachment injury: If you're the one who created the injury (the "wounding partner"), it's essential that your partner gets space to share how they were impacted. For Leah and Max this meant Leah was able to tell Max what it had been like for her to feel second to Max's career and what it was like for her on the day she sat in the hospital alone and in pain. But Leah needed to do that *outside of a negative cycle*, meaning she needed to share her experience from a place of self, of "this is what it was like for me," instead of from a place of blame, judgment, and shame dumping. She also had to do this without minimizing her own feelings or apologizing for her experience ("Maybe I shouldn't be so upset after all," or "I'm probably just overreacting").

Here's how a reparative share doesn't *sound:*

"I can't believe you could leave me there alone like that. How could you be so insensitive? I just broke my leg and you couldn't miss work for two hours? You don't care about anyone but yourself."

Here's how a reparative share does *sound:*

"I was so angry, but underneath that I felt devastated. It felt like the floor dropped out from under me. I felt so betrayed and alone and even humiliated, as if I'm not even worth showing up for."

If you're the wounding partner, it's critical that you're able to take in your partner's message, try to understand it, and then empathize and validate them. Reflect back to your partner what they're telling you about their experience; *let them know you can hear*. Try to step into their world. Maybe the ER experience wouldn't have been as sensitive for you as it was for Leah; maybe you have different emotional experiences around medical events or for whatever reason it just wouldn't have bothered you. But everyone has *something* that might leave them feeling betrayed. Picture a scenario where you might feel betrayed. What would that moment have been like for you? What would have helped you when you felt betrayed? Bring that compassion and openness to these conversations, and remember to *listen with love*. Use whatever experiences of your own you can draw up to feel empathy and use your empathy to validate your partner's feelings: "I remember when I saw you'd texted your ex. I felt very betrayed in that moment. I needed you to hear how upset I was. I'm understanding that's how you feel right now, and it makes sense to me."

Here's how a reparative response does not *sound:*

"I hear you and I'm sorry. Next time I'll try to be more sensitive. . . . But I *wasn't* betraying you. My job depended on that deadline I was trying to meet. You know how important that project was. What about me?"

Here's how a reparative response does *sound:*

"I hear how much this hurt you. I hear how angry and devastated you were when I didn't show up. I'm thinking of moments similar to what you're describing, when I've felt betrayed, and I can feel some of that right now. It hurts me to think of you hurting like that, of feeling so alone. It breaks my heart to imagine you questioning your worth. It makes sense. I get it. I really get it."

As you're having reparative conversations, use nonverbal communication for added support. Delivering messages of empathy and validation with eye contact and gentle touch (if your partner is open to it) can make the process exponentially more soothing and healing.

This conversation might need to happen multiple times for trust to rebuild. It can feel demoralizing to have the same conversation about the same wound over and over, to the point that you wonder if you'll ever get past it and be able to move on. Here are common traps to watch out for that can signal when these conversations are no longer effective or are obstructing healing.

Communicating in a Negative Cycle

When I'm working with a couple with an attachment injury, we're not able to address that injury at the start of therapy. We can talk about it as an event, but we're not going to dive into healing conversations until they're able to talk about smaller problems outside of a negative cycle. When they can do that, it's a signal it's time to move forward. If you and your partner are trying to navigate through an injury repair and you're getting stuck in negative cycles, you might need to back up and first work on your negative cycles around less sensitive material.

Shame Spiraling

Shame spiraling happens when the wounding partner gets triggered and overwhelmed with shame, to the degree that their shame takes center stage, and their partner feels abandoned. Shame spiraling changes the subject from the wounded partner's wounds to the wounding partner's shame. There's absolutely room for healthy guilt when it comes to injuries—guilt feels bad and can contribute to our desire to not repeat the same mistakes—but remember healthy guilt says, "I did something wrong or hurtful," while shame says, "*I* am wrong; *I* am bad." If you find yourself saying things like "I'm so bad, how could you love me? I'm a terrible partner. You don't deserve me," you are shame spiraling.

Also keep in mind that shame spirals aren't shameful. It's hard for anyone to stay present when we're faced with how we've hurt someone we love. But for healing to happen, it's so important to catch them and find your way back to emotional presence. Sometimes the only way to find your way back to emotional presence is to put words to your shame: "This is hard. It brings up so much shame for me. But I'm willing to hold it, so that I can stay present while you say what you need to say," and then move forward with your supportive role.

Making Excuses

If you're the wounding partner, whatever led you to do what you did matters, and we can't ignore it. Eventually you need space to share your experience, too. But making excuses isn't about sharing what was happening for you; making excuses is about trying to convince your partner not to feel the way they do, or to take some of the heat off yourself. Saying things like "I was trying to get a project done," or "My assistant was home sick. I was on my own," or "Traffic was bad," or "I wouldn't have cheated if you'd paid more attention to me," or "How was I supposed to know you needed me right then and there? It wasn't like I never showed up at all," especially when you're interrupting your partner's process, is likely only going to get in the way of the bigger goal, which is moving forward.

Changing the Subject

Again, if you're the wounding partner, your feelings *do* matter. This work is about making sense of the event as a whole . . . all the moving parts. But we can't do it all at once. Responses like "But what about my feelings? What about my stress about the project?" or "Am I supposed to walk on eggshells?" or "Some of this is about you being overly sensitive because of your relationship with your mother. This isn't all about me," are all examples of changing the subject. If you find yourself trying to change the subject, it's not because you're inherently insensitive; it's your way of managing your painful feelings during this process. But we're not trying to help you feel better in the moment only for the relationship to stay unhealed; we're trying for something better.

Trying to Speed Up the Process

Don't try to rush the conversation or process. Saying "I hear you. But how many times do we have to do this? When can we just move on?" shrinks the space needed for healing, and our goal is to expand the space for healing. We don't tell a scraped knee to hurry up and heal. Instead we clean it, maybe put a Band-Aid on it, and trust our body to do its thing in its own time. The more space healing has, the more it can do its job.

Keep in mind, healing an attachment injury should never be avoided, but it also can't be all-encompassing. It shouldn't be the case that it's all you talk about until it is resolved. In fact, that approach will likely obstruct healing. Instead, I recommend going in and out of these conversations. As much as possible (depending upon your unique situation), try to enjoy each other outside of healing discussions. Joy is a vulnerable emotion and a bonding one. Strengthening your bond will help with the healing process.

When you are having your healing conversations, if you can steer clear of the common pitfalls outlined above and practice loving listening, empathy, and validation, the discussions will begin to be fewer and farther between. Why? Because when people get what they're needing, they stop crying for it.

The Wounding Partner: What About You?

The previous sections offer lots of strategies for how the wounding partner can repair with the person they have hurt. They might not be able to right their wrong, but they can use these tactics to help heal and perhaps inspire forgiveness in their partner. But even if you are the person who "wronged" your partner, your feelings matter, too. There is a reason you did whatever you did, so what about your own healing? For a couple to be able to make sense of an attachment injury in a way that fosters understanding and minimizes the chance of it happening again, both partners' experiences matter. When does *your* experience get space? It's all about timing—when your partner feels safe and can take it in, then your experience gets room in these reparative conversations. This can only happen once your partner has felt heard and validated. Being heard and validated creates space and openness for the *whole* of the experience (understanding the whole experience is not the same as making excuses or justifications). If you're not sure if your partner is there yet, ask, "Are you in a place where you can understand what was happening for me?" If yes, share your own experience. Here's how it might sound:

"I'm so sorry I hurt you. I was scared and I put my fear before your need. If I could go back, I would've done it differently. It wasn't my intention to leave you feeling alone. My intention was to run away from my own fear. I recognize this is a pattern for me and it's rooted in my need to be acceptable to you, to the world, and to myself. My shame and fear of failure got in the way of our connection, and I'm so sorry for that. Can you forgive me?"

This, of course, is just a sample script. Every situation is unique and will lend itself to your unique words. My hope is that you can take the spirit and make it your own.

What If We're Not Healing?

When it comes to attachment injuries, it's important to remember that mistrust is a primal response. A survival strategy. It's not a choice. Sometimes mistrust stems from real relationship events, and sometimes it stems from our own personal blocks to trust, which existed before the relationship even started. Often it's a combination of the two. Mistrust is the nervous system saying, "There's a threat. I am not safe. Be careful. Find safety." In the right context, mistrust can keep us alive. So when there has been an attachment injury in a relationship, you might decide you're open to healing and that you're willing to take steps to get there, but ultimately only your nervous system will decide when it's truly ready to trust again. Trust is a felt sense of safety—it can be worked toward, but not forced; it will only come to be when a partner is open to it, and when the right conditions are created for it to grow.

If you're putting all of these principles into practice and you're still saying, "I'm haunted by this event," "I still don't fully trust," "I'm so mad I can't possibly feel close," or "We're putting in the work, but something is still getting in the way," this means something is blocking the healing process. It could be that there have been multiple injuries on one or both sides, and the relationship is so overwhelmed with injuries that it's hard for the couple to trust enough to navigate healing conversations.

It might also be the case that the wounding behavior is *not* ongoing, but the environment that contributed to the wounding behavior is. Let's take an affair, for example. Most of us will agree that affairs are devastating to relationships. At the same time, we might also agree that affairs typically don't materialize out of thin air—they are often (not always) related to a struggling relationship climate. If both partners want to heal from an affair, there needs to be an openness to looking beyond the affair itself and into the overall climate. This might mean that while the partner who was cheated on is the critically wounded partner, we eventually need to make space for the wounding partner's hurts, too.

Consider Ayla and Ari, who were trying to heal from an affair when I began seeing them. Long before the affair, chronic negative cycles were leaving them both feeling shamed, invalidated, rejected, unwanted, and unappreciated, among a host of other unmet attachment needs that bogged down their closeness and their ability to get along. While these smaller ruptures weren't as instantly devastating or visible, they were real. At some point each partner needed to have space to share their experience and be heard and validated. It didn't sound like "I'm sorry I had an affair, but I was unhappy and if I wasn't unhappy I wouldn't have been so vulnerable to falling into the arms of my coworker." Instead it sounded like "I chose to have an affair. You and our relationship problems didn't make me choose to handle our problems in that way. At the same time, I have some hurts of my own and it will help me feel closer if we can talk about it, not as a way to take away from your pain, but as a way to fully heal our relationship." This communication happened deep into the process, when trust was more firmly established because we first had to deal with the more pressing issue of the wronged individual's hurt.

Think of it like waking up in the middle of the night to water seeping in from a leaky roof. You might get the roof patched, which will work for a while and prevent further damage, but eventually you'll need to address why the roof was compromised to the point of leaking to begin with. Otherwise, another problem with the roof is eventually going to show itself. This logic can be applied not just to affairs, but to attachment injuries of all natures.

Sometimes one or both partners aren't sure they really want to heal. They go along with it because it seems like the "right" thing to do, or because they're afraid to be alone. They have one foot in and one foot out of the process. When I have a couple that's stuck and I can't figure out why, much of the time it's because one partner isn't entirely sure they want to go on. If you suspect this might be the case, as hard as it will be, it's important to talk about it. Remember, all the work outlined in this book requires authenticity and vulnerability. The healing process is no exception; it requires full engagement. Without it, your relationship will get stuck in a stale state of limbo.

Some wounded partners find that no matter how they want it, they just can't find a place of forgiveness. Their wounding partner has shown up for them in the best way possible, but still their anger and resentment linger. They might even genuinely believe the injurious behavior won't happen again, but the block remains. What this might be about, on a subconscious level, is how the wounded partner *will feel about themself* if they forgive. They could associate (again, subconsciously) forgiveness with being weak, unworthy, a victim, less-than, and/or humiliated, all of which are shame-based. For them, holding on to the anger that blocks forgiveness can keep them safe from their own shame. Or, holding on to anger might keep them safe from how they might view themselves if they take ownership for their part of relationship problems. If you can relate, it's something to explore and work through.

Finally, some behaviors stem from personal issues on the part of one or both partners, like addiction, and healing can't happen until it's fully addressed. For example, if a partner who has an affair has an untreated sex addiction, the odds are higher that without treatment it will continue to be a problem. In these instances, there are professionals who usher couples through a formal healing program in conjunction with the addicted partner's treatment. If there's a substance abuse problem, we're going to see any number of behaviors associated with addictions: lying, legal problems, draining the bank account to keep up with their use. Anyone in the painful throes of addiction is likely to be causing serious injuries to the relationship, and sadly, it will take help for them or the relationship to heal.

If you can relate to any of these common blocks and you've tried to address them but your relationship still isn't improving, it's time to seek professional help. Attachment injuries can be especially delicate, and sometimes the best way to attend to them is by getting an outside perspective. This does not mean you're broken, weak, not trying hard enough, or that all is lost. It just means that you're experiencing more relationship complications than you can handle on your own—and trust me when I say you are not alone.

Lastly, some wounds cannot be healed. Sometimes the pain is too much. Sometimes the betrayal is so great that it's impossible for trust to ever be rebuilt and closeness to ever be regained. Sometimes there are too many wounds. Sometimes a partner's behaviors were too much of a breach of your value system. If the repair process is going as smoothly as possible, you're having the right conversations and the behavior is ended and communication is improving and you've given it time and still you're blocked, then you might want to consider the possibility that there's too much to overcome. There's no shame in admitting that sometimes trusting your partner again isn't possible. If you think this is the case, I highly recommend seeking a professional to help you talk it through.

Moving Beyond the Injury

How do you know when you've healed? As I've mentioned, healing attachment injuries is a process rather than a one-time event. What I see with couples in my practice is that during our sessions the attachment injury stops being the focus of the conversation. Does their relationship go back to "normal"? No. Relationships that successfully heal from attachment injuries will never be exactly as they were again. Instead, they'll be better because the process of working through injuries is one of deepening connection, personal growth, and relationship growth. What I've experienced is that couples who make it through come out on the other side stronger than ever.

PART THREE

Real-World Considerations

CHAPTER 10

Workable Intruders

When You or Your Partner Struggles with Depression, Trauma, or Addictions

In order to achieve secure love, you and your partner need four basic criteria: 1) commitment, 2) access to actionable information, 3) the ability to self-regulate, and 4) the willingness to consistently do your part to foster an attachment-friendly environment. Since you've read the book this far, that indicates your commitment. It also goes a long way in helping you access the actionable information. But to integrate this information effectively, you need to be able to stay regulated and emotionally present. Your ability to self-regulate and/or emotionally engage in your relationship can be drastically impaired by mental health and addiction issues, and if you have a partner who struggles with these issues, that can impede a connection between you.

My ultimate goal for every couple is to enable them to maintain an attachment-friendly environment as much of the time as possible and co-regulate each other through ruptures. To get there, you each need the capacity to be self-regulated enough to show up as your best self most of the time.

Staying regulated and present is never as easy as simply saying, "I'm going to stay regulated and present." Both take targeted skills (many of which we've discussed in this book) and practice. But some people will have a harder time practicing and implementing these skills than others, often because additional challenges interfere. I call these challenges "workable intruders," and they include (but are not limited to) excessive stress, depression, a history of trauma, and addictions.

Excessive Stress

Stress is distracting and energy draining. While most people probably have more stress in their lives than they'd like, some have *excessive* stress: more than what is manageable without seriously compromising the energy and time needed to devote to self-care and relationship care. If you have to put out fires all day with no break, it makes it that much harder to do what you need to do to prevent the fires in the first place.

For most people, the root of excessive stress is related to finances, parenting, discrimination, taking care of aging relatives, work-related challenges, medical conditions, relationships, socioeconomic issues, or a combination of these. Regardless of the source, such stress is going to make it harder to work on your relationship. But know that by improving the quality of interactions with your partner, you will reduce stress.

Most people don't have the opportunity to overhaul their lives to reduce stress significantly in the short term. Still, usually we can come up with *something*, even if it's small. Do you have the ability to work a little less? Can you add in a ten-minute walk twice a day to move your body and reboot your brain? Can you get into bed an hour earlier? Can you practice breathing exercises five minutes per day? Is there *any* other action that can take the edge off your stress levels in order to open up a little space to focus on relationship work (even just being more mindful of the tone you use with your partner)?

Some people don't have the luxury of making significant changes to the logistical realities of their lives. I understand that. If this is you, see if you can at least take a couple of pauses throughout the day to do three-minute breathing exercises. These will help you ground yourself and be more mindful during interactions with your partner. The smallest pause in the day can help both you and your relationship.

Sometimes three minutes of relaxing breathing at 2 p.m. can impact your reaction to your partner's annoying text at 2:25 p.m. When you get home that day, you might not have time to cuddle on the couch because you're working two jobs and don't get home until too late. But when your partner gives you a hug when you walk through the door, maybe, just maybe, it has something to do with the fact that you took the time to breathe for three minutes, which helped you just enough to refrain from responding to their text with a cynical tone, which was co-regulating to your partner (or at least didn't add bad energy to the mix), and in turn the hug was co-regulating for you. Will you sleep a little better that night without tension between the two of you? How might a good night's sleep affect your ability to manage stress the next day? Small moments add up.

What about when your partner has excessive stress and isn't available in the relationship fully? I don't want to take away from how lonely it can feel when your partner isn't present. Even when it's a situation entirely out of their control and intellectually you understand that, it's still frustrating. Of course it is . . . you miss them and have limited control over the situation. But you aren't powerless. While you might not be able to take the circumstances surrounding their stress away, you *can* be an emotionally supportive presence while they're in the thick of it, which will reduce the overall stress load. If you're the partner experiencing the stressful event, it's important to allow space for your partner's frustration without getting defensive. This might sound like a simple "I understand how hard this is on you, too, and I appreciate you being by my side." This is not to take away from your experience, but it will be much easier for your partner to tolerate situations they can't control when they feel seen for how the situation impacts them, too.

Relationship problems make up at least 30 percent of the average American's stress. So while your stress is real, and I want to validate that some of you can barely keep your heads above water, even the tiniest of actions that will add to an attachment-friendly environment can help reduce stress in an entire one-third of your life.

Depression

Depression robs a person of energy and motivation, leaving them feeling numb, agitated, excessively guilty, often with a lower sex drive, and/ or with their concentration inhibited. If you or your partner is depressed, just getting through the day can be a struggle, which means you might have very little left to give to the relationship. If you are depressed, you might not be able to concentrate on conversations about your own or your partner's attachment needs. Your pain is so big, and your motivation so low, that you cannot give your partner what they're needing no matter how much the "real you," underneath the dark cloud of depression, wants to.

Imagine a voice inside your head that says, "Everything is your fault." You feel sad and unmotivated and maybe even scared; or maybe you just feel numb. Everything seems dark and hopeless, and those feelings consume you. Then your partner comes home and wants to connect, but you have nothing to give. Now the voice in your head telling you it's your fault, that you're a letdown, gets even louder. All you can do is cry, or maybe just shut off. Often depressed clients don't have the emotional capacity to do anything but survive. Even mild depression can be enough of a disruption to your functioning to prevent you from showing up with your full self.

Depression, when not fully understood and talked about, can worsen attachment insecurity. If the depressed partner hasn't been diagnosed, it can leave both partners feeling alone, hurt, scared, and confused. But when someone's depression is diagnosed and they get treatment, the couple can make sense of what's happening and begin the road to recovery.

If you suffer from depression, ideally your first course of action will be to get professional help from a therapist, psychiatrist, or medical doctor. Second, keep in mind the importance of quality connections with others and how it can dramatically improve depression. Attachment-friendly environments are built on the foundation that the space is safe for connection. These environments encourage the release of happy hormones such as oxytocin, and neurotransmitters like serotonin and dopamine—the very neurotransmitters targeted in the drugs that treat depression. So even if you're feeling depressed and the last thing you want to do is funnel energy into connecting with anyone, including your partner, do what you can when you can. Even a tiny amount of engagement can make a difference.

The same skill of sharing your experience that goes into tackling a negative cycle can help when you're dealing with depression: Talk about it with your partner. Let them in. Help them understand your feelings of sadness, guilt, lethargy, and why you're having trouble putting effort into the relationship. Let them see what you're going through. Your partner needs to know that you *do* care about improving the relationship, even if you're having trouble doing the work. If you two can talk about the real, raw parts of yourselves and your life, like depression, you'll feel connected. Sharing is connection, even when sharing the hard stuff.

If your partner is the one who's depressed, it only makes sense that you feel alone and likely out of control of the situation. Try to understand that they are dealing with an illness and that their behavior is not a rejection of you. Providing an attachment-friendly environment that is validating and not shaming *is* something you can control and, believe it or not, is likely to make more of a difference than anything else you can do. Self-care is part of an attachment-friendly environment. Make sure you are attending to your basic needs, like a healthy diet, exercise, sleep, and finding support from others. Maybe seek out a therapist who can help you learn to attend to your own needs while also navigating the relationship. It's easy to neglect ourselves when a loved one is suffering, but over time it takes a toll on both you and the person who is struggling.

For both partners to better understand depression in the context of your relationship and how to find ways to maintain your bond, I recommend the book *When Depression Hurts Your Relationship: How to Regain Intimacy and Reconnect with Your Partner When You're Depressed*, by Shannon Kolakowski, PsyD, and Craig Malkin, PhD.

Other Mental Illnesses and Personality Disorders

While depression is common, it is by no means the only mental health issue which can add a layer of complexity to relationship work. If you or your partner is struggling with bipolar, an anxiety disorder, any other form of mental illness, neurodivergence, and/or a personality disorder such as Narcissistic Personality Disorder or Borderline Personality Disorder (both of which overlap with attachment insecurity and trauma, and pose unique challenges to relationship work), it's important to seek professional help and additional resources.

Unresolved Trauma

Often when we think about unresolved trauma, we call to mind serious events like sexual or physical abuse, or death of an attachment figure. Most people don't need to be convinced that these experiences can be enormously emotionally damaging, and for good reason. What often get missed are the smaller or chronic events that, if never properly processed, also manifest in ways that affect our well-being and relationship health. I often liken those events to a thousand paper cuts—individually they don't seem like such a big deal, but cumulatively they have a major effect.

Unresolved trauma is a more encompassing bucket than you might think and affects more individuals than you might imagine. I regularly work with clients who grew up being subtly emotionally abused, constantly being told things like "if you don't stop crying, I'll give you something to cry about," or "girls are prettier when they're quiet," or "boys don't cry." These phrases represent emotional trauma because they send the message that you aren't safe to feel or show your feelings . . . if you do, you'll be rejected, shamed, sent away, or even physically harmed. Second, it communicates that you aren't even valuable enough to have a voice. These messages fuel self-beliefs that show up in relationship problems throughout life in ways that are often so below the radar that it takes a trained professional to connect the dots.

A highly critical, shaming environment is the perfect breeding ground for the type of trauma I'm describing, which is called complex post-traumatic stress disorder (CPTSD). If you can relate, you might recognize that in your relationship today you'll go to great lengths to avoid the sting of shame you grew up with. Let's say you get a flat tire and realize you don't have a jack and you forgot to renew your AAA membership. The shame wells up inside you, saying, "How could you be so stupid?" This in turn spurs you to snap and lash out at your partner, not because they're at fault but because you'll do anything to deflect the heat that you've put on yourself. Remember, shame tells us to hide the parts of us we don't believe are acceptable to others, so when you don't like being seen as incompetent, or viewing yourself as incompetent, it can feel so much safer to project the incompetence onto someone else, even when this is far from your conscious intention. Your nervous system only knows that it's trying to feel better. But unfortunately the damage is done and your partner feels stunned and attacked, which, depending on how your partner reacts, can incite your negative cycle.

That is a trauma reaction. Someone who didn't grow up with excessive shame will likely not snap. They will likely not shame-spiral and call themselves stupid. Instead, they'll be annoyed with themselves, handle the situation, and make sure they pack the jack and renew AAA as soon as possible, calling it all a valuable learning experience.

Now instead of shame, substitute in traumas related to attachment fears and needs, like emotional invalidation. This kind of emotional abandonment (and invalidation *is* emotional abandonment), when repeated enough during one's formative years, will cause an overarching fear of abandonment. So when your partner doesn't text back after five minutes and you start to feel panicky, convinced they're purposely ignoring you because they don't love you anymore? That's trauma.

What about physical or sexual trauma? These "big-T" traumas can have a profound impact on their victims. This is especially true when they're combined with a generally toxic environment, which is quite often the case. The same is true for PTSD resulting from acute crises such as accidents, being a victim of a crime, natural disasters, and military-related events. PTSD can shake up a person's sense of safety, causing hair-trigger reactions to anything in their environment that might remind them of the traumatizing events. It can cause nightmares and other sleep disturbances, intrusive thoughts, flashbacks, mood swings, and so much more. Being emotionally present when bogged down with trauma symptoms can be so difficult, which is why PTSD not related to your relationship can still have a major impact on your relationship.

Some traumas will need more help healing than others. When I'm sitting across from couples in a session, I can tell this is happening when a partner isn't able to relax into the work we're doing together. For some this shows up as detachment. For others it shows as externalized dysregulation manifesting in escalated emotional outbursts, difficulty staying on topic, lengthy protests, and rants that are more persistent than usual. Many partners, including those without significant trauma histories, will be triggered by therapy especially when painful feelings are at an all-time high. But by providing the safe and validating environment which it's my job to create, both partners will almost always feel heard, and then settle in. When that's not the case, and the trauma in the room is bigger than my ability to contain it, I know it's time for this person to seek help to specifically relieve trauma symptoms. Somatic Experiencing therapy, a type of therapy that is meant to help you feel, process, and manage your feelings as they show up in your body, is a good addition or alternative to traditional talk therapy for the healing of trauma, and I recommend it highly to those who have trouble fully participating in couples work.

While somatic therapy is by no means the only option for healing trauma, it can offer you a break from overrelying on your mind and the invaluable opportunity to start learning from the intelligence of your body. Many people get a lot from talk therapy and then move into somatic therapy when they're ready to address the trauma more deeply. Somatic Experiencing therapists are trained to help people process trauma *without* getting flooded, or overwhelmed, with emotions and unable to "turn them off" when the session is over, which makes the trauma healing more comfortable and less re-traumatizing. It can be more effective for those who haven't been able to heal in other types of therapy. On top of this, somatic therapy is designed to help people self-regulate not just when they're actively processing trauma, but when they're facing the everyday challenges of life and relationships. Being able to self-regulate and find calm within can help a person tremendously when they need that extra bit of support to be able to settle into the work, self-regulate, and stop negative cycles. You can find more about this type of work by visiting www.traumahealing.org.

There's a lot to be said for the ability of attachment-friendly environments to contribute significantly to healing trauma. The shame of trauma says "you aren't worthy of love and care," but secure relationships and attachment-friendly environments send consistent messages through words and behavior that "you *are* worthy of love and care." Additionally, when couples can reduce the frequency and intensity of negative cycles, their home environment feels safer. Safety is the antidote to fear, which is a driving force behind trauma triggers. When environmental stress is decreased, the trauma victim (whether you, your partner, or both of you) will have more energy freed up to devote to their individual healing. For this reason, relationship work is a vital component of trauma healing. To better understand the healing power fulfilling relationships can bring to trauma treatment, I recommend both partners read *The Body Keeps the Score*, by Bessel van der Kolk.

Addictions

It will probably come as no surprise that substance abuse and other addictions will get in the way of a partner's ability to fully show up in their relationship in the healthiest way possible, much less to be able to put new relationship skills to use. Addictions create competing attachments because access to the object of the addiction takes priority over the relationship. Drugs and alcohol alter consciousness, in which case the real person is hidden underneath the intoxication. Porn and sex addiction create competing attachments *and* sexual betrayal.

Getting treatment for substance abuse and addictions is so important. If you have an addiction, you have a real relationship with the activity or substance to which you're addicted, and it will be impossible for you to be fully present in the human relationships that matter most to you, including the one with yourself, until you can cut off or deprioritize the relationship with your vice of choice. But, as science has taught us, cutting that relationship off will be a lot easier if those human relationships are strong.

Rat Park

In the 1970s, drug researchers proved that rats put in small cages alone would, when offered a choice between heroin- or cocaine-laced water or regular water, drink only from the drug-laced bottles until they overdosed or died.

Shortly after these studies, American psychologist Bruce Alexander introduced a new idea that he decided to put to the test with a new version of the rat lab tests. Giving the rats the same choice between drug-laced water or regular water, Alexander added an additional variable: this time the rats weren't alone in a small cage. Alexander created Rat Park. In Rat Park, the rats were surrounded by many other rats, and they could play and socialize all they wanted (rats, like humans, are highly social animals). This time, the Rat Park rats did *not* prefer the drug-laced water; they preferred the plain water. Those rats who did try the drug water only did so intermittently and never overdosed, and never at the expense of food and regular water. Even the rats brought over from the solitary cages who were near death tapered themselves off the drug water and fully recovered from their addiction.

Rat Park taught us that addiction is about much more than chemical dependency; it's also about connection—or a lack of connection. Those who are isolated—and poor relationships are a form of isolation—are missing out on the ability to experience fulfilling connections with other humans. Without connection two things happen: one, a void develops that needs to be filled, and it can be filled by anything that can duplicate the pleasure that comes from connection; two, pain and problems, particularly shame, intensify and so people need to self-medicate to mediate these painful feelings.

The Rat Park study was specifically about addiction, but the logic of Rat Park applies to all the information in this chapter. The same poor relationship environments that play a role in causing and perpetuating addictions are associated with stress and mental illness, so it stands to reason that improved relationships can go a long way in the treatment of *all* of it.

If you're struggling with addiction, my advice is to work on your addiction *and* on your relationship, to the degree to which that is possible. Of course there will be situations when healing from an addiction will leave no room for anything else. In that case there's room for flexibility and prioritizing the short-term need to focus solely on healing the addiction. But when it comes to long-term healing, there is nothing more you can do to ensure recovery than create and foster connections.

If your partner is struggling with an addiction, you probably feel alone in the relationship and can relate to conflicting feelings and a sense of helplessness. If you'd like to learn about providing support to them and yourself in a way that encourages healthy boundaries and self-care, *and* is from an attachment perspective, I'd recommend the book *Beyond Addiction: How Science and Kindness Help People Change*, by Jeffrey Foote.

As I close this chapter, please know that I've by no means addressed all of the extenuating circumstances in life that can make it more difficult to learn and put into practice healthier relationship skills. I've only included the most common, but I've worked with very few couples who don't have something going on in their lives that add a twist to the work. When I work with clients, my mantra is to meet them where they are and try to help them move forward. Whatever your struggles in life, try to do the same . . . meet yourself and your partner where you are, challenges and all, do the best you can with the capacity you *do* have, and focus on moving forward to the best of your ability.

CHAPTER 11

The Sex Factor

Sexual connection provides a uniquely powerful bond between partners. Of course there are always exceptions to the rule, but statistically speaking, couples with great sex lives report the greatest overall relationship satisfaction. It can be easy to take this as "if you want to be a happier couple, improve your sex life," and sometimes that might work. But the truth is there are many layers to a couple's sexual relationship and what needs to be addressed for one couple to see improvements won't always work for the next couple. But we do know this: improving the attachment climate of the relationship is a must, because the only way conversations about creating a happier sex life can possibly go forward is when they can happen outside of a negative communication cycle.

Before diving in, I need to put it out there that when a couple is struggling with their sex life, the very first place any therapist or doctor will start is to have them seek medical testing to rule out problems such as hormonal imbalances, infections, erectile dysfunction, bladder problems, diabetes, cardiovascular problems, and any number of other medical issues that can contribute to pain and low sex drive. Luckily there are treatments, but first you need to know there's a problem, so if you haven't taken that step, start there. And if your problems aren't medically related, or aren't entirely medically related, let's talk about what else might be going on.

By now you know all too well that negative cycles wreak havoc on relationships. They damage emotional closeness and block harmony. It probably comes as no surprise that another very significant side effect of negative communication cycles is damage to a couple's sex life. While there *are* couples who manage to have great sex lives even when they're struggling with communication and insecure-attachment issues, these couples are the exception, not the rule. For some couples, their sexual relationship gets so caught up in their negative cycle that it takes on a negative cycle of its own—now, in addition to their negative communication cycle, they also find themselves in a negative sex cycle.

Most of the couples I treat tell me that at the beginning of their relationship they had good, or even great, sex lives. While it's easy to assume that life circumstances like kids or career get in the way of a couple maintaining a healthy sex life, in my experience and according to research, more secure couples tend to maintain sexual aliveness in spite of their life circumstances (within reason).

The Importance of Physical Connection

From the day you were born, you derived emotional support via touch. Soothing touch from your parents sent messages such as "you are valuable," "you are loved," "you are safe," "you are not alone." Touch soothes the nervous system. Touch is so important to babies that they will fail to thrive and sometimes even die when they don't get enough human touch. This is why skin-to-skin contact is one of the very first acts of bonding between parents and infants after they're born.

Two years ago, my grandma died at the age of ninety-six. I was very close to her, and I had the privilege of being by her side when she passed. By the time I made the cross-country trip to be with her, she was no longer able to speak. I stayed by my grandmother's side for her final days, wiping her forehead with cold washcloths, holding her hand, even curling up in bed with her. I created a makeshift "double bed" by fully extending a recliner, bumping up against her nursing home bed, and lowering the rail. This way, when I had to sleep, I could still hold her hand. Yes, I talked to her, too, but I sensed that touch was just as critical an emotional comfort during what was probably a scary time. She could not talk to me, but she *could* communicate through touch. When I held her hand, she squeezed mine back, and my touch helped her relax, just like it helped me relax to sleep in her arms when I was a tiny baby.

From cradle to grave, humans need physical connection. Touch is as valid and worthy a means to emotional connection as words are, and sex is no exception.

All types of touch between partners is important. Nonsexual touch, like holding hands, cuddling on the couch on a rainy day, and giving a hug when we say goodbye, all powerfully communicate love and safety. But sexual touch *is* different. While all touch releases bonding chemicals like oxytocin, dopamine, and endorphins, sexual touch does so exponentially.

Sex is also vulnerable. It's one of the most vulnerable things we can do in our relationships, because it requires us to show up with our full selves. As we know, vulnerability reigns supreme when it comes to bonding. During a positive sexual experience, each partner gets the message "I see all of you and I not only accept you, but I treasure you." And that message is delivered every bit as powerfully as if it were spoken aloud. Sexual connection is a way to feel chosen and special, and its existence, to the degree it is desired by each partner, is crucial.

Sex in an Anxious-Avoidant Pairing

As I mentioned in chapter 3, the pairing of an anxious partner and an avoidant partner is very common, and perhaps the second most likely pairing to "succeed," after a couple with a secure attachment. This is due, as we know, to the balance in the relationship—one partner is going to turn the heat up, the other is more likely to cool things off; one partner is trying to close the distance by bringing up problems, the other is trying to keep things from getting worse by pushing away conflict. When their opposite strategies collide time and again and the couple becomes bogged down with negative communication cycles, their sex life can easily become collateral damage. Good sex requires connection and vulnerability, and negative cycles degrade connection and discourage vulnerability. They leave anxious partners feeling emotionally neglected, and leave avoidant partners feeling like failures, neither of which creates a recipe for a healthy sex life.

Early in relationships, anxious partners are more likely to seek out sex as a way to feel loved. But as the relationship progresses, when an anxious partner feels like their emotions in the relationship aren't being tended to or validated, they might become *less* likely to want to engage in physical closeness and are more likely to turn down sex. Some avoidant partners are, by virtue of their avoidance, emotionally distant during sex. While at the beginning of the relationship the anxious partner might tolerate this, as time goes on they might start desiring more engagement during sex and "asking for more." If the avoidant partner fears being viewed as a failure and/or already feels like they can't get anything right in other areas of the relationship, the last thing they want to do is feel like a failure in the bedroom, too. To manage the layers of tension, the couple may avoid sex altogether until one day they realize it's been months or even years since they've had sex, at which point it might feel awkward to try again.

Another common scenario between anxious and avoidant partners is that one partner becomes the sexual pursuer and the other becomes the sexual withdrawer. The pursue-withdraw dynamic is one we've seen in this book many times over. When it comes to sex, there is sometimes a role reversal where the avoidant partner is the sexual pursuer and the anxious partner is the sexual withdrawer. It makes sense when you think about it: avoidant partners are less connected to their emotions, which makes it difficult for them to connect intimately by talking about feelings and needs. To make up for that deficit, a lot of avoidant partners feel emotionally connected through sex and physical connection (even when they appear on the surface to be detached). Sex provides the sensory stimulation on which they often thrive, and can even help them get their attachment needs met. When their partner is sexually responsive, it's as if they are being told, "You're valuable, you're a successful partner." If an avoidant partner isn't getting the kind of connection that helps them feel filled up, they often distance from the relationship in other ways.

Anxious partners, on the other hand, can be more verbal than their avoidant partners, and intimacy via words and gestures comes more easily to them. While everyone is unique in the way they feel loved, verbal expressions of love, emotional validation, and supportive gestures that say "I'm here for you" are almost always going to leave an anxious partner feeling loved, valued, and seen. When an anxious partner isn't getting enough of the kind of connection that fills them up, and maybe even feels resentful of the fact that their needs aren't being met, they can become less interested in sex or view sex as transactional.

It's not always the case that the avoidant partner is the sexual pursuer and the anxious partner is the sexual withdrawer. Sometimes the same patterns in the other three Cs of the relationship (cooperation, conflict, and comfort) play out similarly in the sexual relationship (which falls in the category of connection). But regardless of who plays what role, in a sexual pursue-withdraw dynamic, the sexual pursuer is in the rigid position of almost exclusively initiating sex, while the sexual withdrawer rigidly evades the pursuer's advances. Neither is acting as a whole sexual self who takes balanced responsibility for the sexual climate of the relationship. It's not abnormal in any relationship for one partner to have a higher sex drive than the other, but a sexual pursue-withdraw dynamic is much more rigid and exaggerated. Neither the sexual pursuer nor the withdrawer is good or bad, right or wrong. Still, they've created a dance of intimacy that feeds on itself. They've created a negative cycle devoted *specifically* to sex, and anything that gets tied up in a negative cycle fails to thrive.

This is exactly what happened to my clients Monique and Dietlef. Early in their relationship, they had a great sex life. In fact, their sexual chemistry played a big role in their decision to get married. Both of them grew up with parents who weren't happily married or physically affectionate, so in both of their minds good sex was a sign that the relationship was thriving. As time went by, like a lot of couples, they started bickering more often. The content of their arguments changed as their relationship evolved. First it was wedding planning, which evolved into in-law problems, which evolved into all the problems that can arise when two people make a home and life together. Nothing was abnormal about their challenges, but when they couldn't see eye to eye, they easily slipped into negative cycles. Their negative cycles weren't particularly intense or frequent, but the distance they created was enough to take a toll on their sex life. Monique unintentionally adapted to her feelings by losing interest in sex. Dietlef, also without conscious intention, adapted to the disappointment of not getting his attachment needs met by pushing harder for sex and making protests—sex, for him, felt like the *only* way to experience emotional connection. Monique would often go along with sex even when she didn't want to because she genuinely wanted Dietlef to be happy, but in doing so she started to think of sex as a chore, which made her even less interested. Being a good partner was also important to Dietlef—he wanted Monique to be happy—but their attachment issues got in the way of being able to fully connect. Eventually their sex life settled into a sexual limbo. The only reason they ever had sex was that Dietlef continued to pursue, and Monique continued to go along with it, at least enough to keep her husband from feeling entirely deprived. Some couples, however, give up altogether. Monique and Dietlef had unintentionally co-created a negative sex cycle.

When negative sex cycles are deeply entrenched, sex is no longer associated with bonding, fun, and pleasure and instead becomes about pressure, shame, and fear—none of which is a turn-on. The good news? Sure, negative communication cycles outside of sex can cause negative cycles inside of sex, but *the reverse is also true*. Getting a handle on negative cycles in other parts of the relationship can go a long way in improving negative sex cycles. When Monique and Dietlef started learning how to manage their negative cycles around things like chores, reaching for emotional connection, and how they spent their time on weekends—all of which were hot topics for them—they started to feel closer, and instead of the "heat" being tied up in arguments, it naturally transferred over and their sex life got, well, hotter.

The Sexual Stalemate

One partner wanting more sex than the other isn't uncommon and isn't a problem in itself. Issues arise only when this dynamic isn't managed, or if one partner (usually the one less interested in sex) tries to get their needs met by using the mismatch to their advantage, especially if they are feeling shortchanged in another part of the relationship. What does this sexual stalemate look like? "You don't deserve sexual connection unless I'm getting enough verbal connection (or support in whatever way is relevant for the partner)." Using sex as a bargaining chip to get what you want from your partner is not an approach that will help you find the relationship you're longing for. If you *do* enjoy sex, my hope is that you don't deny yourself in an effort to deny your partner.

Early in my career, before I started exclusively working with couples, I treated a woman in her mid-fifties who told me that for years she resisted sex with her partner because the relationship had problems she resented.

She didn't want him to get what he wanted while she wasn't getting what she wanted. Then one day, she thought to herself, "If I choose not to have sex, I might be depriving my husband, but I'm also depriving me," and after that she started having sex with her husband. No, it didn't cure their relationship. But they both enjoyed it, and it gave the two of them something to bond over. It certainly didn't make things worse.

Am I saying that you should ignore relationship problems and try to fix them with sex, or encouraging you to override your sensibilities and have sex even when you absolutely can't stand the idea? No! But there are some situations where it actually can be helpful to put your differences aside and have fun with each other. And what if that fun ends up bleeding over into other parts of the relationship and makes things better?

If you can relate to a sex stalemate in your relationship it's important to start talking about it (without letting the conversation slip into a negative cycle, of course). This is true whether you are the sexual pursuer, sexual withdrawer, male, female, gay, straight, trans, or however else you choose to define yourself. You might try to start with simply stating the facts: "We're in a sex stalemate and it's getting in the way of our closeness. Do you think we can try to honor each other's needs while still honoring our own? How can we meet in the middle?" Think of this as a way to open space for deeper conversations instead of questions with hard answers. This is more about planting seeds of new dialogue than it is about finding instant resolution. If you've followed the advice in this book up to this point and you're able to have attachment-friendly conversations, the kind that prevent negative cycles, you might find that you're able to get somewhere new. And a lot of times when couples start up a conversation about sex, it ends with . . . sex.

Working on Your Sex Cycle

Let's go back to Monique and Dietlef. While they worked hard to stabilize their negative cycle outside of sex, which was enormously helpful in rebuilding their bond, they also did some work specifically on their sex cycle. To start, Dietlef started backing off his tendency to sexually pursue. When one partner is the pursuer, that partner is taking on all of the sexual responsibility in the relationship, which often doesn't allow enough space for the withdrawing partner to recognize or be in touch with their own sexual needs. The more Monique lost touch with her needs, the less longing she had for sex. So I encouraged them to do what I would encourage any couple to do when dealing with any negative cycle: break the established cycle by doing something new. Instead of habitually continuing to push away sex, Monique took the initiative to learn about and celebrate her sexual side. She worked to become more comfortable talking about sex, and began to take ownership of her own sexual needs. Gradually their sex found a healthier, and much more fulfilling, level of balance.

Get Comfortable Being Uncomfortable

I recommend that any couple struggling in their sex life do similar work to Monique and Dietlef. The core problems will be different for each couple, but the solution will always start with each partner's willingness to be vulnerable. For Monique and Dietlef that looked like being vulnerable enough to have uncomfortable conversations and vulnerable enough to move out of their comfort zones in order to shake up the status quo . . . which is what ultimately opened the door to change.

While it's common for couples' blocks to be rooted in negative cycles, many other factors can get in the way of a healthy sex life. You or your partner could also carry a lot of discomfort around sex for various reasons. Certified sex therapists specialize in understanding the complicated world of sex and can bring understanding to sexual problems far faster than what a couple can learn by trial and error.

While this book provides the structure for creating attachment-friendly environments, which will in turn create space for connecting and having emotionally safe conversations, sex is a topic with its own twist: even people who are comfortable *having* sex can be uncomfortable *talking* about sex. Creating secure love requires vulnerability, including the vulnerability to ask uncomfortable questions and even to talk about the discomfort itself, because the deepest moments of bonding happen when we open up about our discomfort.

Instead of pushing through conversations about sex in spite of being uncomfortable, be transparent about the fact that it's uncomfortable for you to talk so directly about sex because of the messages you received, or didn't receive, growing up that may have contributed to your discomfort. Maybe you got the message that getting aroused is shameful and not to be talked about, and this got in the way of your ability to embrace your sexuality. Whatever your insecurities are, it's vulnerable to put words to them and vulnerability is bonding.

If you're on the receiving end of your partner's disclosures about their sexual insecurities, be sure to be emotionally available and validating. If you're this far into the book, you've learned how to be supportive . . . use those skills. Tell your partner you understand them, and that their insecurities make sense to you and why: "Of course you feel uncomfortable talking about sex if you grew up being led to believe it's something to be ashamed of. Anybody would." Understanding and validation create emotional intimacy and emotional intimacy *is* a sexual turn-on.

If you're the sharing partner, tell your partner if there's anything they can say to help you with your discomfort around sex. This part is so important because when couples communicate acceptance of each other, especially in areas where shame is being held (whether it's related to sex or not), they build security and help each other reverse old negative belief systems. You might ask, "Can you reassure me that you accept the sexual part of me and you *don't* see me as shameful?" This is just one example. Some people who grew up believing that sex was "dirty" might need to know their partner can want them sexually and still respect them. Some might need to know their partner doesn't view their sex drive as threatening. Some might need to know that they're still sexually desirable in their partner's eyes even after they've become a parent. Too many couples carry around sexual insecurities without sharing them with their partner, forever walking around with the assumption that what they fear is true.

Keep in mind that when having intentional, exploratory conversations about sex, especially given how sensitive a topic sex is for some couples, all the basic rules of attachment-friendly environments apply. Stay far away from blame, which might sound like "I'm not happy with our sex life because you make me feel insecure," or "I don't understand. All of my exes were comfortable with their bodies." Stay away from criticism: "You're doing it all wrong," "Why can't you just enjoy it?" Most important, stay far, far away from shame, which might sound like something along the lines of "You like that? Ew, that's weird," or any comment that might leave your partner feeling shamed for or embarrassed by their sexual preferences.

Managing the Pain of Sexual Rejection

Sex creates a lot of room for feelings of rejection. Those who find themselves in the role of sexual pursuer, for example, sometimes feel deprived of the opportunity to be pursued, leaving them feeling unwanted. If you're feeling unwanted, broach the conversation directly and from a place of self. Instead of "you *never* initiate sex!" try "I feel sexually unfulfilled. I don't feel wanted and to feel good in the relationship I need to know I'm wanted and that my needs matter to you. I need for us to be able to talk about it." If you're the receiving partner, be sure to do just that: hear, understand, and validate *before* responding with your feelings and perspective about the situation.

Then what? Well, then you try to shine light on the barriers and work through them: What's driving the lack of pursuing? You might already have a hunch about what's getting in the way of your sexual connection and it's just a matter of beginning to put words to it. Here are some common themes I see in my practice when working with couples who feel stuck:

If you're the sexual pursuer, aside from feeling unwanted because you aren't pursued, you might also feel the sting of rejection when your withdrawing significant other pushes sex away. It can be tempting to take the withdrawal as a personal rejection, one that's isolated from overall attachment insecurity in the relationship. Once again, the goal is for you to put on your attachment lens: What is my partner's withdrawal really saying? Are they saying they aren't attracted to me, or could it be that something else is going on? Is the unspoken message that they need me in other ways and they're not getting those needs met? Do I need to work on how I'm showing up in other areas of the relationship? Maybe when they don't feel connected, they pull away from sex. Or, maybe their avoidance of sex says, "I have so much anxiety about all of these other areas of life—parenting, finishing up an education, work, caring for elderly parents, financial hardship—all of which have nothing to do with a personal rejection of *you*." Don't get me wrong: the pain of rejection is very real. It can feel utterly tragic to be turned down for sex even once, not to mention chronically. But if you can talk about the problem in an attachment-friendly environment and look at it through the attachment lens—which provides for many less scary alternatives than your partner simply not wanting you—the conversations can create the kind of connection that can often contribute to sexual desire. Maybe your partner *needs* to be heard and validated for how overwhelmed they feel about life, instead of being told they're a sexual letdown. There's a decent chance that being heard and validated will be a turn-on. (While a simple loss of attraction *can* happen, I've found that this factor alone—isolated from other issues in the relationship—is very rarely the complete explanation.)

If you're the nonpursuing partner, your sexual withdrawing might be driven by any of the above explanations or by self-beliefs like "I can't enjoy sex if I'm the one who asks for it because I can't be sure I'm really wanted." Maybe you had past experiences around rejection that led you to vow that you'll never ask for sex again. Other possibilities could be lingering resentments around sex or other parts of the relationship, or medical issues like hormone-related low libido. There are phases in life when responsibilities and challenges must take precedence, but sometimes there's room to shore up self-care needs in order to be more available.

Sometimes one or both partners have difficulty embracing their sexual sides after becoming a parent, or they simply feel so depleted of energy that sex gets pushed to the back burner. In *Mating in Captivity*, author and sex therapist Esther Perel encourages parents to do their best to maintain their sexual connection, as well as their erotic selves (which have less to do with love and more to do with desire), not in spite of having kids, but *for* their kids. Children, after all, thrive in environments with happy, connected parents.

No matter the cause, if you're the withdrawing partner you do have a responsibility to yourself, your partner, and your relationship to dig in and try to understand more about what's holding you back. Whatever is going on, an explanation exists that makes sense and is valid. Your distancing didn't materialize out of thin air. It could be a personal obstacle you're struggling with, or it could be stemming from something going on in the relationship. Maybe it's a medical issue you don't want to face, maybe you've been doing therapy and you have some old trauma showing up that you're not quite sure what to do with, maybe your self-care needs to be shored up so you can be more available, maybe you have some anger at your partner that needs to be hashed out.

Some partners lose the intensity of their sexual desire as the relationship progresses and they become more emotionally devoted. The same might be true when they have children. This is a way of compartmentalizing their sexual selves and their caretaking selves because somewhere along the line they developed the belief that the two can't coexist.

Sometimes the very shame of being the "rejecting" partner can reinforce rejecting behaviors. Even if you haven't completely lost desire, it might be easier for you to push sex away entirely in order to avoid your feelings around disappointing your partner. If this is the case, try opening up a conversation about it so that you can use the information to move away from shame and toward connection.

Sexual Trauma

Sometimes sexual problems, even ones that may seem like sexual stale-mates or negative sex cycles, are actually trauma related. If you experience feelings of shame around sex (even when a part of you enjoys it), it could be related to sexual traumas from your past. Examples include not only obvious sexual abuse, but even subtle, chronic messages that are body shaming or leave you believing that sex is wrong or dirty. Keep in mind that trauma doesn't have to be overtly sexual to damage your sexuality. Nonsexual physical abuse, for example, can have an enormous impact on the sexuality of sufferers.

Trauma is insidious. It can look different and show up in any number of ways. Signs that sexual trauma might be at play, regardless of the nature or degree of the trauma, include difficulty getting aroused or aroused consistently, difficulty achieving orgasm, erectile dysfunction, porn or sex addiction, feelings of repulsion toward your own or your partner's sexual desire or sexuality, flashbacks to abusive episodes (sexual or otherwise), feelings of anxiety, sadness, or fear during sex, dissociation (a feeling of disconnecting from your body) during sex, or performance anxiety. Even when you don't know it's there, trauma can lead to excessive tension in your body, disrupting your ability to fully enjoy sex and even causing painful intercourse. Keep in mind that these experiences can be so subtle and seemingly so disconnected from your past that sometimes it's tempting to blame bad feelings during sex on yourself or your partner ("I'm not relaxing enough," "I need to be more open," "They aren't doing it how I asked," "I can tell they're just pretending to like it"), when really the enemy is trauma.

If you suspect you have physical or emotional sexual problems that might be related to trauma, or your past in any way, I recommend seeking help from a certified sex therapist, a psychotherapist trained to work with sexually related trauma and anxiety disorders, or even physical or occupational therapists trained to work with sex issues as they impact your pelvic floor and create pain and tension.

Communication about sex and your feelings is critical to overcoming whatever sexual problems might be plaguing your relationship. If you go into sex in a way that overrides your feelings, you run the risk of it becoming an even more negative experience. Instead of pushing through, sometimes it can be enormously helpful to stop and tell your partner what's going on, even in the moment: "I'm starting to feel that sense of shame. Can you reassure me that this part of me is lovable and okay?" I know it might seem strange to have this conversation during sex, but when partners can provide each other with reassurance the moment that these painful feelings arise, it can turn an otherwise negative and disconnecting experience into a bonding one. Putting words to it is also reassuring for your partner. They might sense your distance and assume, without knowing any better, that your retreat is about something they're doing wrong.

The "Healthy Sex Life"

Now that we've addressed what might be getting in the way of a good sex life, let's talk about the other side of the coin: What does a healthy sex life between partners actually look like?

Some commonalities exist in the sex lives of couples who report having the highest overall relationship satisfaction. Of course, all couples have their own unique ways of defining a fulfilling sex life, so keep in mind that all research has exceptions. Couples with good sex lives aren't afraid to open up to each other about their sexual wants, needs, and preferences. Securely attached couples don't have a rigidly entrenched sexual pursue-withdraw dynamic, meaning both partners are relatively in touch with their inner experiences, which contributes to open, honest communication, including putting words to sexual shame and insecurities. Couples with good sex lives also have good sexual boundaries—they don't do anything they aren't comfortable with, but they also don't judge each other for *wanting* to do whatever it is they're uncomfortable with. A healthy response to differences might sound like "I'm not into that, but I don't think less of you for being into it. We're just different in this way. Luckily there are so many other things we both like."

What about sexual "dry spells"? Even couples with great sex lives have dry spells and they view them as normal parts of life and life stages. Their overall sense of security helps them trust they'll get back to it when the timing is right.

Of course, your relationship with yourself is paramount to your sexual relationship with your partner. To start, having a secure relationship with yourself helps with body acceptance, which helps you stay present during sex instead of being distracted by body dissatisfaction. You can learn and experiment with what you like sexually by knowing your own body. By learning to relate to your sexual self in a healthy way, you create an imprint of what will feel good from others. Having a secure relationship with yourself helps with things like relaxation and orgasm, and will help your partner feel better, too. So if you want a more secure sexual relationship with your partner, start with your sexual relationship with yourself. If you're a female, the book *Come As You Are* by Emily Nagoski is a great resource for this.

Lastly, some very happy couples have sex rarely (such as those with medically limiting conditions or simply lower sexual desire), don't have "in-person" sex (such as those who are long-distance), or don't have sex at all (such as those who identify as being asexual). Some couples are polyamorous or have nontraditional arrangements such as open relationships, and that's what works for them. All things considered, there is no statistic or definition of "healthy sex life" from me or anyone else that can override the unique "healthy" experience in *your* relationship.

This is a lot of information to absorb, and my hope is that by learning how to communicate outside of negative cycles, you and your significant other can begin to sort through it all in a way that helps you find each other sexually and strengthen your sexual bond more than ever. But just like all relationship growth, improving your sex life isn't black or white: it's not that you either have a good sex life or you don't.

Instead, it's about the journey toward each other and toward deeper levels of connection.

If you're having trouble finding the sexual closeness you want, don't be afraid to seek professional help or outside resources to help you along. I highly recommend the podcast Foreplay Sex Radio, hosted by certified sex therapist Laurie Watson and EFT couples therapist George Faller, which provides invaluable information on a variety of sexual topics to help couples improve their sex lives from an attachment perspective. The good news about all the work you're doing to foster your attachment-friendly environment, build security, and open up honest conversations about sex is that you can begin to understand what you want, and what your partner wants, in a way that is free of shame, and filled with vulnerability and honesty. Because ultimately no matter what the topic, the goal is the same: connection.

CHAPTER 12

When You Aren't Seeing Results

Let's say you've followed all the advice in this book—you've identified your attachment style, understood your triggers, self-regulated, worked on getting vulnerable, and tried to build an attachment-friendly environment—and still nothing. You and your partner are still fighting. You still feel misunderstood. There's still a hostile energy in your home that you aren't sure how to navigate. "Apparently we're the exception," you might be thinking. "These attachment principles and relationship advice sound great for others, but they don't work for us."

The first question to ask is, how do you define success? Maybe you think you won't be successful until you and your partner live in an attachment-friendly environment where both of your attachment needs are met nearly all the time. When there's a rupture, you can get back on track quickly. You feel emotionally and physically connected and approach life together as a team. This, of course, is the ideal. It's what most insecurely attached couples want. And I hope it happens for you! Hopefully this book has helped you at least get on the right path. But no approach to relationship problems, no matter how logical or scientifically sound, can guarantee this outcome for everyone.

For those of you who aren't quite there, let's explore what might be happening. The first thing to consider is whether or not you have realistic expectations of success. Do you view success as "perfect . . . the exact relationship you've always wanted"? If so, it might be time to scale back and view the work in this book as a launching point. A better question to measure your success is "Have we grown enough to show there's hope?" What I've found is that couples who are growing together can keep growing together. But this doesn't mean growth is linear; it never is. Growth is a two-steps-forward, one-step-back process. The steps back are frustrating and demoralizing, I know, but they're necessary because they provide the most learning opportunities for more growth. In other words, without the steps back there are no steps forward. This is true for all couples, no matter how strong they are.

Speaking of growth, not all partners grow at the same rate. If you're reading this book, and your partner isn't, you're learning new ways to be in a relationship and you have the opportunity to start showing up in new ways, even if your partner isn't initially joining you. In an emotional system such as a relationship or family, the emotional energy of even one person affects the entire system. Your positive changes will rub off. When you, and only you, stop engaging in negative cycles, they can't happen. When you stop showing up with avoidance, you no longer reinforce your partner's anxious attachment, and vice versa.

This will create a safer, more attachment-friendly environment. When an attachment-friendly environment is established—and this takes time—change is inevitable. The change might feel bad at first because change, even positive change, can be uncomfortable initially. It's almost always the case that attachment-friendly environments ultimately end up bringing the best out of everyone in the system, although everybody has different versions of "their best," which can depend on a number of factors. I don't want any two people to be in a relationship where one is "doing all the work"—a relationship can't thrive in that case—but I also don't want to see anyone prematurely give up because one partner isn't initially on board.

When working with couples, time and again I've seen that when we have hard sessions that don't always end in closeness, they come to the next session reporting that it ended up being a great week for them. Yes, the sessions unearthed hard stuff that they maybe didn't know what to do with in the moment, but as each partner had some space to process, they settled into profound growth. What I'm saying is, be careful not to miss the forest for the trees.

But in the worst-case scenario . . . let's say you've put in the work to your best ability. You have work to do, but in the grand scheme you've become more validating, have increased empathy, deliver your messages in a healthier way, respond to your partner in a healthier way, don't get caught up in negative cycles, and can set attachment-friendly boundaries as necessary. You've been growing as an individual. You're getting better at facing your feelings, self-regulating, and self-care. Again, you're not perfect, but your growth is real. Yet, when it comes to your relationship satisfaction . . . it's still low. You're still not feeling close, responded to, or a felt sense of met attachment needs. In this case, and it's a terrible one, it's important to let yourself feel the disappointment, and even anger, anyone would feel. At the same time, while the overriding goal of *Secure Love* is to help you find a securely attached relationship with your partner, the benefit of finding a securely attached relationship with yourself *cannot be understated*. The one relationship in your life that will last forever, from birth to death, which will be with you twenty-four hours a day, the relationship you have first and foremost, no matter how much you need connection with others, is your relationship with *you*. And every time you validate your partner, self-regulate before acting out, shore up your empathy, get vulnerable, set healthy boundaries, communicate from self instead of from blame and shame, advocate for your attachment needs, and on and on, you are showing up for yourself, loving yourself, building self-trust, building self-confidence, and building self-care . . . all of which are the major components of self-security. You are not only trying to gain a better relationship with your partner, you're learning how to be in a healthy relationship at all. No matter what your partner is doing, you are building a better life for yourself, even when it might not be evident right away. Your growth is an investment in your future self and other relationships outside of your romantic partnership, including your children, which will pay off in dividends. And we all know that, unfortunately, life happens and circumstances change beyond our control. If you ever are in a new relationship, your level of growth is not only going to inform what you look for in a partner, but it will heavily inform how healthy the relationship will be from the start. So while this book is focused on relationship growth, it's just as much about self-growth.

Consulting the Professionals

If you feel like you've done everything you can and nothing in your relationship is changing, that in itself is information. If that's the case, I might say that this approach *did* "work," because you have clarity today—about yourself and your partner and your relationship—that you might not have had before. From that clarity comes options. You have choices to make, presented in this chapter, most of which will require self-exploration that you can do on your own. But before we dig into those, I want to address your first option: getting professional help.

Some of you have your own unique extenuating circumstances and will need a higher level of help than this book alone can provide. Some circumstances are simply harder to navigate than others, especially when there aren't easy answers for what resolution even looks like. These circumstances could include having a blended family, dealing with a military deployment, having a partner with a personality disorder, managing neurodivergence, surviving a natural disaster, having a sick child, managing chronic illness, and so much more. When this is the case, I recommend getting professional help from a couples therapist who works from an attachment perspective and who directly works toward stabilizing a couple's negative cycle. If possible, try to find one who specializes in working with your particular challenge. (The truth is, any couple can benefit from couples counseling, but for couples who fall into the aforementioned categories, it's especially key.) Emotionally Focused Therapy for Couples is especially effective. Formal studies on the effectiveness of EFT reflect the same progress I see with couples in my practice: at least 70 percent of couples are symptom free at the end of treatment (and continue to be at a two-year follow-up) and an even higher percentage have seen marked improvement. Fortunately there are therapists who practice EFT worldwide (visit ICEEFT.com for an EFT therapist in your area). I recommend EFT because that's how I've been extensively trained and so I know for certain that this type of work will most closely align with the philosophy of the material in this book.

What Now?

So, what if you've done your absolute best to put the ideas of this book into practice, you've given time, but your partner doesn't seem to be moving with you, you're not happy in the relationship, and you have very little hope things will ever change? You feel stuck, frustrated, and alone. Now what?

You have three viable options: 1) maintain the status quo, 2) keep working on you and your side of the relationship, or 3) part ways.

But before we get into those options, let's look at what is *not* viable that many of you are doing but that is keeping you stuck: working on the relationship in a negative cycle.

When "Working on the Relationship" Becomes Its Own Negative Cycle

What's missing from our three options above is the very thing you might be *most* tempted to do: trying to force change.

Trying to force, coerce, or pressure your partner to change (or vice versa) can become part of its own negative cycle. Some signs this is happening include if you or your partner find your primary motivation for changing is to "get the other partner to change" instead of growing as individuals or making long-term investments in the relationship; being hypervigilant to anything the other partner says or does (or doesn't say or do) to determine whether or not they're changing; feeling driven by fear and anxiety instead of driven toward deeper connection; and/or are being excessively threatening or demanding.

Let's say you and your partner are both having minor health issues that will likely respond well to a healthier diet. Your partner has an interest in nutrition and has decided the two of you need to adopt a healthier diet. You're not entirely opposed to the idea—you recognize the need—but do you really want to dramatically change the way you eat? Your partner, on the other hand, is *very* enthusiastic. In fact, what starts as enthusiasm quickly escalates into pressure: "Did you have your green smoothie today?" they might text you after lunch. "Have you read that article I sent you?" they ask later in the evening. "Oh no," you think, "not another conversation about food."

Your partner senses your distance from the topic, which causes them to exert even more pressure: "How could you not want to be healthy? These changes aren't just to help me, they're to help *us*. This is about our future together. What if we end up with diabetes? It runs in both of our families. This is serious. How could you not want to do whatever we can?"

You want to be supportive, so you try to be a team player. You listen to health podcasts with your partner, when you just want to watch Netflix. You swap out sugary snacks with veggies and nuts. You start packing salads for lunch. But the second your coworkers invite you to the highly raved-about specialty cupcake shop that just opened up in your building, you're first in line.

You don't mention the treat to your partner because you don't want to deal with the long conversation about how you're not putting in the work like they are. But they end up seeing a picture of you on your coworker's social media account: "Cupcakes with the BEST coworkers ever!"

Eventually you stop going along with the plan. You're no longer interested in keeping the peace. What's the point anyway? Your partner mostly just emphasizes your failures to "stick to the program." So you start pushing back. "This is ridiculous," you protest. "Eating doesn't have to be so complicated!" You try to argue details about the legitimacy of different ways of eating, but your partner only doubles down and tells you that you must not even care. Finally, you shut down and refuse to talk about food.

What just happened? Food now has its own private negative cycle in your relationship.

This exact scenario can happen with couples when it comes to relationship work, and it's a very common explanation when relationship change doesn't seem to be working. Maybe Gianna wants her partner Luca to stop blaming her for not being emotionally available, but the way she communicates her feelings of rejection is by telling Luca, "You're constantly criticizing me; it gets old. If you ever want us to grow as a couple, you need to stop doing that." Or maybe Tanny wants her partner Gavin to be less defensive. When she brings up concerns, and Gavin starts telling her why she's "seeing it all wrong," Tanny responds with "See . . . we'll never get out of our negative cycle because you just don't want to change." Gavin and Tanny are both meeting fire with fire, and when that happens, relationship change takes on its own negative cycle. One partner (usually the anxious partner, who is more likely to bring up problems) recognizes there's a problem, a very legitimate problem, that needs to be addressed. They take the lead, do the research, roll up their sleeves, and get a plan in place. The effort is truly commendable, but the way they approach the problem and try to implement the plan can easily turn into a situation where the solution becomes part of the problem.

The second partner (usually the avoidant, who is more likely to try to maintain the status quo to avoid shame and conflict) reacts to the pressure by distancing. After all, the current plan isn't working so it's best to just avoid the topic. In reaction, the first partner keeps pressing. The more partner one pushes the topic of relationship help with pressure, the more partner two distances; partner one feels alone, partner two feels like partner one's demands only make things worse. Nobody's needs are met; nobody is happy.

If you are the person reading this book, trying to make change, you might be wondering why partner two can't just "go along with it." But sometimes it doesn't work that way. And sometimes partner two's resistance is warranted—they aren't resisting relationship change as much as they're resisting how bad all of this is making them feel. My goal is to make the space for change, without it having to feel bad. The way to do this is to work to change the *environment,* not change your partner.

Here's what healthy environment change might look like in our diet example: Partner one talks to partner two about making dietary changes. Maybe partner two agrees there's a problem, maybe not. At any rate, partner one says, "I'm going to be keeping healthier foods in the house and I am going to try to eat healthier and cook at home more." Then partner one starts to make changes. They stock the fridge with healthy snacks. When they are cooking for the family, they don't go to extremes but instead integrate the new style with the old style. Most important, they model healthy changes, inviting the other partner to come along but without the pressure of "you must do what I do or else," or "if you really love me you'll do it this way," or "when you fail to do it right, we're going to have lengthy conversations about what you need to be doing better." They also don't say, "If you don't get healthier with me, I won't get healthy either."

Of course partner one *wants* partner two to join them in being healthier. But taking any of these pressuring or controlling approaches is, for most couples, the fastest way to ensure it doesn't happen. In fact, this is true for people in general. Most people will rebel when they feel controlled—it's an understandable human need to maintain a sense of dignity.

This is what it takes to create an attachment-friendly environment. You can't force your partner to change, but you can decide that you are going to do your best to help make a new way of communicating easier for both of you. You can interrupt the cycle. You can empathize. You can model healthy changes. You can do all this without saying, "You need to change, too . . . or else."

When one partner is pushing hard for change and the other is distancing from the topic, it's a reflection of the very imbalance already plaguing the relationship: the anxious partner's understandable quest to close the distance (or avoid loneliness) by hyperfocusing on immediate change, and the avoidant partner's understandable quest to keep the peace (or avoid shame) by avoiding tough topics. Remember that secure attachment comes from relationship balance, and in moments of growth the balance comes from each partner acknowledging the need for change and taking responsibility for their own part (even if it takes time to get there). If you're the partner initiating relationship change, you have to be willing to stay the course and get out of your own extremes (for anxious partners, that's usually pressure and control) long enough for your partner to begin making the same shifts as a response to the new environment. If you're the avoidant partner, you need to take the risk of opening yourself up to new information.

If pressure and controlling for outcome aren't going to get your partner to open up to change, what might? In addition to creating an attachment-friendly environment, I like to start by trying to meet our own needs, and then following up with modeling, like in our food example. Think about what you want from the relationship, see if you can give it to yourself, and then model it for your partner. Do you want your partner to be more validating? Instead of demanding validation from them, validate yourself first by saying to yourself, "My feelings are real and they make sense." It will never be enough from your partner if you aren't able to first self-validate. If you can't, you're going to try to pull more from them than any other human, even the most loving partner, can realistically give. Next, show them what validation looks and feels like by validating *them . . . even when it means validating their resistance to relationship work.*

What do I mean? Well, if your partner is resistant to relationship work, they might have a very good reason for feeling that way. Here are some common reasons some of my clients resist getting relationship help: they see it as a sign of weakness or incompetence; they see it as the final option for a relationship, only useful if it's going to prevent a breakup; they have doubts it will be effective; they see it as a surefire way to get accused of being wrong, not just by their partner but now by a therapist; they see it as a way to be controlled. Some partners might see relationship work as an opportunity for them to be bulldozed as if their ideas aren't relevant. They see it as a threat to the status quo, which might not be ideal but is at least safe in its familiarity. They see "working on it" as a threat to their authenticity or to the ability to just enjoy each other instead of working all the time. They are too tired to think. They can't come up with the "right" things to say and will feel like a failure. Maybe they've seen friends and family get couples therapy only to divorce soon after. They're worried about finances, and it can sometimes be cost-prohibitive (one of the reasons I'm writing this book). Again, I'm not justifying the reasons, I'm seeking to understand them through the lens of attachment.

Consider this example of the dynamic with Victor and Dahlia: Victor recognizes himself as an anxious partner and his partner Dahlia as an avoidant partner. He recognizes their negative cycles and is committed to working toward secure attachment. When he brings the idea of seeing a couples therapist to Dahlia, she responds by telling him they don't need couples therapy, that they're doing better than most other couples she knows, and that couples therapy is for couples on the verge of divorce, not for couples like them who have normal problems. Victor is shattered. He doesn't think they're on the verge of divorce, but he *knows* there's something better—that they could fight less and feel more connected.

But Victor also knows that while he can't control whether Dahlia will go to couples therapy, he *can* control how he shows up in the relationship. His urge is to tell Dahlia how wrong she is about couples therapy and to convince her that prevention is the best medicine, but he resists.

In their negative cycle, Dahlia does a lot of responding to Victor's emotions with "Why are you so upset? It's not that big a deal," and "Do we have to talk about this right now? Can't we just enjoy the day?" Victor, as the anxious partner, is in touch with his need for more emotional validation in the relationship.

Victor also recognizes that Dahlia, as an avoidant partner, is not as in touch with her emotional needs, but that doesn't mean her own need for emotional validation doesn't exist. Piecing this together, Victor starts responding to Dahlia's resistance to couples therapy with curiosity and validation, as if sending her the message "I see you. You make sense. Your fears are understandable." He might directly communicate this by saying, "Okay, I'm hearing you. Tell me more about your concerns," or "I can see why you wouldn't want to identify us as a 'broken couple,' that makes sense to me," or "I like the idea of couples therapy because I'd like to improve our communication, but at the same time I can respect your feelings about it, too," or even "Maybe to you couples therapy represents failure and the last thing you need is to feel like we're failing." After letting Dahlia know she's safe to have her own ideas and feelings held as worthy, Victor might decide to share more directly about his needs: "I get where you're coming from. I wouldn't want to go forward with something I wasn't sure about, either. I just ask you to at least keep an open mind because it might be something that can really benefit us."

What happens next? Ideally when changes like this are put into place over the course of time, Dahlia will get the emotional support she's likely never had before and will naturally begin to give it back, without coercion, and without inserting more of what's not working into the relationship.

When you are tempted to pressure or control your partner in order to enact change, consider this instead: *be* the change you want to see. If you want understanding, understand. If you want curiosity, be curious. If you want change, change. If you want to be heard, listen. If you want your partner to change, notice the times when they do. In other words, reflect what you want to grow.

Finally, your relationship with yourself is fundamental. How you treat yourself will show up in how you treat your partner. You aren't putting on the heat and approaching your partner from a place of control because you're maniacal or unempathic. You have very good reason for taking this approach, whatever that reason might be. The chances are high that you grew up being motivated in the same way, and it only makes sense that that's how you might approach your partner. Also, the pain of a strained relationship is real—it hurts, it's lonely, frustrating, and maddening. The temptation to feel better in the best way you know how is so compelling. Give yourself this validation and understanding. But don't forget to balance it out with the idea that just because everything you do makes sense on some level, and your feelings are valid, that doesn't mean what you're doing is going to help you get what you need.

Moving Forward: Three Viable Options

Option One: Maintain the Status Quo

In my opinion, maintaining the status quo is the least desirable of the three options, but let's explore what it means. Maintaining the status quo essentially means giving up on any more self-work and deciding, "Well, I guess this is as good as it's going to get." Someone who takes this route might think that change can only happen when both parties commit, and decide to accept the relationship the way it is. This might be the easiest option—after all, it requires the least amount of effort, and sometimes it feels safer to not try at all than to try and be disappointed. Maintaining the status quo often results in partners keeping each other down because they decide that "if you're not going to change, I'm not going to change"—nobody changes. The partners hum along in mediocrity at best, misery at worst.

For some people the status quo might seem incredibly safe because your relationship environment might not be great, but it *is* familiar. Sometimes the devil you know really does seem better than the devil you don't. If you decide to go this route, nobody has to leave their comfort zone. Doing the work by yourself probably seems daunting, and possibly like a setup for feeling disappointed, and leaving the relationship might seem downright terrifying. At the same time, doing nothing comes with its own risk: staying stuck.

Everybody has their own reasons for maintaining the status quo in their relationship. Relationship work is work: it takes time and a lot of emotional energy, especially if you feel you're the one doing the bulk of it. Maybe you just don't have the energy right now to work too hard. Trying to raise kids and keep food on the table is just about all you can handle. My hope is that at the very least you choose to maintain the status quo with intention: "Our status quo might not be ideal, but it is what it is for now." That level of consciousness is growth in itself.

Option Two: Keep Working on You and Your Side of the Relationship

If you and your partner aren't equally invested in working on the relationship, change will undoubtedly be more difficult, but it's not at all hopeless. If you choose to work on your own side of the street, the worst that can happen is still a huge success: you grow as an individual.

As I mentioned earlier in this chapter, time and again, I've observed that when one partner starts to make changes and an attachment-friendly environment is set into motion, all kinds of space gets opened up for change. But change is about so much more than what your partner is up to; for change to be real, it has to be foremost about *you*. You can keep exploring the attachment patterns you picked up in childhood so you can use the insight to better understand yourself in the service of making better choices for your own peace of mind.

Moving away from the status quo *will* be uncomfortable. Even in the best of circumstances, when both partners are fully on board from the start, your brain circuitry has a system in place that does not want to rewire. It will do everything in its power to resist change and will interpret, faster than you know what's happening, something as a threat. In the beginning, every consideration of a new move will feel weird. If your partner tells you something you don't want to hear, even just considering saying something like "Tell me more, I'm not sure I understand what you mean" instead of "What are you talking about? I never do that!" will make your neural pathways scream, "What are you doing? Are you crazy! Don't *ask* for more criticism, that's not safe!"

But the benefits of pushing through your discomfort and taking risks even when your nervous system is giving you a hard no will pay off in dividends for you as an individual. For one, choosing to take new action to avoid negative cycles will defuse conflict in a way that will lower your overall stress because heated negative cycles are stressful and exhausting. When you can look back on your day, week, month, year, and say, "Wow, I'm doing things differently! I'm not getting sucked into rabbit holes and it's all because of *me*," your confidence will only grow. And with confidence you'll learn to trust yourself. You'll learn to trust that you can rely on yourself to show up in a way that is healthy and self-compassionate instead of that old drive to fight or avoid. Self-trust is self-esteem is self-security is *your secure attachment with yourself*.

It's my experience and belief that somewhere deep inside all of us is a drive to grow. We all truly want to be our best selves and manifest our inherent goodness, although sometimes, for some people, they either don't know where to start, or they feel hopeless, or they have so much shame they can't bear to face. This is where partners can have an enormous impact on each other. If you're the healthier partner right now, I encourage you to create that de-shaming, attachment-friendly environment as much as you can on your own. Do it for you, for your family, and for the fact that it just might be enough to kick-start your partner's drive for growth.

If you choose this option, and you've taken this advice and you've given it time, and your partner still isn't changing? Maybe you decide to stay, or at least stay for now. Some people choose to stay in less-than-fulfilling relationships for many different logistical reasons (not wanting to split up a family or finances, maybe), continue to do their part to create a healthy environment, learn to appreciate the relationship for what it is, both strengths and shortcomings, and find other ways to get their emotional needs met. In this case, your acceptance of "what is" might take some grieving. You might have to let go of the idea of what you wanted your relationship to look like, and that's a loss.

But staying in a relationship that isn't exactly what you hoped and planned for doesn't mean all is lost. Even when things aren't perfect, better is a really good step. If you do all this work and the relationship still isn't ideal, but you've seen improvement, then your hard work isn't in vain. You might have to step back to see it. Our brains are wired to be biased toward what *isn't* working so sometimes we need to be intentional about getting some perspective to be able to make an accurate assessment. Ask yourself, "If things have truly improved, how might that be?" See what you come up with. I'm not asking you to view things through rose-colored glasses, but to give it time for improvement to be seen. Just as it can be difficult to recognize the physical growth of the children you may have in your life on a day-to-day basis until it hits you one day that your teenage son has imperceptibly lost two inches on his pant cuffs, it can also be hard to see positive relationship growth on a day-to-day basis. Rarely do I have clients come in saying, "We're cured!" Rather, after weeks or months of therapy they come to their sessions casually saying, "Yeah . . . we had a great week," as if that's just the new norm. What I'm saying is that you might have to intentionally focus on areas of growth to recognize in the short term when the bad times might still be more pronounced than the good ones. Intentionally assessing for improvement can give you the momentum you need to continue this important journey.

Finally, while the focus of this book is on romantic relationships, relationship work doesn't end there. All relationships, including the ones you're in outside of your partnership, and also any future relationships you may find yourself in, benefit from the principles in this book: validation, empathy, active listening, self-regulation. All these foster connection, and connection feels good.

Option Three: Part Ways

As hard as it can be to face, sometimes after a significant period of time (the length of which is different for everyone), you make great strides with your personal growth and start showing up in the relationship in the healthiest way possible, but you're still miserable. Maybe your partner is not changing, or maybe getting your negative cycle in better shape has clarified for you that some of the problems in your relationship really are about incompatibility rather than communication. The reality is that sometimes two people aren't a good fit. Sometimes two people used to be a good fit but have grown apart. Healthy communication can go a long way in creating compatibility, but it can't guarantee compatibility.

If that's what you're finding to be true and you have little hope of getting the relationship you're hoping for, then what? At this point, you might need to decide that the healthiest path forward is to end things and move on. That is not just okay; it might just be the best option for yourself and all involved. I've worked with couples who've done great work to manage negative cycles—couples therapy gold medalists!—but ultimately, it made sense for them to end the relationship. Some have wanted different things out of life; some have determined that they are better friends than lovers; some have had other reasons. As paradoxical as it might sound, my job as a couples therapist is not to save a relationship; my job is to make it healthy for the partners to go forward together, or apart, from a place of clarity that can only be found in safe communication.

When your relationship isn't improving after you've put in hard work and started changing, it's a tender spot to be in. Give yourself some love and compassion, and know you don't have to figure anything out immediately. Commit to yourself and this process of healing.

CHAPTER 13

Instead of This, Do This

When you see me _____ *shutting down* _____

inside of me I'm feeling ___ *overwhelmed* _____

because _*I don't always know what my feelings are*_

and I can see how that leaves

you feeling _____ *left in the dark* _____ .

From my work in my private practice and on social media, I've learned that people want words. It's one thing for me to tell you what to do conceptually, but giving you the words is what will make this work come alive for you. This is exactly what I do with the couples I treat. I help them find their real, authentic inner experience and then I give them the words to share it. The experience is theirs, and eventually the words become theirs, too, but at first they need more guidance to learn the new language of attachment.

This chapter is full of phrases you can use with your partner in tough

situations. They are very generically written because, as you can imagine, it's not possible to reflect the vocabulary and style of speaking for
each of you. So, while they might not feel authentic to you, see if you
can try them anyway. Play around with them. Get vulnerable. Take the
principles of attachment-friendly communication we've covered and
make them your own. And remember, this work is about authenticity,
so if you feel awkward, say it: "I might sound silly, but the old way
isn't working so let's try something new anyway." Also keep in mind,
so many factors go into the way partners speak to each other: cultural
factors, gender factors, generational or regional factors, and on and on.
Some couples are more comfortable being edgy with each other in a
way that would make other couples gasp. Some couples speak to each
other so formally that if you were watching them, you might wonder
if they were in a romantic relationship at all. I don't even use many of
these phrases with my husband, and I'm the one writing this book! (I
do, however, use the principles.) My point is, take the principles I have
to offer, make them your own, take what works, and leave the rest.

Hopefully you and your partner have already worked through this
book, in which case most of these phrases should land well. If not, my
guess is that they'll at least land better than whatever else you've been
doing that has launched you into the negative cycle. If you keep practicing speaking from a place of "self" and through an attachment lens,
over time the words will start to take on a more authentic flavor and
will become more of your own.

Before approaching a tough topic, self-regulate to calm and prepare
your nervous system. Use your breathing skills, mindfulness and mentalization skills, or any other self-regulation techniques you find useful
(revisit chapter 5 for more ideas) to find clarity, feel grounded, and have
more ability to say to yourself, "I've got this, everything is okay. I'm
safe. I'm strong. I can be vulnerable. I'm learning new ways to be in my
relationship, and that feels really good."

Then, when you talk to your partner, don't underestimate the emotionally regulating and connecting power of nonverbal communication
and touch. As you say these phrases, try to make eye contact, turn your

body toward your partner, open up your stance, use physical touch, hold their hand, or do anything else that can help you physically connect to them, co-regulate, and send the message "You're important to me." Sometimes even moving to the same side of the table helps show you're on the same side. Find what works for you both.

This work is not about "walking on eggshells" in order to keep your partner from reacting poorly, but rather about doing your best to create emotional safety and to help each of you feel more confident about your communication skills. The following phrases come from a place of self, vulnerability, transparency, curiosity, and/or are embedded with attachment meaning. They are free of blame, shame, criticism, defensiveness, or any other potential triggers.

Lastly, the spirit of this work is planting seeds and creating shifts, not getting exactly what you're hoping for in a moment. It's about progress over perfection. If you start speaking in a new way, you might not get the response you want, and you might even get pushback. Change, even good change, can feel threatening when it's new. If you get pushback, stay the course and be honest: "Here's what I'm trying to do and here's why—I'm trying to show up differently in this relationship because of how important it is to me, and because I want to be proud of who I am."

Also, I've given examples of specific topics, but most of the examples can be used in different contexts unique to your relationship.

When You're Feeling Lonely or You Want to Spend More Time with Your Partner

Instead of:
"You never want to spend time with me."

Try:
"I appreciate how hard you work *and* I also really miss you. I think both of us will feel better if we carve out some time to connect. What are your thoughts?"

Protest elicits defensiveness. "Never" and "always" create arguments because it's usually easy to find exceptions, in which case the real issue—I miss you—gets sidetracked. The alternative version is attachment-friendly in that it includes met attachment needs ("I appreciate you"), which create safety. It speaks to the bigger meaning, "I miss you," rather than creating arguments over facts. It speaks from a place of self ("here's what's happening for me"), which will prevent the need for defensiveness. Inviting your partner to share their thoughts sends them the message that they matter to you, which is another met attachment need.

When You're Feeling Overwhelmed with Life and Need Help

Instead of:
"I do everything around here."

Try:
"It's important for me to feel like we're a team; that's one of the ways I feel close to you. Here's what's going on with me and what would feel better . . ."

Or:
"Let's talk about our different standards around the house so we can work together where we see eye to eye, and try to meet each other where we don't."

Or:
"When it comes to our chores around the house, I know I've given you the message in the past that your way of doing things isn't the right way, and that maybe that's felt bad for you. If so, I'd like to try reaching each other in a better way."

The original statement invites arguments over facts; it's a me-versus-you approach, and is delivered as a global protest. Also, it shows that you may have lost sight of what your partner *does* contribute, and their experience, which can get lost when we're triggered. The alternative statements I've suggested own past behaviors that may have impacted you and your partner, and that creates safety and trust. Placing a focus on "team" and "closeness" maintains the attachment lens, instead of the "you-versus-me" lens, while being clear about what will help you feel safe and open to more focused solutions.

When You're Annoyed About Something That's Important Enough to Bring Up

Instead of:

"I'm tired of being late everywhere we go because you can't be ready on time."

Or:

"It drives me crazy when you bring up my work problems in front of other people. Why do you have to do that?"

Try:

"I value our time together more than anything, but it makes me anxious to be late. I feel sick inside in those moments. I need to talk about it and know it matters to you. "

Or:

"I know you're trying to engage and I love that about you, but when you bring up my work problems in front of other people, I get embarrassed. Can you be more mindful of that?"

The first options are protests, shaming, and take a me-versus-you approach. It's easy for someone to tune out protests, or experience them as a threat, because they don't reveal vulnerability. But owning your needs instead of judging your partner's behavior is nonshaming and attachment-friendly. The latter options are solution-focused and validating to your partner's experience, which creates safety and is good modeling. When you share with your partner more about how their actions emotionally impact you, it's more likely to inspire empathy. Empathy is a better motivator than shame and protest.

But I want to point out, not *everything* needs to be brought up. Sometimes feeling annoyed is less about what your partner is doing and more about your mood or unhealed wounds haunting you from your past. You might decide to simply take a walk, "shake it out," jot down a gratitude list, journal, or trust that this one moment doesn't define the entire relationship and that "this too shall pass" because, truthfully, that's just how relationships work. You choose your battles.

When You Need to Know There's Space for Your Way, Too

Instead of:
"Why does everything have to be your way?"

Or:
"Stop telling me what to do."

Try:
"I like to be tidy but I'm never going to have the same standards as you. How can we meet in the middle?"

Or:
"I get it. I know you feel most comfortable when things go the way you want them to. But as an adult, I need to be able to do things my way, even when sometimes it's different from your way."

The original statements are critical protests, which risk shutting down the other, or inspiring them to get defensive or counterblame you, all of which will start a negative cycle. The alternatives, however, set gentle boundaries around what you *can* do, without creating shame or judging your partner's way or feelings about it. They offer the opportunity to talk about solutions instead of getting stuck in accusations. They are validating and speak through an attachment lens by seeking to protect closeness in the relationship. They say, "I care about you. I care about us. You're not the enemy."

You Want to Bring Up a Difficult Topic

Instead of:
"We need to talk about . . . " (in a demanding tone)

Try:
"I have something I need to talk about and it's going to be hard for both of us because we haven't had a lot of luck with this topic in the past. Our relationship is too important to me to get stuck in a negative cycle. Do you have any ideas on how we can prevent that from happening?"

Or:
"I'm so proud of all the work we've done to communicate better with each other, and it keeps getting better. Can I bring something up that might be hard and see how we do?"

Or:
"I'd like to sit down and talk about our budget because financial safety is extremely important to me. At the same time, it's also really important to me that we talk when it's a good time for you. Can we make a plan?"

Or:

Use the DEAR MAN technique, created by Marsha Linehan. You can find more information about the DEAR MAN approach online.

D escribe the problem
E xpress how it affects you
A ssert what you need
R einforce the message
M be Mindful of staying on topic
A ccess confidence
N egotiate

For example:

We have too much credit card debt (D). That's a problem for me. It causes me anxiety. I can't feel close to you if we can't talk about it, and I don't want that to happen (E). I need a commitment from you that we can take some time to talk about it soon (A). It's a problem I can't live with and I need for us to try to meet each other on this (R).

If your partner changes the subject with "why do you always bring this up when we're having dinner/going to bed/on our way to work/having a nice walk/etc.":

"It might not be the best time to mention it, but I need a plan." (M) As you speak, don't second-guess yourself. Remember that it's good for you and the relationship for you to advocate for your needs (A). "Here's when I'd like to talk. When is it a good time for you?" (N)

Demands send the message that your partner is "less-than" instead of your equal. Chances are they won't be inspired to collaborate if they don't feel like an equal. The alternative approaches use a teamwork mentality. Leading with the positive is motivating—it provides reward for effort. Acknowledging it will be hard makes it easier to manage, and making a plan allows each partner the opportunity to feel a sense of control over when the conversation will happen, instead of feeling blindsided, and will give each partner space to reflect on their thoughts and feelings so they are more likely to respond instead of react.

The DEAR MAN approach is effective because it helps you stay organized as you speak, prevents the topic from going off course, and encourages solutions.

You Don't Agree with Your Partner

Instead of:
"You're wrong."

Try:
"Tell me more about how you came to see it this way."

Or:
"Being able to disagree while still respecting each other is really important to me. Would you be willing to work together to get us to that place?"

Or:
"Your feelings about this make a lot of sense to me. I feel afraid of bad things happening, too. I have a different idea about how to approach this, but that doesn't mean I can't see and hear you."

Nobody reacts well to being told they're wrong. It's invalidating, when we all need to be respected as worthy humans with a right to our thoughts and opinions. In contrast, curiosity sends the message that your partner's opinion matters, and that you view them as worthy and respect their separateness. Being open means you might learn something new and grow as a person. It also makes it more likely that you'll be heard and your partner might learn something new, because feeling safe gives people room to step back and reflect instead of clinging to ideas out of fear. This makes for rich, stimulating, intellectual connection, and that kind of connection is bonding. These approaches open up intentional dialogue about how to approach disagreement, instead of blindly going into negative cycles.

When You're Feeling Defensive Because Your Partner Is (or You Perceive They Are) Overly Critical

Instead of:
"That's not true, I'm doing my best and you refuse to appreciate anything about me . . ."

Or:
"You're the one that yells. I only yell because you yell."

Try:
"I want to start defending myself right now, but I don't want to do that to our relationship. I'm committed to staying present and hearing you out."

Or:
"What you have to say is important to me, and you have good reason to be afraid you won't be heard because of all the negative cycles we've been stuck in. I want to hear you but when it comes at me like that it just hurts. Can we try this in a different way?"

Or:
"When you say I'm inconsiderate, what are you really needing for me to know/what feelings are you really trying to tell me about/ what are you really needing right now?"

The first options are invalidating negative cycle behaviors that escalate instead of defuse. The original topic will get lost, and nobody will be heard. They don't address the criticism, or perceived criticism. When you name your urge, put words to it, you can relieve some of the pressure to act on it. Telling your partner that you're willing to do something new sends the message that you care about them and your relationship so much that you're willing to be vulnerable and step out of your comfort zone. That meets an attachment need. Sharing vulnerability inspires empathy, which makes it more likely they'll be willing to deliver their concern in a more attachment-friendly way, and being curious gives them the opportunity to clarify so they don't feel misunderstood.

When You Feel the Urge to Disengage or Shut Down

Instead of:
Shutting down

Try:
"I'm afraid if I don't shut this down, it's going to become a big fight, but I also know if I do that it will leave you feeling abandoned. What can we do differently right now?"

Or:

"Everything in me just wants to fix this, but since I don't know how, I can feel myself getting overwhelmed and tuning out. I want to let you in on what's going on inside of me, so we can try something new."

Or:
"I know we haven't been able to do this well in the past and you worry you aren't going to be heard. Your concerns matter to me and I want to try to meet you. At the same time, I feel unseen when it comes at me like this. Can we start this over?"

Shutting down leaves your partner feeling abandoned, unheard, alone, and frustrated. It won't solve problems and even if the topic gets dropped in the moment, it will continue to come up until there's enough attachment safety (both partners feel valued, seen, respected, etc.) to address it. These verbal responses show vulnerability, which is the very emotional engagement that helps your partner not feel alone. They send the message that you aren't protecting yourself from your partner by shutting down; you're protecting yourself from shame and relationship threat. At the same time, they say that the relationship matters so much to you that you're willing to face your fears and step out of your comfort zone.

When You Feel Emotionally Shut Out

Instead of:
"What's going on? Why won't you talk to me about how you're feeling?"

Try:
"I understand it's hard for you to talk about your feelings. I'm not here to judge you for that and I know you're not trying to hurt me. At the same time, when I can't reach you it's lonely for me. I want to know you."

Or:
"I'm understanding more about how overwhelmed you get when you don't know what to do. Conflict can be different from what we both experienced in our childhoods. I want to try a new way to do this that will help us reach each other."

Or:
"I learned that my feelings show up in my body in tension or heavi-

ness. Do you ever notice that? If so, maybe you can share that with me. I need to be able to connect with you to feel close. Otherwise I feel out here on my own."

People who are out of touch with their feelings will feel overwhelmed by a simple "why won't you talk to me?" because they don't know how to answer. The alternative examples are meant to validate your partner's struggle, use curiosity to open a deeper conversation, and use an attachment lens: "I want to know about your feelings in order to be close" as opposed to "You're letting me down by not sharing your feelings." They are meant to create room for deeper conversations, in the moment or in the future. Go slow . . . people who shut down do so to stay safe from feelings of shame. Too much too soon can be overwhelming. It's also important for your partner to know what you need and how you're impacted by disconnection.

When Your Partner Says, "I'm Not Mad, I'm Fine," but Obviously They *Are* Mad

Instead of:
"Why can't you just admit you're mad?"

Try:
"I feel some tension and I can give you space right now. At the same time, the tension is stressful for me, so at some point I need for us to be able to have a conversation."

Or:
"I can understand why you might not feel safe saying you're mad because in the past it's only made things worse to talk about it. At the same time, my body can feel the tension and I need to know we can address this at some point."

Or, if you think it might land:
"What would help me right now is to know whether your distance is about me or not. If it is, I can handle it and we can talk now or later. Either way, unspoken distance can't work for me. The tension is too much."

Or, if they aren't fully in touch with their anger and have a hard time putting it to words:
"If you were mad earlier today, what might you have been mad about?"

Or:
"Maybe you shut down like that because you're afraid it's wrong to be mad, or shameful or dangerous. Does any of that fit?"

Sometimes it can help to bring it up in the moment, but sometimes it's better to bring it up later. When someone is mad and unable to own it, it's usually because they're afraid of their own anger and they're doing everything in their power to hold it in, even when they might not consciously recognize that they're angry to begin with. While it might not be obvious on the surface, inside they are experiencing uncomfortable and conflicting feelings, and they aren't going to be able to take in reason or answer questions.

Later, when the dust has settled, share how their anger impacts you, and make a plan for the next time. Don't expect immediate results. Most of the work in this book takes time to create shifts, but in this case it's especially true. For someone who's been trying to hold anger in for a lifetime, there needs to be a lot of safety and trust in place before they're going to feel safe recognizing it and owning it.

Also, keep in mind that anger *needs* to be heard and validated. You don't have to tolerate bad behavior like yelling, or name-calling, and you don't have to agree with *why* they're mad (although you can make sense of how they got there), but do validate the anger because unvalidated anger doesn't disappear. If you do bring it up in the moment, and you're self-regulated enough, come from a place of co-regulation instead of questioning.

Keep in mind, your partner might not even know they're mad. Some people had to learn to stuff their anger so far away—because they learned anger is wrong, dangerous, or shameful—that they genuinely lose touch with the awareness of the feeling, even when it's there. Others might not want to admit they're mad, so they can't answer the question, which will possibly leave them feeling more frustrated. Giving them space to own and feel their feelings is validating. Reflecting the physical signs you observe, when done safely, will help them recognize signs of anger they might not be aware of. Asking them, hypothetically, what they might be mad about allows them to answer with an "out" if it doesn't fully resonate. While it's important to allow their feelings to be their own instead of a construct, nine times out of ten their answer ends up being accurate and they can start working toward owning it and talking about it. Being curious about their relationship with anger (fear, shame) allows for recognition, reflection, and deeper conversation, planting seeds of awareness.

When You Aren't Feeling Validated

Instead of:
"You don't even care about my feelings. Why can't you just tell me you understand my feelings?"

Try:
"I don't need for you to agree with me about anything. I just want to feel seen for the fact that I feel sad/angry/alone. It will help me feel safe and close to you."

Or:
"You have your reasons for thinking I shouldn't feel the way I do. I want to know more about them. Whatever they are, they're understand-

able. At the same time, I can't feel safe and close to you if I don't feel validated. Both of us need validation, not just me. Let's work together."

Or:
"I understand how uncomfortable my anger can make you. I think it might feel threatening to you when I'm mad, but I need to know there's space in the relationship for all of me, including sometimes my anger. I'm responsible for how I express it to you, but I can't feel close to you if I have to hide it."

Telling someone they don't care and must validate you is itself invalidating. But the other responses are validating, which model the very thing you're wanting in return. By validating your partner, you're teaching them both how to validate and how good it feels to be validated. These responses create safety by telling your partner they don't need to agree, which helps them maintain their sense of self and equality. They can plant seeds of awareness to help your partner recognize they never received validation and help them make sense of why it's so hard, instead of leaving them feeling like a failure.

When You Need to Know You're Appreciated

Instead of:
"I'm tired of you putting me down all the time."

Try:
"The only way I can truly feel safe and close to you is to know you appreciate what I bring to this relationship. Even when I can't be perfect, I need to know you see my strengths."

Or:
"Your concerns are real and I know I've done things in the past that have let you down. At the same time, sometimes I feel like I hear

much more about what I'm getting wrong and it leaves me feeling demoralized and alone. How you view me is so important to me and I'm needing to hear about the good things, too."

Protests are unlikely to be heard, and "all the time" is going to leave your partner feeling misunderstood or invalidated for their concerns. The alternative responses, on the other hand, set gentle, attachment-friendly boundaries: "I want to feel close" instead of "you versus me." They are clear about asking for needs to be met, while still validating that your partner's concerns matter to you.

When You Feel Disappointed

Instead of:
Sulking, being passive-aggressive, getting defensive

Try:
"I'm disappointed that we're not going on the trip. It feels bad, but I know I'll get past it. It's better for me to put words to it than to hold it in."

Or:
"I know it can be hard for you when I'm disappointed about something and I can relate to that. It feels awful. At the same time, I need to know I can have space for all of my feelings."

Disappointment can be anxiety-provoking or even scary for people who were mistreated or given the silent treatment when their parents were disappointed. These behaviors can create abandonment fear and even can be re-traumatizing. That said, disappointment is a part of life. Making safe space for it is invaluable. The suggested responses will help your partner know you'll come back, that you aren't going away forever. It sets gentle boundaries around your right to be disappointed.

When You Need Reassurance

Instead of:
Not asking for reassurance in order to avoid feeling rejected

Try:
"Can you help me feel reassured that even if I say no, you'll still see me as a good partner?"

Or:
"Can you help me feel reassured that if I talk about my own needs, you won't see me as needy?"

Or:
"Can you help me feel reassured that if I share my emotions with you, you won't see me as 'too much'?"

Or:
"Can you help me feel reassured that if I talk about my feelings, you won't see me as weak?"

Avoiding rejection obstructs connection. Not asking for reassurance misses an important opportunity to reverse negative beliefs created during childhood (or other impactful adult relationships). When partners consistently reassure each other when they're experiencing issues that trigger core fears of abandonment and shame, they will help reverse each other's core fears on a deep level. As this transformation takes place, the need for reassurance will dissipate. It likely won't disappear completely—we all need reassurance from time to time—but consistent reassurance will help you be braver to risk vulnerability, which will help you feel connected.

When You're Feeling Grumpy and It's Not About Your Partner

Instead of:
Taking your anger out on your partner

Or:
Not sharing your feelings and leaving your partner wondering if it's about them

Try:
"I had a bad day and it's hard for me to be present right now, but it's not about my feelings toward you. I just need some time to decompress."

Taking your anger out on your partner is destructive and doesn't give you the opportunity to work through your feelings, while leaving your partner in the dark is anxiety-provoking. They are much more likely to tolerate your feelings and show up compassionately if they aren't left in the dark and anxious. They need reassurance you'll come back in order to feel safe.

When Your Partner Is Feeling Grumpy and You're Feeling Anxious

Instead of:
Walking on eggshells

Or:
Being mad at them for being grumpy

Or:

Taking it personally

Try:

"I'm sensing distance from you right now and I feel really uncomfortable. Can I just check it out with you to see if this has something to do with me? It will help me feel less anxious."

Or:

"It's important to me that you get the space you need to sort it all out and I know I haven't been able to give you that space in the past. I can do that now, but I need to know you'll talk to me about it when you're ready."

Walking on eggshells takes away from your own peace of mind and blocks the opportunity for compassion. Thinking your partner's mood is about you when it's not creates misunderstanding and disconnection. The alternative approaches directly communicate your need, and set gentle boundaries, while still allowing space for your partner to have their feelings. They are not shaming.

When You Need to Set a Boundary Around Yelling, Name-Calling, Being Mean

Instead of:

"You're violating my boundaries and I won't reinforce this behavior. You have no right to throw these tantrums and act like a big baby."

Try:

"I can't live with being yelled at and called names because it will affect my good feelings toward you and I want to protect myself, you, and the relationship from that. I'm going to need to leave the room if I'm being yelled at, and we'll have to come back to it later."

Or:

"I can't feel safe and close when you're yelling. Help me be open to you by saying what you need to say in a way that I can hear you."

Or:

"The real you is hiding underneath your words right now. I can see you're hurt. Let's not do this. Can I hold your hand?"

Or:

(*if things aren't changing*) "I can't stand here being talked to like that. (*firm tone*) Your feelings are real and matter, but the way you're expressing them is not okay. It feels horrible. If it continues, I'm going to need to . . ." (*whatever you need to do to take care of yourself*)

Boundaries are necessary, but when they are shared in a way that leaves your partner feeling like the enemy, they disrupt attachment security. Nobody thrives when they feel like the enemy. If you can co-regulate your partner (which isn't always easy when they're being mean), it's probably going to be the most effective option. These responses also validate your partner's feelings without approving of or encouraging their behavior. Some partners weren't raised with healthy boundaries so they will need a firmer approach. Boundaries create clarity and safe parameters, and for many people, setting boundaries is very vulnerable because it brings up abandonment fears ("If I set limits, I'll be seen as mean, unreasonable, or undeserving, and I'll be rejected"). But nothing moves forward in a relationship without them. Boundaries help teach people how to treat us, and that's only fair to both parties. Some people don't initially respond to boundaries in the most supportive way because it might feel threatening. In the end most people appreciate having clarity about where they stand. Boundaries eliminate the guesswork and are safe for all. It will take consistency and follow-through but if you want the relationship to work, it's necessary.

When Your Partner Is Sad

Instead of:
"Don't be sad, look at the bright side . . ."

Try:
"I'm so sorry you're suffering. I can feel how hard this is on you. I'm right here. You can talk about it or we can just sit in silence . . . whatever you need."

The only way out of hard feelings is through. Give yourself a moment to take that in. Instead of trying to go around the bad feeling, or make it go away for someone else or yourself, we need to give it space to exist. Try to breathe and move through it instead of fighting it. Listen to it and learn from it. If you try the first approach, it might get in the way of your partner's ability to work through their sadness. It's also invalidating and sends the message "it's not okay to feel" or "your feelings are too much for me to handle." By being a supportive presence, you can help them feel less anxious about having the feelings to begin with. They'll feel less alone, which is healing.

When You Want to Bring Up the Topic of Getting Help for the Relationship or Working on the Relationship

Instead of:
"We have to go to therapy and if you won't go that means you don't care about our relationship as much as I do."

Or:

Anything that sends the message "We need therapy so you can see what you're doing wrong."

Try:

"I understand your resistance to therapy. Of course you don't want to feel ganged up on and feel worse. At the same time, what we're doing isn't working and I feel shut out and alone."

Or:

"I can see how you think therapy can make things worse, and I agree that risk is real. At the same time, I don't feel okay with how things are going between us. I feel sad, alone, and frustrated a lot of the time, and I believe that not getting help is also a real risk."

Or:

"You're right. It's a sacrifice of time and money and I know you need to protect us from any more stress. I appreciate the cautious part of you. That makes sense to me and I appreciate your cautiousness because in so many ways it helps me feel safe. At the same time, I don't feel safe right now because I'm worried about our relationship, which is the most important thing we have. I feel protective of us, too."

Or:

(*if you've decided therapy is necessary for you to stay in the relationship*) "I'm not happy with the way things are. I would like to get help. If you're not willing to do that, I'm not sure I'm willing to stay in this. It's too painful to fight so much and feel so far away. This is not how I want a relationship to feel."

The truth is that most people avoid therapy for reasons other than simply not caring about the relationship. Demanding, even demanding healthy things, sends the message that your partner's ideas or free will don't matter. If your partner associates therapy with a demand, it won't be a safe topic. If your partner has any reason to believe the goal of therapy is for them to be fixed, they might feel shamed or invalidated by both you and the therapist, and won't feel safe to go. Ultimately, it's impossible to *make* someone go to therapy. Trying to force them to go becomes part of the problem. But you can create the right environment, validate their resistance, and influence them. You need to share how you and the relationship will be impacted, especially from an attachment perspective—"If we can't improve things, I can't feel close"—but ultimately you can't control them. If they feel there's space for their feelings and they aren't being forced, they will more likely be open to the idea eventually.

Another piece is trying to understand more about *why* they are closed off to the idea of therapy. How is their resistance a misguided attempt for them to feel safe? If the explanation is narrowed down to "you just don't care," the opportunity is missed to better understand what's really going on.

When You Perceive Your Partner Is Taking Your Concern as a Criticism

Instead of:
"Stop being so sensitive."

Try:
"I know in the past I've delivered concerns to you in a way that has left you feeling attacked. I'm committed to sharing things in a new way so you don't feel that way. I also need to know you're willing to hear me."

Or:
"You're a good partner and I appreciate you for more reasons than

I can list. *And* I don't like this (*certain behavior*) and to feel close I need to know there's space for me to be heard."

Telling someone they're "so sensitive" is invalidating, and sends the message that their feelings don't matter, are too much, or stem from the fact that they are flawed as a person. But acknowledging how the past has contributed to insecurity is validating and healing. Holding two truths at once—that your partner needs to feel safe *and* that you need to be heard—encourages teamwork and collaboration.

When You Feel Misunderstood

Instead of:
"That's not what I said!"

Or:
"That's not what I meant."

Try:
"I think we're missing each other. Let's take a pause and try to understand each other. I'm right here."

It might be true that you were misunderstood, but when that message is delivered as a protest, before emotional safety has been established, it will block the ability to reach each other.

Taking time to connect *before* clarifying will create the emotional safety needed for your message to land. This approach sends the message that your goal is to understand them. Adding "I'm right here" is simple enough to reach your partner's nervous system and can be co-regulating.

When You Say Something in the Most Perfect Way Possible and Your Partner Still Becomes Reactive

Instead of:

"No matter how I say it, you refuse to listen. Why should I even bother?"

Try:

"I completely understand why it's hard for you to take in what I'm saying. Given our history it's probably hard for you to believe it's heartfelt. But our relationship is important to me and I know that if we can't reach each other we're both going to feel awful. Would you be willing to try to let me in even when part of you doesn't want to?"

Or:

"I can tell something big came up for you. What are you hearing me say?"

When you communicate in an open, loving way, and aren't received, it's enormously frustrating because your vulnerability is being dropped. But you'll undo that work if you follow it up with a protest, like the first option, which lacks vulnerability and validation. Providing validation for your partner's block can be a powerful way to get in. The new approaches might not get the response you're looking for immediately, but you will probably be heard (even if it's not apparent), planting seeds for future growth and connection. You will model to your partner what you're hoping to get in return, to build as your communication style together. The second approach, in particular, can be co-regulating. It allows space for your partner to build awareness around their trigger and your curiosity will send the message you care. It will give you an opportunity to validate their feelings. This can create the safety needed for you to be heard.

It bears repeating that conversations like this do not always solve the problem right then and there. It's like choosing an apple over a donut because you want to eat healthier. Rationally it makes sense, but emotionally everything in you wants the donut. And while you might notice feeling better right away by choosing the apple, you might not. Your body might not respond immediately with positive feedback. You might feel worse. You might have to battle hard feelings of deprivation. You might think, "Why bother? I don't feel any better and one apple won't make a difference." And you're right, one apple won't make a difference in your overall health. But if you keep choosing the apple over and over, day after day, it will start to make a difference.

Words, along with comforting touch, can help you address tough issues, while creating a new way of relating to one another over time. Getting vulnerable and reacting differently than you have been, and were raised to, can be challenging, especially when triggered. But if you can take a moment to check in with yourself, regulate, and validate your partner, while using attachment-friendly language, you create more safety for you both and more room for secure love.

Conclusion

Going Forward in the World with Secure Love

As an avid skier, I love living in Montana, where the powder is often fresh . . . but the temps are low. I can bundle up easily, except for my toes. This year, I tried out electrically heated socks. After a couple of wears, I called the ski shop to see if I was doing something wrong because they didn't seem to be heating up. "You won't feel the heat in your toes," they explained. "You just won't feel the cold anymore."

When you have a secure attachment, you'll feel a strong sense of connection to your partner, but a lot of the time security is less about what you *do* feel and more about what you *don't* feel. In other words, the room you're in together won't have a chill in the air; there won't be a palpable sense of hostility or a palpable sense of negative energy. Most of the time your toes won't be cold. Being less distracted by discomfort so much of the time will create space for moments of heightened connection. What is most of the time? I think a good rule of thumb is that at least 80 percent of the time you are either consciously aware of positive feelings about your partner and the relationship, or you have a subconscious felt sense of "all is well." It's a sense of security that's just *there*, hovering in the background. The other 20 percent of the time isn't awful per se, maybe there's some anxiety or tension in the air, you're in an active negative cycle, or you're trying to find your way back to each other via the repair process. If 80 percent sounds too low for you, that's okay, too. This book is predominantly written for couples in distress, so for a lot of readers 80 percent is a major improvement. Ideally I'd like to see all couples achieve this "felt sense of security" closer to 90 percent of the time, but I also like to set up realistic expectations. Putting consistent effort into practicing the principles of this book and doing the work to maintain an attachment-friendly environment will help that happen, but, of course, all couples start their journey at different places.

Another way to assess your emerging attachment security is to take a look at your negative cycles. Negative cycles are a great way to gauge relationship growth. To start, you'll notice that you're having fewer negative cycles, and by fewer I mean *fewer*, not none. Fewer matters because fewer negative cycles leads to fewer bad feelings leads to fewer negative cycles leads to fewer bad feelings leads to more space for good feelings, and on and on it goes, building upon itself. You might have to step back and eye the relationship from afar to really notice the change. Take a moment and ask yourself, "Are we fighting less? Are we talking through our hard topics with greater ease? Are we better at finding solutions to our problems outside of negative cycles?" Better yet, have this conversation together.

When I'm working with a couple, I don't define their success by perfection; I define it by signs of growth. As I was explaining this concept to a couple I used to treat, one of the partners said, "What you're saying is you want to see a positive trend with peaks and valleys."

That was exactly right. From that day forward I've shown my patients the growth I'm looking for in this graph:

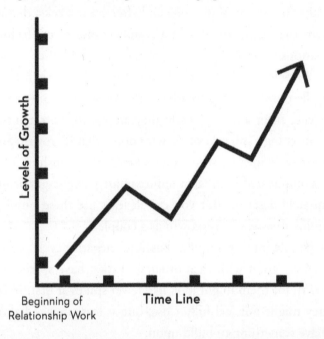

Beginning of
Relationship Work

Time Line

As you can see, and as I've already mentioned, growth isn't linear. And I don't mean growth isn't linear sometimes; I mean growth isn't linear *ever*. It simply doesn't work that way—humans are far more complicated, with too many variables at play, many of which are out of a couple's control, such as bad moods or global pandemics. If you notice on the graph, once couples start growing, even when they backslide, they never go back to square one. Square one is awareness. Once you become aware of the concepts of attachment, it's not something you can unlearn—even when things seem to completely unravel, you'll still have your foundation of awareness to draw upon when you're ready. Another thing you might notice is that the down spurts are almost always followed by growth spurts. The downward spurts are often opportunities to work on deeper problems that finally feel safe to surface—it's as if the relationship is saying, "We're strong enough to work through this now." Once it's worked through, the couple experiences greater growth.

If a couple is experiencing consistent growth of positively trending upward with peaks and valleys, I consider this success. And all couples start at different places. If a couple comes to me feeling good in the relationship 60 percent of the time and after a few weeks, they're up to 70 percent, that is growth. But if a couple comes to me feeling good in the relationship only 10 percent of the time, and after a few weeks they're at 20 percent, that's growth, too. Or perhaps when I start seeing a couple, they're having negative cycles anywhere from one to three times a week. After a few weeks, if they are getting through the week with one, or going a full two weeks with none, that is growth. Success is at least in part defined by where they started. Relationships, of course, are more complicated than what approximate percentages or numbers can adequately describe, but you can at least use these numbers as a general guide to assess your growth as a couple.

Some couples are always in a "baseline" negative cycle, never really feeling entirely good with each other, and then have spikes of escalation. Growth for them might look like fewer spikes at first. In between spikes they might not feel fully close, but at least they're fighting less and we have something to build upon.

This brings me to another common scenario. Most of the couples I treat will report to me that they're fighting less, but feeling even more distant. I liken it to a bucket of water: When we start doing the work, their bucket of is full of dirty water. As we work to stabilize negative cycles, we slowly empty the bucket. Long term, we want to fill the bucket up with clean water: closeness, increased trust, higher levels of emotional and physical intimacy, and closer friendship. But there is a period between emptying the bucket and filling it back up when the bucket is just empty. There's no fighting, but there's not really any bonding, either. If you've experienced this, it's normal. We need to use this space to continue having deeper repair conversations around old wounds (go back to repair in chapter 7) and building bonds.

Speaking of repair, couples who are moving toward secure attachment will notice they repair faster than in the past. Some couples at the beginning of their journey toward healing will not talk for days, or even weeks, after a rupture. For them, a faster repair might look like a couple of days instead of a week. For some couples, they might find they can repair after an hour, or even after a few short minutes. Another way to assess repairs is seeing if they are more complete, deeper. Do you feel a stronger sense of resolution? Are you holding less resentment?

Vulnerability is necessary for repair, but it takes time, and practice, to work up the courage to be vulnerable. Nobody can go directly from "I'm terrified my vulnerability will be too much for you and I'll feel rejected" to "I'm putting it all on the table, I need to know my needs matter to you." You have to work up to it. When you talk about what happened and try to repair, are you being *more* vulnerable than in the past?

Another way to assess your level of growth is by how "negative" your negative cycles are. Are you still getting escalated, but not as high? Are you staying engaged longer than you used to? Are you calling names or yelling less? Are you noticing more validation and listening before getting defensive or deflecting criticism? Are you feeling less yucky when it's all over? Again, we're looking for improvement, not perfection. And you might still backtrack and have ugly cycles—but are they overall less ugly?

Finally, think about problem-solving. Are you finding it easier to work through decisions both big and small? Are you able to better understand and respect each other's perspectives? Are you allowing time for decisions to be made instead of taking the approach of "we need to make this decision right this second"? Are you better able to tolerate the unknown? Are you finding it easier to bring up difficult topics, even just a little, *or* are you bringing them up anyway despite your fear? Have you noticed any evidence of growth and do you have hope the growth will continue as you continue to work at it?

I hope that by now, you're able to look at your relationship and see that you and your partner have fewer negative cycles, they're less miserable when you do have them, and you're able to make repairs faster. If this is the case, this is no small feat. Celebrate that! You have done really difficult work, and it speaks volumes about your emerging attachment security. Remember, negative cycles are fueled by insecure attachment, so if your negative cycles are improving, you and your relationship are becoming more secure. The two go hand in hand.

Beyond Secure Attachment

Securely attached partners spend far less time working on their relationship, and far more time *enjoying* their relationship—which *is* working on the relationship if you consider how much resilience is created when two people take time to enjoy each other. Secure attachment isn't just about "not fighting," or "not having negative cycles."

Again, no relationships, even the ones with the most trust and security, are perfect. I think of my own relationship. My husband and I love to do certain things together, especially outdoorsy activities, but on any given late evening, you might find him downstairs watching foreign films and me upstairs watching football or reading a mystery novel with a strong, British female lead. That's just us. There are no rules about what a secure relationship should look like—as long as they have an attachment-friendly environment, secure couples find all sorts of ways to thrive.

With that said, here are some things securely attached couples are doing—what you might find yourself doing now that your energy isn't being drained by the negative cycles.

Just Being

Because you now have a felt sense of security, you may just be going about life not even consciously thinking about your partner. Without the constant swirling fears or insecurities or worries, you are freed up to focus on other things. That doesn't mean you ignore your partner, but relationship anxieties aren't a constant undercurrent or distraction. Maybe you're engaged in work or a hobby. Maybe you're with other friends or family. Maybe you're in the same room as your partner doing separate things. You're fine. You both know you can reach each other if you need to, that you are loved and cared for, and that you will have plenty of moments of engagement when the time comes.

Having Fun

As a securely attached couple, you will have your own unique ways of having fun together. Some couples might love going to art galleries and concerts, having family and friend time, watching or playing sports, laughing and joking, having sex, going to dinner, getting out in nature, shopping, watching movies, playing with pets, taking long drives, taking long walks, listening to music, traveling, playing video games, and doing anything else under the sun. It doesn't have to be anything fancy, just shared moments of joy. I recently asked social media followers what brings joy to their relationship. One woman has a husband who prints out tiny animals for her from his 3-D printer. Another follower and her partner love to work through crossword puzzles while they cook (impressive). Most happy couples like to have fun in separate ways, and that's important, too, but they have at least a few ways in which they have fun together, and they make time for it. Also, they don't compare themselves to other couples in this sense or any other, which gets in the way of enjoying what you have.

Sharing Experiences and Feelings

Securely attached couples talk to each other about their experiences in the world. You might talk about your day at work, or events from your childhood, or about your dinner with a friend. It could be anything. The happiest of couples go out into the world and have experiences to come back and share with their partners. This is one reason the Covid-19 pandemic was especially hard on couples—they weren't having separate experiences to share with each other. As a securely attached couple, you don't just talk about details and facts; you share your feelings about events: "It really hurt my feelings when my boss said . . ." instead of a long story limited to surface details, which can be overwhelming and, without emotional significance, sometimes boring. You also know how to share in a way that is considerate, you have good listening skills, and you can set boundaries when needed: "Honey, what you have to say is so important to me. Right now I'm just too tired to be a good listener. Would you mind telling me about this tomorrow?" or "Let's put a pause on this and pick it up tomorrow when I can listen better."

Connecting with Other People

Securely attached partners have other people in their lives to talk to and connect with. Sometimes your best friend, family member, or coworker will be the one to give you the emotional validation you're needing in a moment. Or sometimes you stick with self-validation because that feels good, too. Sometimes a certain story you want to tell will be better appreciated by another person in your life than by your partner.

Securely attached partners meet most of each other's needs, most of the time. You are each other's *primary* support, but you aren't each other's *only* support. And just to clarify, I'm not saying if you don't have strong relationships with other people, or if you don't share private details about your relationship or partner with others, that means you're insecurely attached. Remember, every couple is different.

Nurturing the Relationship

Securely attached partners spend more time nurturing their relationship than they spend repairing it. The nurturing you will put in now that things feel better will prevent you from having to do a lot of repairing. Examples of nurturing include: being considerate of each other's space and boundaries; doing little things for each other, like remembering to grab oat milk creamer at the market because you know that's what your partner likes in their coffee; being tolerant of minor mistakes; speaking to each other respectfully and lovingly; helping each other out around the house; sharing chores and responsibilities; making time for physical touch and connection; sharing emotions; having good manners; asking about each other's day and taking the time to listen; being curious; being each other's biggest fan.

Protecting the Relationship

Securely attached partners are cognizant of protecting the relationship. Now that you've put in all this work, you are far more likely to think about what you do or say and how it might land with your partner. You've learned to prevent negative cycles and you'll probably continue to actively practice doing so. You won't do things behind your partner's back that might interfere with their sense of trust or teamwork. You won't try to control each other. You will protect the relationship from damage in the same way you would protect your material goods from damage. And hopefully, once you've reached this security, protecting the relationship in this way isn't necessarily work; it's more of a natural state of consideration.

Go Be Secure; Go Be Imperfect

Congratulations, you're on a path toward healing. Just by reading this book you've shown your commitment to creating a better relationship and a better environment for you and your loved ones. You've grown, you've connected, you can move forward in security, happiness, and meaning. The journey is never over but you've done something brave— you've chosen vulnerability. By choosing vulnerability, you've opened yourself up to the experience of real love, real connection, and lasting growth. Relish it! Maybe celebrate with your partner, together.

Years ago, I was treating a client in her early twenties who was struggling with perfectionism. At the end of our session, I grabbed a Post-it note, jotted down "Go be imperfect," and pinned it next to my door, telling her, "This is for you; go be imperfect." I left it there and all my other clients liked it so much that I eventually put it in a tiny little frame and made it permanent. To this day it still hangs next to my office door. So, just like all the clients who leave my office at the end of their session, I will leave you with this: make secure attachment your goal, but don't let a quest for the perfect relationship get in the way of the "good-enough" relationship. Make "good-enough" your goal and you might find that "good-enough" is exactly what you've been looking for. So . . . go be imperfect.

Appendix

Childhood Experiences of Avoidant Attachment

Caregiver Behavior	Avoidant Child Strategies	Benefit of Child's Strategy (subconscious)	Downside of Child's Strategy
Caregiver ignores or shames child's expression of emotions.	"It's best to not acknowledge my emotional self. What's the point? It's better to push it out of my awareness."	"If I don't have feelings I'll never have to feel rejected or shamed."	Child becomes disconnected from their emotional self. Without awareness of this part, child can't learn to communicate and manage feelings.
When child is emotionally distressed, caregiver focuses on "fix it" approach.	"The best way to manage painful feelings is to use logic and reason to fix my problems."	"If I'm good at fixing my problems, I'll never have them. If I never have problems, I'll never have to feel painful feelings."	Child doesn't learn to seek comfort from others or to understand and comfort their own feelings when upset. As they age they'll have problems connecting with the inner worlds of others.
Caregiver sends the message (verbally or nonverbally) "don't talk about your feelings."	"It's not safe to talk about my feelings. People who talk about feelings are weak and less-than."	"If I keep my feelings to myself I'll be acceptable."	Child learns to hide parts of self, which can cause feelings of emptiness. They might develop disdain of self or others for showing feelings.

Caregiver Behavior	Avoidant Child Strategies	Benefit of Child's Strategy (subconscious)	Downside of Child's Strategy
Caregiver overly focuses on success and appearance, with little focus on child's feelings and thoughts.	"My worthiness wholly depends on whether or not I can do a good job, get it right, and how others view me."	"If I can get it right in the eyes of others, I'll be viewed as worthy."	Child doesn't learn to connect to their inner world. Child might become anxious about being successful. Child might paradoxically become an underachiever ("I can't keep up so why bother?").
Caregiver creates an environment that heavily rewards independence.	"I have to know how to do everything on my own. Asking for help is weak."	"Being able to do it all on my own and figure things out on my own is how I feel competent and acceptable."	Child doesn't develop healthy interdependence. Child develops the idea that asking for help is a sign of weakness. Child associates interdependence with a loss of self.
Caregiver shames child for making mistakes or misbehaving. Sends messages that "you're bad, you're failing," instead of labeling the *behavior* as wrong, and instead of using missteps as learning opportunities.	"Worthy people don't make mistakes or mess up."	"If I work hard to get it right all the time, I won't have to feel unacceptable in the eyes of others. I can only feel good about myself if I never mess up."	Child will become defensive to real or perceived criticism. Child will struggle accepting their own imperfections, which can be anxiety provoking. Child might struggle to accept the imperfections of others, which can get in the way of closeness and connection.
Caregiver is emotionally intrusive: doesn't have good boundaries, overshares with child, tries to coerce child into sharing their feelings, or becomes upset when child shares their feelings.	"Close relationships are smothering." "My feelings make others upset."	"If I want to maintain my sense of self, I need to push away closeness." "I need to keep my feelings to myself so I don't upset others."	Shutting out all closeness blocks child from experiencing fulfilling connection with others.

Childhood Experiences of Anxious Attachment

Caregiver Behavior	Anxious Child Strategies	Benefit of Child's Strategy (subconscious)	Downside to Child
When child is upset, caregiver doesn't give predictable responses. At times they might respond positively. Other times they respond with anxiety, overwhelm, or anger.	"I have to fight to be seen, heard, understood, and comforted."	"If I keep fighting to be responded to, maybe I'll get my needs met. Getting big and protesting gives me hope I won't end up feeling rejected and alone."	Child's nervous system is chronically activated; child develops conflicting feelings of longing for connection yet anger at having to fight so hard.
Caregiver's emotional and/or physical presence comes and goes.	"I have to learn to pay close attention to any signs my caregiver will go away and I'll be left alone."	"If I stay close and keep them in eyesight, I won't feel abandoned."	Child's energy is put toward maintaining safety with the caregiver, and taken away from learning and growing.
Caregiver is too overwhelmed with their own feelings to be emotionally present with child or meet child's emotional needs.	"I can't trust that my caregiver can show up for me emotionally. I have to make my feelings bigger than theirs so they will see how much I need help."	"I've learned that if I get big enough, my caregiver will finally be able to see me."	Child gets stuck in an exhausting pattern of protesting to be heard and responded to. Child isn't modeled self-regulation.
Caregiver overreacts or becomes anxious or dysregulated when child is upset.	"If my big feelings are enough to trigger my caregiver, that must mean I'm too much for others to handle."	"Maybe I should try harder to keep my feelings to myself so I'm not viewed by others as too much."	Child develops a conflict between the fear of being "too much" and the longing for being responded to. The conflict is exhausting and leaves them unsure of how to reach for their needs to be met. They are torn between being "too much" or being ignored.
Caregiver's emotional closeness is inconsistent. Sometimes they can connect, sometimes they can't connect.	"It feels so good to connect but then it goes away and I feel dropped. Connection can't be trusted because it's always followed by disappointment."	"I long for closeness but at the same time I don't trust it when I get it, so I subconsciously push it away to protect myself from disappointment. Sometimes when I do get the closeness I long for it reminds me of how angry I am that it's not predictable."	Child carries a mistrust of closeness that blocks their ability to relax and fully enjoy the good moments in relationships out of a legitimate fear that "good things eventually go away."

Childhood Experiences of Disorganized Attachment

Caregiver Behavior	Message Received by Child	Response of Child
Overall climate that is punitive/hostile/rejecting/abusive	"The very people I need for love and protection are also dangerous. I'm so confused and I don't know where to turn."	Child has to manage their human longings for connection, protection, and care alongside feelings of fear and mistrust. This leaves child feeling inner confusion and chaos. Child is left to manage their problems and big feelings on their own. The loneliness creates feelings of despair.
Caregiver dissociates (appears to "go blank," "go away," to child)	"I'm alone. At any moment my caregiver might disappear. I see them but I don't feel them. I'm confused and scared."	Frightening experience for child to manage the conflict of physical presence, but emotional absence.
Caregiver has unresolved trauma (trauma that isn't being managed or healed)	"I never know when my caregiver is going to get triggered and take it out on me."	Child can never feel fully safe because at any given moment a situation can become frightening, or because the environment is so chaotic. Child gets stuck between needing comfort and safety, but being too afraid to reach for it.
Caregiver is afraid of child	"I overwhelm my caregiver and push them away. I'm threatening. I don't have a 'wiser, stronger' helper to protect and guide me. I'm alone."	Child has nowhere to turn when they need help. Child feels alone and a deep sense of shame.
Caregiver uses child as attachment figure	"I'm responsible for my caregiver's feelings. Who is responsible for me? Being responsible for an adult is too much. I don't know how."	Child feels overwhelmed, unsupported, and alone. Child feels like a chronic failure for not being able to keep caregiver happy.
Chronic marital conflict and/or domestic violence	"My environment is unsafe. Nobody is here to protect me from fear and harm."	Child doesn't feel valuable enough to be protected. Child is modeled fighting and violence and will learn to behave in this way. Without anyone to help them make sense of the situation, child will blame themselves.
Predatory behavior toward child (glaring, baring teeth)	"My caregivers are terrifying. If I mess up I'll be harmed. My environment is never really safe."	Child learns to fear what should be the source of comfort. This creates intense confusion, distress, lack of safety, and apprehension about reaching for support.

Common Relationship Feelings

💔 Sad

empty	despairing
demoralized	hurt
powerless	unheard
longing	unseen
lost	dismissed
heartbroken	misunderstood
dejected	undervalued
lonely	

🔥 Angry

annoyed
frustrated
enraged
critical
irritated
hostile
indignant
resentful
mad
fuming

🐱 Afraid

terrified
confused
anxious
insecure
overwhelmed
nervous
panicky
agitated
worried
alarmed

👧 Ashamed

inadequate
stupid
less than
embarrassed
rejected
devalued
humiliated
guilty
not enough

❤️ Positive Feelings

close	appreciated
connected	supported
seen	loved
understood	accepted
cared for	calm
valued	worthy
warm	competent
safe	empowered
secure	

Negative Cycle "Moves" of Avoidant-Attached Partner

Avoidant Strategies to Manage Emotions	Perceived Benefit (subconscious)	Downside
Stuffing down painful feelings; pretending they don't exist	Partner can partially and/or temporarily protect themselves from being overwhelmed by painful feelings, or from creating conflict.	Can't access or express feelings; feelings will be acted out in unhelpful/ destructive behaviors; doesn't recognize the need for emotional comfort; doesn't learn to communicate and manage negative emotions in ways that can lead to bonding.
Sees childhood experiences through "rose-colored glasses"; minimizes negative childhood experiences	By maintaining an imbalanced view, partner doesn't have to see family in a negative light, which might bring up shame from the idea that "if my parents are broken, that makes me broken," or might bring up painful feelings of being disloyal to family they love.	Partner can't see how negative childhood experiences have impacted their present circumstances. Problems remain a mystery or someone else's fault. Simplistic view of relationships: can't view families or others as "whole" with both strengths and weaknesses.
Thinks that all their problems would be solved if only they could get it right	Partner uses shame as a way to motivate themselves to do better, a strategy that relies on a supply of toxic shame. Partner believes that if they're the "bad guy" they can be the one to change; everything will be okay and they won't lose their partner.	Taking on shame can lead to stress, anxiety, mental illness, addictions, and substance abuse. Trying to take on all the blame in the relationship (whether in the big picture or in moments) can get in the way of setting healthy boundaries and blocks authentic connection. Shame blocks vulnerability.
Verbalizing and/or believing the relationship is "fine," even when there is evidence to the contrary	In the avoidant partner's mind, if the relationship is "fine," they don't have to face conflict, which is uncomfortable and overwhelming. If they can convince their partner that the relationship is "fine," their partner will stop bringing up concerns and/or is more likely to stay in the relationship.	Denying real relationship problems keeps problems from being addressed and resolved. Denial of problems leaves their partner feeling alone, confused, and desperate for connection and resolution.

Avoidant Strategies to Manage Emotions	Perceived Benefit (subconscious)	Downside
Viewing or accusing anxious partner as "overly emotional or sensitive"; minimizing partner's feelings	If the avoidant partner can convince the anxious partner they are the problem because they're too sensitive, they can make sense of the situation and/or not have to face their own flaws and shame.	Putting blame solely on the anxious partner blocks uncovering deeper unmet needs in the relationship and blocks healing.
Avoiding conflict	Avoid feelings of shame, overwhelm, anger, or fear of losing partner. Avoid big fights that will harm the relationship.	Relationship problems aren't addressed or resolved; no opportunity to learn how to manage conflict in a way that is safe for both partners. Bonding opportunities are missed because healthy conflict makes space for vulnerability.
Distancing from relationship	As negative cycles damage the relationship, avoidant partners will distance from the relationship in order to distance from the pain the relationship has come to represent, including feelings such as shame from feeling like a failure, despair, and/or fear.	"Checking out" doesn't make space for healing; creates feelings of emptiness; adds to distance; leaves both partners feeling alone.
Seeking comfort elsewhere (excessive work, hobbies, addictions, other romantic or nonromantic relationships, etc.)	When avoidant partner associates the relationship with pain, failure, and emotional overwhelm, they can fill their void of emptiness and distract from the pain by seeking out other pleasurable activities.	Seeking comfort elsewhere creates distance and blocks the opportunity for real problems to be addressed and healed.
Getting defensive against real or perceived criticism	Avoid being seen as a failure by self or partner.	Defensiveness blocks healthy self-reflection, blocks healthy boundaries, masks deeper feelings, blocks resolution of problems, and leaves partner feeling unheard and invalidated.
Denying their own relationship needs	Won't have to face disappointment if needs aren't met; doesn't want to burden partner and make things worse. If they minimize/deny their relationship needs, they won't have to risk feeling engulfed.	Can't self-advocate for needs; inability to respond to self needs can contribute to inability to respond to needs of others; denying one's own needs breeds resentment.

Avoidant Strategies to Manage Emotions	Perceived Benefit (subconscious)	Downside
Deflecting partner's concerns; counter-blaming when partner brings up concerns: "I'm not the problem, you're the problem and here's why . . ."	The avoidant partner can feel safe, the subconscious logic being "If I can get you to see that you're the one in the wrong, to see your flaws, it will take the heat off me and I'll feel safe. I won't view myself as wrong and shameful and neither will you."	Their partner feels invalidated, attacked, and unsafe.
Handles anger with passive-aggressiveness and/or biting humor	Doesn't have to own or take responsibility for their anger, which they perceive as threatening.	Their anger doesn't get the attention it needs to be addressed, validated, and worked through.
Excessive use of reason and facts to "win" arguments	If they can provide the right evidence, their partner won't see them as bad or failing, and the problem will have an easy solution.	Overreliance on reason and facts comes at the expense of emotions and deeper meanings. If one partner is "right," that makes the other partner "wrong," which gets in the way of the attachment needs to feel respected and understood, which will block emotional safety, vulnerability, and resolution to problems.
Appeasing partner; "keep the peace" at all costs	When avoidant partners appease (say or do what their partner wants them to say or do even when they don't want to) and work hard to "keep the peace," they can keep the relationship stable, avoid conflict, and prevent their partner from being disappointed with them.	Relationship issues don't get addressed or resolved, partners sacrifice authenticity and true intimacy, they carry resentment, and they are at risk for eventually "blowing up" over small events, or over things unrelated to the relationship.
Overvalues their independence	Can avoid feeling "dependent," weak, and smothered.	Too much independence blocks healthy interdependence, vulnerability, and intimacy. Partner feels pushed away.

Avoidant Strategies to Manage Emotions	Perceived Benefit (subconscious)	Downside
Pushes away emotional closeness	By pushing away emotional closeness and/or partner's reaches for closeness, the avoidant partner doesn't have to feel like a failure for not knowing how to respond, or engulfed and feeling as if they are losing self to the relationship.	Pushing away connection blocks intimacy and relationship closeness. Even when the avoidant partner doesn't recognize it, it leaves them feeling empty and alone. It leaves their partner feeling unfulfilled and alone.
Shutting down during conflict	"I'm afraid of conflict and the negative impact it will have on the relationship." "Shutting down helps me escape feeling overwhelmed."	Partner feels alone and unsure that the relationship even matters to the partner shutting down. No resolution to problem.
Distancing when their partner asks them about their feelings	"Feelings are weak. If I show them to you, or even to myself, that means I'm weak. If I'm weak, I'm not worthy."	Partner can't feel connected; feels alone. Relationship lacks vulnerability and emotional intimacy.
Stonewalling	"I can show you how hurt I am without having to own and express my hurt directly, because that doesn't feel safe. Then you'll see me. "	Partner feels powerless, anxious, and left in the dark.
"Fix it"	"If I can make the problem go away by fixing it, we'll be okay."	Usually doesn't address the real problem, which is emotional and attachment issues.
Avoiding difficult topics	By avoiding difficult topics they can avoid difficult feelings or they can avoid conflict and "ruining the moment."	If there isn't ample space to address difficult topics, their partner feels unheard and unseen, and nothing gets resolved.
"Moving target" (when someone says they feel a certain way, then quickly shifts and says they don't feel that way)	If they own their feelings they fear they will be used against them later, or that their feelings might be viewed by themselves or partner as "weak" or "wrong."	Not being able to own and talk about feelings blocks vulnerability and connection.
Making hurtful comments	If they can get their partner to feel the pain they're feeling inside, their partner will understand them. Or, making their partner feel "less than" can temporarily help them feel secure within themselves.	Hurtful words are destructive to the relationship because they erode safety and trust.

Negative Cycle "Moves" of Anxious-Attached Partners

Anxious Behaviors	Perceived Benefit (subconcious)	Downside
Protesting when feeling unheard, invalidated, un-responded to, and/or misunderstood	Fighting to be heard and seen. If the anxious partner keeps fighting, there's a chance they'll get their needs met and won't have to face feelings of despair and powerlessness.	Protesting decreases the odds they'll be heard, pushes partner away, and blocks their ability to self-regulate and learn to sit with vulnerable feelings of grief, fear, and shame.
Expressing emotions with "big" intensity	Discharging feelings in a big way releases painful energy, which can feel like a second-best substitute for self-regulation. Can temporarily numb the pain of lack of co-regulation in the relationship.	Is exhausting to their own nervous system and overwhelms their partner's nervous system. Decreases the odds the real problem will be addressed. Leaves anxious partner feeling ashamed and alone.
Being overly controlling of environment and/or partner	Keeping their environment "perfect" or under control keeps them from feeling anxious when things go wrong and provides a false sense of safety.	Exhausting, can leave partner feeling resentful and/or incompetent, blocks opportunity to learn to regulate through inevitable hard moments and to develop self-trust.
Blaming, criticizing, judging partner	Blaming keeps them from having to face the shame of being too much, wrong, and invalidated for their suffering. It will help them get their partner to see how they're the problem and they'll change. If their partner changes they'll feel safe.	Creates resentment from partner, blocks intimacy; doesn't create space for self-reflection.
"Filtering for the negative"	Focusing on what is wrong can keep them on alert for what needs to be changed. They won't feel blindsided when something bad happens.	Focusing on the bad gets in the way of experiencing the good; leaves partner feeling unappreciated for the strengths they bring to the relationship and they will feel demoralized.
"Peppering with questions"	They believe that if they can get enough information somehow they'll end up feeling safe and reassured.	When reassurance stems from a core fear of being unlovable or from a relationship rupture, no matter how many answers a partner gives it won't be enough. Partner might feel frustrated by being unable to give the "right" answers.
Testing partner's love and responsiveness	If their partner can pass the test, they will finally feel loved.	If they have a core fear of being unlovable, even when tests are passed, there will always be more tests.

Anxious Behaviors	Perceived Benefit (subconcious)	Downside
"Lots of words," repeating self again and again in conversations	By saying the same thing over and over, they believe they'll finally be heard.	Overwhelms partner; partner feels no space to be heard; "looping" is a way to defend against vulnerable feelings that need to be faced and addressed. Repeating gets in the way of resolving real problems if partner isn't listening.
Difficulty ending or taking breaks from arguments	Doesn't have to be alone with painful feelings; fighting is better than being alone.	Continued fighting in escalated states often leads to behaviors that harm the relationship; blocks opportunity for self-regulation and co-regulation.
Presenting excessive details and "proof," often repetitively	If they present enough "proof," they'll get the validation they're longing for, and their partner will finally change.	Overfocusing on details can mask bigger meanings and patterns; presenting details can leave partner feeling blamed and misunderstood and invites arguments.
Silent treatment (out of protest; different from avoidant version of silent treatment)	If they "abandon" their partner, their partner will feel how mad and alone they feel and they'll want to comfort them and change.	Maintains climate of unhealthy communication.
"Raising the bar"	Since "good things" can't be trusted, anxious partners continue to seek perfection and maintain unreasonable expectations in order to help them feel safe and that one day everything will be okay.	Anxious partner never gets to experience "good enough." Their partner becomes demoralized because they think that no matter what they do to change or get it right, it will never be enough.
Being emotionally or physically "clingy"	They believe that if they keep their partner close they won't have to face their abandonment fears.	No amount of closeness or proximity will be enough to cure the fear of abandonment. The fears cannot be worked through when they're avoided. Partner feels suffocated and pushes away in order to maintain their sense of individuality.

Anxious Behaviors	Perceived Benefit (subconcious)	Downside
People-pleasing	If their partner is always happy they can feel lovable and safe. This is a way to "soft-control" partner.	Both partners will likely harbor resentment.
"One foot out the door" (when there's a fight, making threats to leave the relationship as a protest, not an authentic plan to leave)	"If I can scare you into thinking I'm going away, maybe you'll hear me;" or, "I'm in so much pain all I can do is think about escaping."	Partner feels confused and hurt, and might take threats seriously. Or, partner might stop taking the threats seriously.
Poking to get partner's attention	"If I can get a response, any response, I won't feel alone and disconnected."	Partner feels scared and abandoned, and doesn't learn how to respond to healthy reaches for comfort and connection.
Overfocus on partner's behaviors and growth	Overfocusing on partner keeps them alert to how their partner might let them down. If their partner is "perfect" they will finally get to feel safe.	Pushes partner away; keeps partner from having the space to take ownership of their own growth.
Difficulty recognizing their part of the problem and how it impacts the relationship	They've had legitimate experiences of being repeatedly let down, which has left them in a state of blame and the need to change what's outside of them in order to feel safe inside of them. They might work hard on the relationship, but without realizing some of what they do to help is making things worse. Since they're "working" so hard and things aren't changing, they make sense of it by assuming the partner is the problem.	Stuck mindset. Gets in the way of focusing on self. Blocks vulnerability and self-regulation. Blocks them from seeing and working on their part of the problem that keeps relationship stuck.

Acknowledgments

First and foremost, thank you to my husband, Mario, for supporting me in more ways than I can ever list. You are my rock. You've reached for the stars with me and yet you've kept me grounded. We've been through a lot together and I'm proud of us for never giving up on growth in our partnership and in our parenting. You've been telling me for ten years to write a book and when I threw my hands up and said, "There's no way I can do this," you were the one to say, "You *have* to write the book." The message I received at that moment on the front porch was "I believe in you and I'm here. I'm on your team." I love you more than words, and I'm looking forward to sharing the rest of our lives together.

Thank you to my children. This project has been a team effort, and each of you has made sacrifices in your own way for this to have worked. How many times have you heard over the last three years, "Once I finish the book . . . ?" I thank you with everything I have for your support and for believing in me. My journey to attachment theory began with my unyielding desire to be the best mom I can be to each of you. I plan to create a legacy of emotional support for our family that will live on through the generations.

Jamie, for thirty years you've been the other rock in my life. I admire and value so many things about you. Your unwavering support brings tears to my eyes, and your solidness has kept me going in life in ways you will never know. And you do it all with impeccable style.

Thank you to my mom for believing in me beyond a shadow of a doubt. Thank you to my dad for giving in all the ways you knew how to give. You lived in the stars, too, and often I feel that my life is an extension of a journey you didn't have the resources to complete on your own. Thank you to my grandma for modeling the combination of warmth and strength I aspire to, and thank you for all the laughs.

And for my team:

Thank you to Katrina, my work rock. You are very special to me. Thank you for your loyalty, and for tirelessly helping me make all of this logistically possible.

Alexandra Machinist, thank you for believing in me and in my work. I'm so grateful for all the inspiring skills you possess as a person and as a professional that set *Secure Love* into motion.

Stephanie Frerich, you are a gift. You've brought a purity to this project that has helped me stay true to the spirit of *Secure Love*, and I know that doesn't always happen in the publishing world. I value your friendship and the raw insight you bring to my work. Thank you to everyone else at Simon & Schuster who has believed in and supported this project. I intend to make you proud to have taken me on.

Rachel Bertsche, you are a genius. I'm in awe at the speed at which you can digest information and help me turn it into something more approachable for readers. You helped me take *Secure Love* from a great book to a phenomenal one, and I'm beyond grateful to have you on my team for this book and beyond.

Thank you to Helen and the UK Penguin/Cornerstone team. Helen, I appreciate the feedback you've given me that has helped *Secure Love* maintain nonshaming inclusivity for all. Thank you for believing in this project.

And of course, where would this book be without my teachers?

John Bowlby, you created something beautiful . . . a theory of attachment that has the potential to change the course of humanity by moving us backward to go forward.

Sue Johnson, your brilliance is undeniable. I try to imagine the patience, intuition, and intelligence it took for you to sculpt EFT out of the deceptively simple theory of attachment. Your work has profoundly impacted my life personally and professionally and I thank you from the bottom of my heart for what you've tirelessly contributed to the field of psychology.

George Faller. You took the concept of EFT to new heights, and when I started learning from you everything changed. You brought a realness and grit to EFT that hasn't taken away from the innate softness and empathy of our beloved modality, but has expanded it to something even more human and more relatable. By dedicating yourself to the exhausting task of traveling around the world and being our teacher, you are touching an unprecedented number of lives. Thank you, thank you, thank you. I feel proud to consider you a teacher, a mentor, and a friend.

Wendy, you are my EFT sister. Thank you for all the growth as therapists we've experienced together, for tolerating this book process even when it interrupted our weekly hikes, and for teaching me how to be a "strong Montana girl," which is obviously still a work in progress.

Thank you to all the couples I've worked with. You have made it possible for me to bring this work to life and never could this book have been written without your willingness to trust me and take a journey through your vulnerability with me by your side. I have the utmost respect for anyone who is willing to be vulnerable and face the most painful parts of themselves, to commit the time, energy, and money to working on their relationship. This is not easy work, and each and every one of you is special to me. I never forget your stories.

Thank you to my Instagram followers, for whom this book was written. I never intended to grow such a large, loyal following, and I never intended to write a book. But consistently from day one of this journey you asked for it, and here it is for you, especially those of you with all the motivation in the world but with no access to couples therapy. I write for you.

Notes

Chapter Two

18 50 percent of the time: Susan S. Woodhouse, Julie R. Scott, Allison D. Hepworth, and Jude Cassidy, "Secure Base Provision: A New Approach to Examining Links Between Maternal Caregiving and Infant Attachment," *Child Development* (2019).

18 *Alexander Thomas and Stella Chess*: Alexander Thomas and Stella Chess, *Temperament and Development* (New York: Brunner/Mazel, 1977).

19 Good Inside, *by Dr. Becky Kennedy*: Becky Kennedy, *Good Inside: A Guide to Becoming the Parent You Want to Be* (New York: HarperCollins, 2022).

20 *one foster mother to another*: John Bowlby, "Forty-Four Juvenile Thieves: Their Characters and Home-Life," *International Journal of Psycho-Analysis* (1944).

20 *in order to seek food*: John Bowlby, *Attachment and Loss*, vol. 1, *Attachment* (New York: Basic Books, 1982).

21 *disorganized attachment*: Mary Ainsworth, *Patterns of Attachment: A Psychological Study of the Strange Situation* (New York: Lawrence Erlbaum Associates, 1978).

21 *attachment theory to adult relationships*: Cindy Hazan and Phillip Shaver, "Romantic Love Conceptualized as an Attachment Process," *Journal of Personality and Social Psychology*, 1987.

27 *attachment behavioral system (ABS)*: Bowlby, *Attachment*.

32 *attachment needs, longings, and fears*: Ainsworth, *Patterns of Attachment*.

33 *75/25 male/female*: Rainer Weber, Lukas Eggenberger, Christoph Stosch, and Andreas Walther, "Gender Differences in Attachment Anxiety and Avoidance and Their Association with Psychotherapy Use: Examining Students from a German University," *Behavioral Sciences* (2022).

34 *75/25 female/male*: Weber et al., "Gender Differences."

Chapter Three

57 *disorganized-oscillating*: Joseph E. Beeney, Aiden G. C. Wright, Stephanie D. Stepp, Michael N. Hallquist, Sophie A. Lazarus, Julie R. S. Beeney, Lori N. Scott, and Paul A. Pilkonis, "Disorganized Attachment and Personality Functioning in Adults: A Latent Class Analysis," *Personality Disorders* (July 2017).

59 *the avoidant spectrum*: Beeney et al., "Disorganized Attachment and Personality Functioning in Adults."

Chapter Four

76 Hold Me Tight, *by Dr. Sue Johnson:* Sue Johnson, *Hold Me Tight: Seven Conversations for a Lifetime of Love* (New York: Little Brown Spark, 2008).

Chapter Ten

210 The Body Keeps the Score, *by Dr. Bessel van der Kolk:* Bessel van der Kolk, *The Body Keeps the Score: Brain, Mind, and Body in the Healing of Trauma* (New York: Viking, 2014).

Chapter Eleven

213 *the greatest overall relationship satisfaction:* Bianca Acevedo and Arthur Aron, "Does a Long-Term Relationship Kill Romantic Love?," *Review of General Psychology* (2009).

225 Mating in Captivity, *by Esther Perel:* Esther Perel, *Mating in Captivity: Unlocking Erotic Intelligence* (New York: Harper Collins, 2007).

228 Come As You Are, *by Emily Nagoski:* Emily Nagoski, *Come As You Are: The Surprising New Science That Will Transform Your Sex Life* (New York: Simon & Schuster, 2015).

Chapter Twelve

234 *have seen marked improvement:* Paul M. Spengler, Nick A. Lee, Stephanie A. Wiebe, and Andrea K. Wittenborn, "A Comprehensive Meta-Analysis on the Efficacy of Emotionally Focused Couple Therapy," *Couple and Family Psychology: Research and Practice* (2022).

Index

About the Author

JULIE MENANNO is a licensed marriage and family therapist with a passion for helping partners build deeper connections, lasting love, and secure attachments. She founded and runs Bozeman Therapy & Counseling and The Secure Relationship Coaching.

In addition to her therapeutic work, Julie shares her invaluable insights and advice with a wide audience through her popular Instagram account, @TheSecureRelationship. With over one million followers, she has become a trusted source for couples seeking guidance on fostering secure and fulfilling partnerships.

Julie resides in Bozeman, Montana, where she spends her free time hiking and skiing. She shares her life with her loving husband and six wonderful children, who remind her daily of the importance of nurturing and cultivating strong bonds.